The Book of Home Finance
2006 Update

2006 Conforming Limits

	1-Unit	2-Unit	3-Unit	4-Unit
2006	$417,000	$533,850	$645,300	$801,950
2005	$359,650	$460,400	$556,500	$691,600

2006 FHA Limits

	1-Unit	2-Unit	3-Unit	4-Unit
Base Limits	$200,160	$256,248	$309,744	$384,936
High-Cost Limits	$362,790	$464,449	$561,411	$697,696

High-Cost Areas—(CA) Los Angeles-Long Beach, Napa County, Orange County, Oakland, Riverside, Sacramento, Salinas, San Diego, San Francisco, San Jose, San Luis, Santa Barbara, Santa Cruz, Santa Rosa, Stockton, Vallejo, Ventura; (CT) Stamford, Bridgeport; (DC/MD/VA) Washington; (FL) Ft Lauderdale/Miami; West Palm Beach; (HI) Honolulu ($544,185); (MA) Boston, Cambridge; (NH) Rockingham/Strafford Counties; (NJ) Newark, Bergen, Edison, Cape May; (NY) New York, Nassau-Suffolk, White Plains

Other Notable Areas Above Base Limits—Anchorage, AK $255,050; Juno, AK $294,000; Phoenix, AZ $254,600; Tucson, AZ 230,200; Bakersfield, CA $244,150; Fresno, CA 263,150; Modesto, CA $334,875; Denver, CO $261,609; Hartford, CT $254,600; New Haven, CT $293,075; Wilmington, DE $270,750; Jacksonville, FL $209,000; Orlando, FL $248,200; Tampa, FL $202,800; Atlanta, GA $227,905; Blaine, ID $312,895; Chicago, IL $275,200; Gary, IN $275,200; Baltimore, MD $308,750; Springfield, MA $206,700; Portland, ME $256,025; Detroit, MI $226,100; Minneapolis, MN $244,625; Kansas City, MO $201,638; St. Louis, MO $213,750; Trenton, NJ $334,058; Camden, NJ 270,750; Las Vegas, NV $297,400; Reno, NV $332,500; Santa Fe, NM $290,319; Buffalo, NY $209,057; Poughkeepsie, NY $308,750; Rochester, NY $201,400; Syracuse, NY $203,300; Wilmington, NC $208,950; Cincinnati, OH $228,000; Cleveland, OH $221,006; Columbus, OH $233,700; Portland, OR $284,600; Philadelphia, PA $270,750; Pittsburgh, PA $243,200; San Juan, PR $247,000; Providence, RI $316,350; Charleston, SC $251,750; Nashville, TN $226,100; Salt Lake City, UT $232,750; Burlington, VT $237,975; Norfolk, VA $285,093; Richmond, VA $237,025; Seattle/Tacoma WA $312,895; Milwaukee, WI $208,700; Madison, WI $211,700; Jackson, WY 312,895;

Note: These limits were published December, 2005 and are subject to change. This list is not inclusive of all areas above the minimum base limits.

2005 Indices

	Jan	Feb	Mar.	April	May	June	July	Aug.	Sept.	Oct.	Nov.	Dec.
COFI	2.18	2.32	2.40	2.52	2.62	2.68	2.76	2.87	2.97	3.07	3.19	3.30
6 mo LIBOR	2.96	3.15	3.39	3.42	3.53	3.69	3.92	4.08	4.22	4.45	4.58	4.69
1 Year T	2.86	3.03	3.30	3.32	3.33	3.36	3.64	3.87	3.85	4.18	4.33	4.35
3 Year T	3.39	3.54	3.91	3.79	3.72	3.69	3.91	4.08	3.96	4.29	4.43	4.39
5 Year T	3.71	3.77	4.17	4.00	3.85	3.77	3.98	4.12	4.01	4.33	4.45	4.39
30 Year/	5.71	5.63	5.93	5.86	5.72	5.58	5.70	5.82	5.77	6.07	6.33	6.27

Mortgages (Freddie Mac Primary Mortgage Market Survey—Average 0.5 to 0.7 points)

Prime Rate 7.50% as of Jan 31, 2006

This Financial Update Is Provided To My Valued Customers By—

*Published by the Hershman Group. For more information regarding ordering the 2005-2006 edition of the **Book of Home Finance**, call 1/800-581-5678 or visit us at www.originationpro.com and download a free copy of Chapter One—The Home as an Investment, Tax Deduction and Inflation Hedge.*

S0-EQZ-781

Federal Housing Administration (FHA)

- Mortgagee Letter (ML) 2005-2 clarified FHA requirements regarding verification of seller concessions and sales data.
- ML 2005-14 implemented FHA's interim rule allowing 5-year adjustables with a 2.0% annual cap and a 6.0% life cap. The final rule was published in December, 2005;
- ML 2005-15 allowed minor changes without requiring rescoring in TOTAL, including small changes in escrows, income and cash reserves.
- ML 2005-16 changed FHA qualifying ratios from 29/41 to 31/43 and allowed the "grossing-up" of child support income since it is non-taxable.
- ML 2005-19 introduced the "Streamline K" program allowing $15,000 of minor repairs to be financed into the loan.
- ML 2005-21 clarified FHA's procedure for underwriting energy efficient mortgages. EEMs allow the borrower to finance up to $8,000 of energy efficient improvements into the loan.
- ML 2005-27 announced that FHA would be validating Social Security Numbers.
- ML 2005-34 announced that FHA would begin accepting the new Fannie appraisal forms on January 1, 2006. Concurrently, FHA "retired" the VC condition form and Notice to Homebuyer/Homebuyers Summary and updated their "Appendix D," Valuation Protocol.
- ML 2005-38 announced that effective December 28, 2005, up-front mortgage insurance will be charged on rehab mortgages (203k) and condominiums (234c)
- ML 2005-39 adopted the revised Fannie Mae application forms.
- ML 2005-43 revised refinance transaction requirements to allow cash-out up to 95% of the value, limiting cash-back on no-cash-out mortgages to $500, allowing a 20.0% in the payments that shorten the term or refinance from an adjustable into a fixed rate.
- ML 2005-44 announced an expanded network of HECM (reverse mortgage) counselors
- ML 2005-48 announced revised repair requirements for existing property appraisals.
- ML 2005-50 announced enhancement to limited repair, Streamline (k) Program, including raising the maximum repair amount to $35,000 and eliminating the minimum $5,000 repair threshold.

Department of Veterans Affairs (VA)

- 05-03-05 VA reaffirmed the need for subterranean termite treatment for new homes.
- 01-01-06 The VA maximum mortgage amount was raised to the conforming limit of 417,000

Freddie Mac and Fannie Mae

- Fannie Mae revised its condominium approval guidelines, adding the acceptance of FHA-approved condominiums as well as creating a category for expedited review of established projects.
- Fannie Mae and Freddie Mac issued revised forms: Credit Verification Authorization, Loan Application, Transmittal Summary and The Residential Appraisal Form.
- Freddie Mac introduced its home-possible mortgages for low-to-moderate income borrowers. The program has reduced MI requirements as well as assessment for those without usable credit scores
- Fannie Mae began purchasing mortgages with 40-year terms.
- Freddie Mac expanded the acceptance of employer assistance homeownership benefit programs.
- Freddie Mac also expanded acceptance of interest-only mortgages.
- Freddie Mac also revised its condominium guidelines.

For more information regarding these changes, contact your mortgage representative who provided you with this update.

Published by the Hershman Group. For more information regarding ordering the 2005-2006 edition of the **Book of Home Finance**, call 1/800-581-5678 or visit us at www.originationpro.com and download a free copy of Chapter One—
The Home as an Investment, Tax Deduction and Inflation Hedge

Book of Home Finance

David L. Hershman

Finance ◆ Education ◆ Consulting

Edited by Beth Fisher

©2005 - The Hershman Group

ALL RIGHTS RESERVED. No part of this publication may be reproduced, stored in a retrieval system, or transmitted by any means, electronic, mechanical, photocopying, recording, or otherwise, without the prior written permission of the publisher and the copyright holder.

This publication is designed to present, as simply and accurately as possible, general information on the subject. It should be noted that the information presented is not all inclusive. Processes may have altered due to rapid changes in the industry. This publication should not be used as a substitute for referring to appropriate experts and is sold with the understanding that the publisher is not engaged in rendering legal, accounting, or other personalized professional service. If legal or other expert assistance is required, the services of a competent professional should be sought.

Library of Congress National Serials Data Information

Hershman, David L.
    Book of Home Finance/David L. Hershman
ISBN 0-9645939-4-7
I. Mortgage Loans. II. Real Estate. III. Hershman, David L. IV. Title

ISSN 1081-6720

Printed in the United States of America

The Book of Home Finance

Introduction

The world of mortgages is certainly different than it was ten or fifteen years ago. It was not so long ago that a real estate agent would sell a home and send the purchaser to their community savings bank to apply for a mortgage. Qualification was never a question and neither was the choice of mortgage products. The purchaser had a relationship with the financial institutions which offered only one or two mortgage alternatives.

Now there are many mortgage products and institutions from which to choose. The qualification guidelines and mortgage alternatives are increasingly more complex. To make real estate finance even more interesting, one can apply for a mortgage with a mortgage broker, a mortgage banker, a bank, a credit union, a savings institution or even through your home computer!

It is clear that mortgage bankers, real estate professionals and home buyers need to be able to navigate through this maze of real estate finance in order to be a success in today's challenging market. This book is a step toward bringing this complex world into perspective and focus. It will not answer all questions, but it will give a base of knowledge so that one can master the process. Invaluable time will be saved by using the charts which compare mortgage products, down payment formulas and qualification guidelines.

Good luck in your efforts towards mastering the world of mortgages and real estate ownership!

Dave Hershman

Table of Contents

Chapter 1: A Home as an Investment, Tax Deduction and Inflation Hedge 1

Real estate as an investment—the concept of leverage 2
Calculation of the tax savings of a mortgage payment 4
The mortgage payment as an inflation hedge 6

Chapter 2: Sources of Mortgages 9

The Federal Housing Administration (FHA) 9
Who is eligible to obtain FHA mortgages? 9
Types of transactions financed under FHA 10
Types of properties eligible for FHA 11
Mortgage types offered under FHA 12
Costs to obtain an FHA mortgage 13
FHA qualification requirements 18
The Department of Veterans Affairs (VA) 20
State and local bond issues 27
Rural Housing Service 30
Conventional conforming mortgages 31
Conventional non-conforming 42

Chapter 3: Types of Mortgages 45

Fixed rate/fixed payment mortgages 45
Computation of an amortization schedule 46
Fixed loan alternatives 47
The bi-weekly mortgage 50
Interest-only programs 51
Fixed rate hybrids 51
How much does a buydown cost? 54
Lender subsidized buydowns 56
Adjustable rate mortgages 59
Reverse mortgages 68

Chapter 4: Qualifying For a Mortgage: Ratios and Residuals **71**

The ratio method of qualification 71
The housing ratio 72
The monthly mortgage payment (PITI + HOA) 72
The debt ratio 73
The debt ratio calculation... 73
Pre-qualification using ratios 74
Credit Scores and Underwriting Systems 76
The residual method of qualification 79
Residual method example 81

Chapter 5: Comparing Mortgages **85**

Comparing mortgage payments over the life of the mortgage 85
Comparing mortgage payments for different mortgage terms.. 88
Comparing points on mortgage programs... 91
Comparing mortgage combinations 92
Comparing cash requirements for each mortgage 93
Comparing qualification requirements for each mortgage source 94

Chapter 6: Refinancing a Mortgage.. **95**

What is a refinance?... 95
Why would someone want to refinance a home? 96
Mortgage sources and refinancing 102
Other considerations for refinances 107
How much is it going to cost?.. 108

Chapter 7: Applying and Packaging Your Loan for Approval **111**

Preparing the documentation 111
Application.. 114
Processing 116
Underwriting 120

Chapter 8: Mortgages, Home Ownership and Taxes **123**

Purchasing a Home 123
Deduction of Regular Mortgage Payments... 124
Tax Deductions and Refinances... 126
Rental Property Deductions 126
Taxation Upon Sale of Residential Real Estate 127
Special IRA Provisions 129

Appendix A: Federal Withholding Tax Tables
Appendix B: Estimate of Settlement Costs of a Mortgage Transaction
Appendix C: National Real Estate Transaction Taxes and Title Insurance Costs

Glossary

List of Tables

Table 1-1	Return on Investment	3
Table 1-2	Principal Reduction	3
Table 1-3	Net Return on Investment—10 Year Holding Period	4
Table 1-4	Net Return on Investment—Varying Holding Period	4
Table 1-5	Rental Tax-Equivalents	6
Table 1-6	Inflation Effects on Rent and Mortgage Payments	7
Table 1-7	Inflation, Tax, and Principal Reduction Effects on Rent and Mortgage Payments	8
Table 2-1	Refunds of One Time FHA MIP	14
Table 2-2	FHA Mortgage Insurance Chart	15
Table 2-3	National FHA Maximum Loan Limits	16
Table 2-4	FHA Monthly MIP Factors	19
Table 2-5	History of VA Entitlement	27
Table 2-6	30 Year Mortgage Rate Changes -- A 50+ Year History	28
Table 2-7	A History of Conforming Mortgage Limits	33
Table 2-8	HUD Estimated Median Family Income Limits	34
Table 2-9	Private Mortgage Insurance	40
Table 2-10	Major Mortgage Source Comparisons	44
Table 3-1	Annual Amortization Table—20 Year Term	46
Table 3-2	Annual Amortization Table—15 Year Term	46
Table 3-3	Annual Amortization Table—30 Year Term	47
Table 3-4	Fixed Rate Monthly Payments	47
Table 3-5	Comparison of Fixed Rate Mortgages	48
Table 3-6	Effect of Monthly Payment	49
Table 3-7	Annual Amortization Table	51
Table 3-8	History of Major ARM Indices	57
Table 4-1	Interest Rate Factors	75
Table 4-2	Mortgage Amounts for Given Payments	76
Table 4-3	Mortgage Qualification by Income and Interest Rate	78
Table 4-4	VA Family Support	79
Table 5-1	Interest Rate Increases for Variable Mortgages	88
Table 5-2	Mortgage Term/Prepayment Comparison	89
Table 5-3	22 Year ARM Performance -- Historical Method	90
Table 5-4	Annual Percentage Rates	92
Table 5-5	Cash Necessary for Home Purchase	93
Table 5-6	Qualification Requirements for Mortgage Sources	94
Table 6-1	Months to Break Even After Refinance	97
Table 6-2	Points and Refinance Savings	98
Table 6-3	Effects of Monthly Payment on Typical $100,000 Loan	98
Table 7-1	Items Needed for Loan Application	122

List of Graphs, Figures, and Worksheets

Graph 1-1	Median Price of Existing Homes	2
Graph 1-2	Median Rent Paid in the United States	6
Figure 3-1	The Bi-Weekly Advantage	50
Figure 3-2	I-0 Buydown	53
Figure 3-3	2-1 Buydown	53
Worksheet 4-1	Purchaser Qualification Sheet	82
Worksheet 4-2	Conventional Pre-Qualification	83
Worksheet 4-3	VA Pre-Qualification—Residual	84

1

A Home as an Investment, Tax Deduction and Inflation Hedge

Security, privacy, freedom—the American Dream is to purchase a home. Ownership of property is the bastion of capitalism. There is no doubt that owning a home is the goal of the average American today. Why? Is it the ability to have no landlord? Is it the freedom to stay or move? There are many emotional benefits to home ownership. However, the cornerstones of our capitalistic society are financial in nature. The reason we all aspire to own real estate is simply this: we desire to accumulate wealth. Time and time again, we hear of riches built with a real estate foundation. This book focuses on the financial aspects of home ownership as opposed to the emotional. Accordingly, this Chapter will address the financial reasons for owning and financing a home.

Even so, we do not want to play down the importance of the *psychological*, rather than economic reasons for owning a home. In 1992, the Federal National Mortgage Association (Fannie Mae) released a survey indicating 78% of all Americans think owning a home is a good investment. More than one-third of these gave *security* and *sense of permanence* as the reasons for wanting to own.

There are three basic economic reasons for purchasing a home:

1. *Real estate is an investment.* Using the concept of leverage, we will learn exactly why real estate constantly outperforms other investment vehicles—even during periods of low inflation.

2. *Real estate is a tax deduction.* Every year it seems that Congress opts to cut more and more tax breaks from the menu in the interests of tax simplification and preserving the progressive nature of the tax system. The mortgage interest deduction has suffered nicks and scratches and has emerged as the major survivor in the world of tax strategies.

3. *Real estate is an inflation hedge.* It has been several years since double-digit inflation numbers have raised their ugly heads. Even in times of low inflation, monthly rents move upward much more quickly than a mortgage payment.

Chapter 1

Real estate as an investment—the concept of leverage

Early in the decade, financial experts predicted low appreciation rates for housing in the 1990s and beyond. For those who have dreamed of the 25.0% appreciation rates some areas experienced in the 1980s, these predictions must have been a major source of disappointment for those years. In fact, most of these *experts* predicted housing would not be as solid an investment as it had been in the past. In reality, home price appreciation picked up as the century came to a close and real estate's long-term record of 7.0% average rates of annual appreciation was more than supported.

Any prediction of the future is just that—a prediction. We do not aspire to be any more accurate in presenting a scenario for the future of housing appreciation in any part of the country than the so-called economic experts. We feel the best approach is to assume a low rate of appreciation to be conservative. We also feel the concept of leverage has been missing in the experts' comparison of other investments to housing. It is the concept of leverage that makes housing an excellent investment in any inflationary environment.

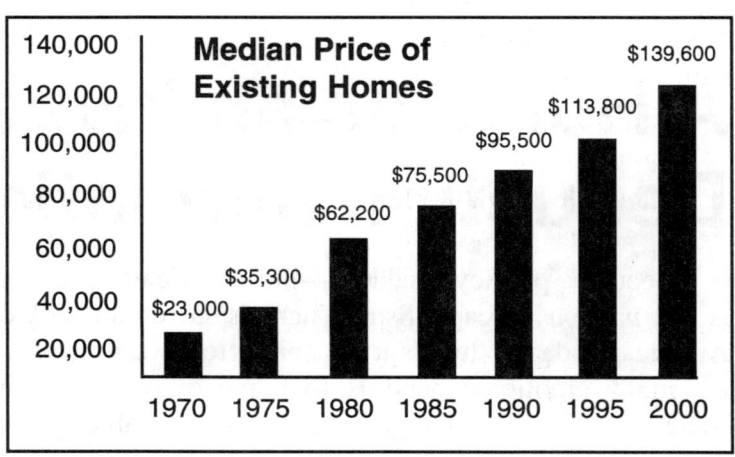

Source: National Association of Realtors
Graph 1-1

What is the concept of *leverage*? Leverage is defined as the ability to control a large asset with a smaller asset. For example, you can purchase $100,000 in real estate using $5,000 in cash assets. You can leverage real estate highly because of several factors:

Leverage

High-powered finance for everyone

a. Real estate assets have a long history of appreciation, this means security for those institutions that would lend against the asset.

b. There is a complex system to record ownership of property—older than the United States itself. It is unlikely that the purchaser of real estate will be challenged by someone who is the *real* owner of the property from years gone by. This is also security for the lender.

c. There are consistent national standards for qualifying purchasers of real estate. These standards reduce the risk that a real estate loan will default and allow the loan to be easily *liquidated* (sold for cash) in case the lender needs to raise capital in the future.

d. Some mortgage programs are directly sponsored, subsidized, or insured by federal and local governments, resulting in smaller down payments than would otherwise be necessary through conventional lenders.

Let us compare a simple example in which we invest a cash asset of $10,000 over a number of years, either by leaving it in the bank or by purchasing $100,000 of real estate. The table assumes a 6.0% rate of interest in the bank for a total gain of *$7,908* after ten years. It also assumes a 6.0% appreciation rate for real estate during this time period. Factored in are a $5,000 cost of purchase (closing costs) and 10% cost of liquidation (sales costs). It should be noted that, assuming the property is sold after ten years, these costs are $15,000, which is more than the original asset. Yet the gain after ten years is *$64,085, or a 22.2% annual rate of return*!

What we have developed in this Chapter is a more in-depth look at the concept of leverage as it relates to residential real estate. What if the rate of home appreciation slows down to 2% per year? What if you try to sell the real estate after two years? What if the down payment is 20% of the purchase price? Generally, these rules apply:

Return on Investment

Years	$10,000 Cash	$100,000 Property
3	$1,910	$4,102
5	$3,382	$18,823
10	$7,908	$64,085
15	$13,966	$124,656
20	$22,071	$205,714
30	$47,435	$459,349

Assuming 6% rate of gain, 5,000 down payment, $5,000 closing costs, and $10,000 selling costs.

Table 1-1

a. *Low rates of appreciation*. The effect of leverage will lessen with lower rates of appreciation. However, in the long run, real estate will still outperform savings based instruments. It makes sense that low rates of housing appreciation will be accompanied by low rates of inflation, which will also lower savings rates.

b. *Holding periods*. Because of the cost of real estate acquisition (figured in our examples to be 10%) and the cost of real estate disposition (also figured as 10%), there must be a reasonable holding period for gain on real estate. During periods of moderate appreciation (5% to 7%) real estate must be held at least three to five years to be more profitable than savings accounts. Higher appreciation rates will allow for shorter holding periods. When we consider the fact that real estate also may serve as our home, the holding period required becomes less of an issue.

c. *Increasing the down payment*. Generally, the larger the down payment, the smaller the percentage-return on real estate. Remember the concept of leverage requires that we control as large an asset as possible with the smallest asset possible.

d. *Mortgage principal reduction*. In addition to the leverage principle, the gain on real estate is increased by a reduction in the principal amount of the initial mortgage on the property. In simple terms, as one owns a house, one builds up additional equity because each mortgage payment reduces the amount of the principal balance outstanding.

Table 1-2 shows the amount of principal reduction on a $100,000 loan. In this example, the cumulative principal reduction after ten years would be $14,187. This would be added to the gain calculated due to leverage and appreciation, as presented in the previous table. The table also shows how the most common type of mortgage loan, the *positively amortized* mortgage, has *accelerated* principal reduction properties. That means that the amount of principal reduction increases with each monthly payment. Note the table shows the first year's reduction is only $1,015.79, while the tenth year's payments reduce the principal by over $1,900.

Principal Reduction

30 Year Term
$100,000 Loan Term
7% Fixed Rate Loan

Year	Annual Principal Reduction	Cumulative Principal Reduction	Outstanding Principal Balance
1	$1015.79	$1015.79	$98984.21
2	$1089.21	$2105.00	$97895.00
3	$1167.94	$3272.94	$96727.06
4	$1252.39	$4525.33	$95474.67
5	$1342.91	$5868.24	$94131.76
6	$1440.00	$7308.24	$92691.76
7	$1544.08	$8852.32	$91147.68
8	$1655.73	$10508.05	$89491.95
9	$1775.41	$12283.46	$87716.54
10	$1903.76	$14187.22	$85812.78

Table 1-2

Chapter 1

With these concepts in mind, let's take a look at a comparison table that takes our money in the bank and compares its earnings with those from a purchase of $100,000 in real estate over ten years. We have varied the appreciation rates, interest rates on savings, and down payments. We also assume 5% closing costs and 10% selling costs. Thus, the *total investment* is the down payment plus the 5% closing costs. The net returns are then calculated from the appreciation of the property, plus the principal paid, minus the closing costs, the selling price, and the income that could have been received had the investment been left in a savings account. That means the returns shown are over and above what the money would have made in the bank.

Net Return on Investments
$100,000 Home
With Principal Reduction and Equity Gain
Assuming a Mortgage Held for 10 Years

Down Payment		20%	10%	5%
Total Investment		$25,000	$15,000	$10,000
Loan Amount		$80,000	$90,000	$95,000
Home Appreciation Rate	Savings Interest Rate			
2%	3%	$6,758	$11,254	$13,502
3%	3%	$19,250	$23,746	$25,994
4%	3%	$32,883	$37,379	$39,627
5%	5%	$40,623	$47,969	$51,642
6%	5%	$56,819	$64,165	$67,838
7%	5%	$74,449	$81,795	$85,468
8%	6%	$89,578	$98,543	$103,026
9%	6%	$110,421	$119,387	$123,870
10%	7%	$128,652	$139,380	$144,744
12%	8%	$175,068	$187,714	$194,037
15%	9%	$263,828	$278,559	$285,924

Table 1-3

The result is an interesting comparison of returns. Note the returns are actually greater when a lower down payment is used. This becomes an enormous difference if viewed in terms of the percentage return on the investment.

Next, let's look at the impact of varying the number of years you own your home. Since you only have to pay closing and sales costs once, you will benefit most from a longer ownership period. As table 1-4 shows, the financial benefits of longer homeownership periods are even more impressive. A long holding period assures positive returns, even at low appreciation rates.

Calculation of the tax savings of a mortgage payment

The concept of rental equivalency

This section will focus on the tax savings of a mortgage payment. Recent changes in the tax code leave mortgages as the only major write-off still available to the average citizen. Other sections of this book will focus on whether a purchaser can qualify for a mortgage loan. This section will focus on whether a purchaser can afford a mortgage loan. We do this by comparing the present rent payment of the purchaser with the proposed mortgage payment.

Net Return on Investment
$100,000 Home
With Principal Reduction and Equity Gain
Assuming a 7% Mortgage and 10% Down payment

Number of Years Held		3	5	10
Home Appreciation Rate	Savings Interest Rate			
2%	3%	($8,247)	($3,273)	$11,254
3%	3%	($5,095)	$2,246	$23,746
4%	3%	($1,881)	$7,984	$37,379
5%	5%	$421	$12,192	$47,969
6%	5%	$3,760	$18,386	$64,165
7%	5%	$7,163	$24,819	$81,795
8%	6%	$10,129	$30,567	$98,543
9%	6%	$13,661	$37,497	$119,387
10%	7%	$16,747	$43,721	$139,380
12%	8%	$23,620	$57,902	$187,714
15%	9%	$34,685	$81,764	$278,559

Table 1-4

We make this comparison by calculating the rental equivalency of the mortgage payment. The term rental equivalency refers to the amount of the mortgage payment after the effect of taxation. A discussion of rental equivalency should enable a real estate professional to demonstrate the concept of affordability to a first time homebuyer. The concept can also be applied to move-up buyers because the increased mortgage payments can also be reduced by the amount of tax savings.

Let us take an example of someone who is paying $900 each month in rent. Let's also assume the same home would cost $150,000:

Rent	Owning		Mortgage Payment (PITI)	
$900	$150,000	Sales Price	$948.52	Principal & Interest (PI)
	142,500	Mortgage	150.00	Real Estate Taxes (T)
	7.00%	30 Year	30.00	Homeowner's Insurance (I)
			58.19	Private Mortgage Insurance
			$1186.71	PITI

In this example the mortgage payment is $287 more than the rental payment of $900 each month. It is natural for a prospective purchaser to say:

"I can hardly afford my rent. How can I afford $287 more each month?"

In order to answer this question, we must compare the rent payment with the mortgage payment after the tax benefits have been calculated. To do this, we must answer the following:

- How much of the mortgage payment (PITI) is tax deductible?
- What tax bracket is the borrower in?

Fortunately, most of the mortgage payment carries tax benefits, because the interest and real estate tax portions can be deducted from one's income. The calculation is as follows:

$142,500 mortgage x 7.00% = $9,975 annual interest, or $831 monthly

Therefore, $831 out of the total PI payment of $949 is interest and is deductible, along with the real estate taxes—

	$831	Interest
	150	Real Estate Taxes
Total deductible portion of payment:	$981	83% of total PITI

Now that we know the deductible portion of the payment, we can determine the tax bracket of the borrower and calculate the tax savings. Using the Federal Monthly Withholding Tax Charts in the Appendix, we find the following:

Borrower's Income (Single):	$60,000	annually, or $5,000 monthly
Borrower's Present Federal Tax:	$863	
Borrower's Income after Deduction:	$4,019	($5,000 minus $981)
Borrower's New Federal Tax:	$613	
Tax Savings:	$250	
Rental Equivalent:	$1,187	Total Mortgage Payment
Tax Savings:	(-) 250	
Rental Equivalent:	$937	
Actual Rent on Same Property:	$900	

Chapter 1

A few things to note on the previous calculations:

1. There are also state and local tax savings for most borrowers. They are not shown because many times the borrower will need the deductibility of state taxes paid to exceed the standard deduction given to tax payers who do not itemize deductions. Those who do not have enough itemized deductions to reach the standard deduction without the mortgage payment will not fully realize the tax savings for mortgage deductibility. Eliminating the analysis of state and local tax savings minimizes this effect.

Rental Equivalency

Rental Tax-Equivalents

Assuming married filing jointly, no standard deduction, and 85% of PITI is deductible

	Total Mortgage Payments (PITI)						
Monthly Income	$800	$900	$1,000	$1,200	$1,500	$2,000	$2,500
$3,000	$696	$783	$870	$1,045	$1.307	$1,743	$2,179
$4,000	$610	$686	$762	$915	$1,177	$1,613	$2,049
$5,000	$610	$686	$762	$914	$1,143	$1,524	$1,919
$6,000	$610	$686	$762	$914	$1,143	$1,524	$1,905
$7,000	$610	$686	$762	$914	$1,143	$1,524	$1,905
$8,000	$589	$663	$738	$891	$1,119	$1,500	$1,881
$9,000	$589	$663	$737	$884	$1,105	$1,473	$1,851

Table 1-5

Note: This table will vary as income tax rates change as well as by variations in property taxes

2. There are additional savings for homeowners. The portion of the principal and interest payment that is not interest ($949 PI - $831 I) is principal which goes to pay down the loan. This is equity the homeowner is building up even without housing appreciation—a forced savings plan. In this case the rental equivalency with the additional factor would be $937 minus $118, or $819.

To save you the steps of these complex calculations, we have devised a chart that calculates the rental equivalency of mortgage payments. The chart assumes that 85% of the typical mortgage payment will be tax deductible. It also assumes the tax bracket of a married couple with no children. The savings for single individuals will be slightly larger. You can use the table to extrapolate to other mortgage payments. For example, the tax savings for a $950 mortgage payment would be one-half of the difference between $900 and $1,000.

The mortgage payment as an inflation hedge

We have discussed the investment aspects of a home purchase; clearly the use of leverage causes real estate to be a superior investment at any level of appreciation. The concept of rental equivalency makes the investment affordable in the short run. But what about the affordability of a home in the long term? How does the home stack up against renting five, ten, and twenty years from now? As time goes on, home ownership becomes more and more affordable because a home is an *inflation hedge*.

What is an inflation hedge? We all know what inflation is. It is the tendency for expenses to rise over

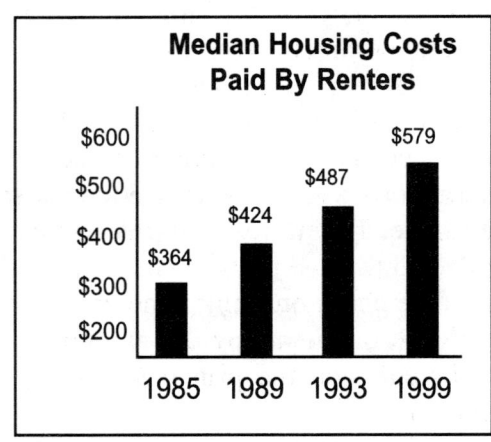

Source- U.S. Bureau of the Census

Graph 1-2

time. We know that rent is subject to inflation. If your present rent payment were $800, a 5% rate of inflation would make the payment *$1,303* in ten years. A *hedge* is an instrument of financial protection. Sophisticated investors protect their investments from erosion by using hedges. For example, someone holding a large stock portfolio may purchase futures, betting that the stock market will go down. If we then have a stock market crash, the person can offset the loss in the value of his stocks with the gain in the futures. An inflation hedge protects one against future costs of inflation. The reason for this is simple—a mortgage payment resists inflation.

Why does a mortgage payment resist inflationary pressures? Because the largest portion of the mortgage payment is the loan repayment (P&I). (Note: The payment on adjustable rate mortgages may increase independently of inflation.) The remainder of the payment will be subject to inflation. Specifically, real estate taxes, homeowners insurance, and association dues will tend to move up with inflation. However, since these are only a small portion of the payment, the overall payment will not increase as fast as rent.

A Typical Mortgage Payment

$100,000, 30 Year Mortgage at 7%

Principal and Interest (P&I)	$665
Real estate taxes	101
Homeowner's insurance	35
Total PITI	$801
Portion subject to inflation	$136
Percentage subject to inflation	17.0%

In the example, only $136.00 or 17.0% of the total mortgage payment is subject to inflation. We will use 20% as an even number. This will reduce any effective inflation by a factor of five, i.e., an inflation rate of 5% will become 1%. In other words, the rent payment will move up at a speed of five times the amount of the mortgage payment. Let's see what the effect is on long-term numbers.

Using Table 1-6, we can see that even low rates of inflation (3% to 4%) will cause the mortgage payment to become virtually equal to rent in ten years time. These are conservative measures; the average inflation rate in the United States for the period from 1978 to 1999 has been over 4.0%.[1]

Our analysis of inflation hedging is only partially complete. We have merely compared the actual payment increases over a period of time in accordance with various imputed inflation rates. We have not factored in the effects of tax deduction and principal reduction of the mortgage. In ten years, the rent payment is still projected to have no tax benefit. Table 1-7 repeats the same chart, only this time we are reducing the mortgage payments by the amount of the federal tax benefit and the principal portion of the P&I payment.

Inflation Effects on Rent and Mortgage Payments

Assuming 20% of mortgage is subject to Inflation

	$1,000 Rent		$1,400 Mortgage	
Inflation Rate	After 5 Years	After 10 Years	After 5 Years	After 10 Years
3%	$1,159	$1,344	$1,443	$1,486
4%	$1,217	$1,480	$1,457	$1,516
5%	$1,276	$1,629	$1,471	$1,546
6%	$1,338	$1,791	$1,486	$1,577
7%	$1,403	$1,967	$1,501	$1,609
8%	$1,469	$2,159	$1,516	$1,641
9%	$1,539	$2,367	$1,531	$1,673
10%	$1,611	$2,594	$1,546	$1,707
11%	$1,685	$2,839	$1,561	$1,740
12%	$1,762	$3,106	$1,576	$1,775
13%	$1,842	$3,395	$1,592	$1,810
14%	$1,925	$3,707	$1,607	$1,845
15%	$2,011	$4,046	$1,623	$1,881

Table 1-6

---

[1] U.S. Department of Labor, Bureau of Labor Statistics

**Inflation, Tax, and Principal Reduction
Effects on Rent and Mortgage Payments**

Assuming $120,000, 30 Year mortgage at 7%
Interest, with 20% of mortgage subject to
Inflation, real estate taxes starting at $150 per month

	$1,000 Rent		$1,400 Mortgage	
Inflation Rate	After 5 Years	After 10 Years	After 5 Years	After 10 Years
3%	$1,159	$1,344	$1,052	$1,055
4%	$1,217	$1,480	$1,066	$1,087
5%	$1,276	$1,629	$1,080	$1,122
6%	$1,338	$1,791	$1,095	$1,161
7%	$1,403	$1,967	$1,110	$1,203
8%	$1,469	$2,159	$1,126	$1,249
9%	$1,539	$2,367	$1,142	$1,298
10%	$1,611	$2,594	$1,160	$1,352
11%	$1,685	$2,839	$1,177	$1,411
12%	$1,762	$3,106	$1,196	$1,474
13%	$1,842	$3,395	$1,215	$1,543
14%	$1,925	$3,707	$1,235	$1,617
15%	$2,011	$4,046	$1,255	$1,698

Table 1-7

2

Sources of Mortgages

The Federal Housing Administration (FHA)

The Federal Housing Administration has long been a player in the mortgage industry. The Federal Housing Administration is a federal agency within the Department of Housing and Urban Development. The loan program was created in 1934 to assist homebuyers in acquiring property with small down payments. It is important to note that under the most prevalent mortgage program, FHA does not lend money. Lenders are given protection against default[2] by the borrower. This protection is in the form of *mortgage insurance* and FHA is considered an insurance program. An FHA borrower actually pays for this insurance and these insurance premiums are called *Mortgage Insurance Premiums*, or *MIP*. Simply stated, FHA mortgages are mortgages made by private lenders that are insured by the Federal Government through premiums paid for by the users. Having insurance provided by the Federal Government enables the program to offer lower down payments, and allows more liberal qualification standards than comparable private mortgages.

The lenders actually can approve the mortgages for FHA under the *Direct Endorsement Program*.[3] Lenders deal with FHA through the FHA Connection automated system. Through this system they can get case number assignments (for new appraisals under the CHUMS system), borrower credit watch (under the CAIVRS system), and access to MIP refund information for refinances. FHA-approved condominiums and appraiser lists are also available from this system.

Who is eligible to obtain FHA mortgages?

Any borrower of legal age can participate in FHA Mortgage Program. Citizenship is not required, though physical evidence of a social security number and picture identification must be presented at loan application. The lender must determine residency status for non-U.S. citizens. There are no income restrictions, however maximum mortgage limits ensure the program will serve primarily lower and middle income homeowners. In addition, all parties to the transaction must be

---

[2] In this context, default simply means non-payment of the mortgage by the borrower. Technically, when a mortgage is more than 30 days past due, it is *in default*. The vast majority of notes carry provisions of a late payment penalty if the mortgage is more than 15 days late (the first 15 days is called a *grace period*). The 30-day period is not in addition to the 15-day grace period, rather it includes the 15 days so that the total is 30 days.

[3] When approved under the *Direct Endorsement* or *DE* program, the section of FHA would be referenced as *703b*, rather than *203b* (*734c*, not *234c*, for condominiums). Participation in the direct endorsement program also allows the utilization of *staff appraisers* to appraise properties for FHA mortgages. Staff appraisers are employees of the mortgage company as opposed to independent FHA *fee panel appraisers*.

checked through the Denial of Participation List and the Federal Government's List of Excluded Parties. The validity of the social security number will be verified as well.

Two or more borrowers, or *co-borrowers*, can finance a house under FHA program. These co-borrowers need not be related, but they must have a family-type relationship if one of the co-borrowers does not occupy the house. In this case the *co-borrower* is defined as a *non-owner occupant co-borrower*.

FHA currently limits one FHA mortgage per borrower that can be outstanding at any one time. Prior to 1992, each borrower was limited to one *high balance* (defined as above 75% loan-to-value) FHA mortgage outstanding at one time. Currently, there are exceptions to the one FHA mortgage rule for hardship situations (for example, transfers in which the home currently owned and financed by FHA cannot be sold, a new home is mandated by an increase in family size, or the home being vacated will be occupied by a co-mortgagor). In the price range of FHA mortgages, borrowers retaining more than one FHA mortgage are not common—especially now that assumptions are restricted to owner occupants.

In May of 2003, FHA released its ban on financing when the property is being "flipped" as defined a by resale in the first 90 days after a home is purchased. Resales within 91-180 days may require additional documentation if the original value increases significantly. The sale must also be from the owner of record. Rules released in December of 2004 specifically exempt property acquired through inheritance or properties bought and sold through FHA or other governmental agencies.

Types of transactions financed under FHA

FHA finances the following types of transactions:
- *Owner-occupied purchase transactions* (203b). The vast majority of FHA financing is for purchases of primary residences (must be occupied within 60 days of settlement). Investors cannot finance purchases through FHA and the financing of second homes is restricted to *hardship* situations. FHA is prohibited from insuring a mortgage on a second home that is a vacation or investment property.
- *Owner-occupied rate reduction[4] refinance transactions (203b)*. Homeowners can refinance their current mortgage through FHA program. If the homeowner currently has an FHA mortgage on the property and the new FHA mortgage will result in a lower payment, the homeowner can participate in *FHA Streamline*, or *FHA Rate Reduction*, refinance program. This program requires no income re-qualification as long as there is a good mortgage payment history. Although FHA does not require an appraisal if the original mortgage amount is not exceeded through including the costs of the refinance in the new loan amount, a lender may require that an appraisal be provided. A borrower may not receive cash back under this program except for minor adjustments that may occur at closing; these adjustments may not exceed $250. Under the *FHA Streamline Program*, a homeowner who no longer lives in the property but has an FHA mortgage can obtain an FHA mortgage with a lower payment through a refinance as long as no closing costs are financed. Though one can refinance a conventional mortgage to an FHA with full processing, this option is not popular due to the need to pay FHA mortgage insurance.
- *Owner-occupied cash-out refinance transactions (203b)*. An existing homeowner can refinance his/her primary residence to *take cash out*, or *pull equity out*, up to 85% of the *appraised value* of the property if purchased more than one year prior or up to 85% of the *sales price* if the

---
[4] A *rate reduction* refinance transaction is a refinance of only the existing mortgage balance and allows an increase of the new mortgage amount over the existing mortgage balance only to finance, or *roll in*, the closing costs of the refinance transaction.

property was purchased less than one year prior. In other words, if a homeowner had a property worth $100,000 and a present mortgage of $50,000, the homeowner could obtain a new mortgage of $85,000. Cash-out refinance transactions are limited to homeowners who have had their present mortgage for at least six months. This is also referred to as six months *seasoning*. The growth of conventional cash-out alternatives, including second mortgages, has caused the popularity of this option to decrease.

- *Rehabilitation mortgages (203k)*. These mortgages are used for the acquisition of properties that need repairs or *rehabilitation*. The cost of rehabilitation can be included in the mortgage amount with no additional down payment required. The eligible improvements must amount to at least $5,000 under this program. Minor improvements amounting to less than $5,000 are not eligible. The lender loans enough money to acquire the property and places the excess necessary to complete the repairs in *escrow*[5]—the estimate of which is determined by plans submitted at the time of the loan application. The repair money is then released in increments, or draws, as the work is accomplished in stages. Fixed rate and adjustable rate mortgages are available under this program. Previously, investors could finance properties under this program with a larger down payment, but in October 1996, FHA declared a moratorium on the financing of investor properties using 203k. Late in 2002, FHA proposed limiting the total improvements to 20% of the maximum FHA loan amount, but this rule has not been implemented as of early in 2005.
- *Qualified veterans (203b Vet)*. FHA finances purchases for qualified veterans. This program does not differ from any other FHA program except that the minimum 3.0% cash contribution does not apply. Therefore, the seller can pay all closing costs up to the maximum of 6.0% allowed by FHA without an increased down payment required. The program is open to all veterans, but is not for active military personnel. A *Certificate of Veterans Status* from the Department of Veterans Affairs must be provided.
- *Assumptions*. FHA mortgages closed before December 1, 1986 are fully assumable by owner occupants and investors for a $125 fee. FHA mortgages closed from December 1, 1986 to December 14, 1989 are fully assumable by owner occupants but investors must pay the loan down to 75% LTV. Mortgages closed after December 15, 1989 require buyer qualification for a fee of $500. Investors cannot assume these mortgages.

Types of properties eligible for FHA

Generally, FHA programs include all properties that contain up to four units. Condominium projects must be approved by FHA for properties within the developments to obtain FHA financing. In January 2003, FHA announced it would no longer require approval of planned unit developments (PUDs). For new homes, FHA must approve the plans and specifications of the home to be financed. If the plans and specifications of the new home are not approved by FHA, the home must be covered under an FHA approved warranty program of at least one year, or the borrower must provide a minimum down payment of 10 percent. FHA does not finance farms and the land upon which the property is located cannot exceed what is necessary for *livability*.

The issue of condominium project approval is the most complex property issue associated with FHA mortgages. In general, condominium projects must adhere to the following rules:

- 70% of the project must be *sold* (the developer cannot hold more than 30% of the project, whether the project is complete or not);

---

[5] The term *escrow* refers to holding money aside in a third party account.

Chapter 2

- 100% of the common areas must be complete, or there must be approved financial protection such as *bonds* or *escrows*;
- 51% of the units must be the primary residences of the occupants (no more than 49% investor-owned units). FHA local regions have the authority to increase this requirement to 70%;
- The legal documents must be in compliance with local, state, and federal laws, with a specific reference as to compliance with FHA regulations;
- The annual budget and insurance coverage must be acceptable to FHA;
- There will be a site inspection by FHA to determine the acceptability of the facilities of the project (for example, is the roof in good maintenance?);
- If a new project, the sales must be governed by a Fair Housing Plan;
- If a conversion from rental units has occurred, the units must have been converted for at least one year before FHA lending can take place (except for existing tenants);
- An *environmental assessment* of the project must take place;
- If the project is built in legal phases, compliance may take place phase-by-phase;
- If the project is approved by the Department of Veterans Affairs (VA), an abbreviated approval process may be acceptable, but the 51% owner-occupancy and 70% presale requirements will still stand.
- In August of 1996, FHA issued procedures for condominium units to be approved on a spot basis when it appeared that the association could not make changes in the legal documents. Projects are limited in the number of units that can be "spot" approved.

FHA appraisals are called *conditional commitments* and lenders can hire staff appraisers (appraisers employed by the mortgage company) to issue the *conditional commitments*. These appraisals are valid for six months and approvals issued are called *firm commitments*, which expire when the *conditional commitments* expire. A blanket appraisal can be accomplished for a new subdivision and this is called a *master conditional commitment*, or *MCC*. In this case, FHA approves the plans and specifications for each model in the subdivision and a final inspection is accomplished when each home is completed. FHA regions no longer approve builders within a particular jurisdiction.

If the lender is *Direct Endorsement* (which means the lender approves FHA mortgages without sending the mortgage to FHA for the decision), the designated appraiser sends the appraisal directly to the lender and the lender issues the conditional commitment. Appraisers approved by FHA are said to be part of the HUD Appraisal Roster. In late 1994, FHA approved rules allowing lenders to choose their appraiser from the roster without *employing* the staff appraiser.

In 1999, FHA implemented new appraisal rules designed to increase the accuracy and thoroughness of FHA appraisals. The Valuation Condition (VC) form filled out by the appraiser clearly indicates areas that must be inspected, including: potential hazards, mechanical systems, roofs, foundations, and more. In addition, any deficiencies must be noted in a *Summary Report* prepared for the purchaser.

Mortgage types offered under FHA

FHA Mortgage Program offers several types of mortgage instruments:
- *Fixed rate mortgages.* FHA will insure fixed rate mortgages that carry anywhere from a 15 to 30 year term, although the 30-year fixed mortgage is by far the most prevalent FHA financing instrument. It is typical for FHA fixed rate mortgage pools to be securitized and sold through Ginnie Mae, which is also a Division of HUD. Until November 30, 1983, FHA published an

interest rate ceiling that was set in tandem with VA's maximum interest rate. On that date, FHA deregulated the interest rate and the rate and discount points became negotiable between the borrower and the lender. For the first time, the borrower was eligible to pay discount points.

- *Fixed rate buydowns.* FHA allows the temporary buydown of FHA fixed rate mortgages. As of July of 2004, qualification must be at the note rate of the mortgage. Increases are limited to no more than 1.0% each year. Ginnie Mae securitization requirements are different for these mortgages, therefore, the price of the FHA mortgage with a buydown may be greater than a comparable FHA fixed rate mortgage.
- *Adjustable rate mortgages (251).* FHA annually insures a limited amount of one-year adjustable rate mortgages with caps of 1.0% each year and 5.0% over the life of the mortgage. The down payment and qualification guidelines mirror those of FHA fixed rate programs. As of March 1998, FHA borrowers applying for 1-year adjustable rate mortgages must qualify at the start rate plus 1.0% if the LTV is 95% or greater. The volume of adjustable rate mortgages that FHA can insure are allocated through guidelines set up through Congress. FHA began insuring hybrid adjustable mortgages with a minimum fixed period of three years in 2004 under a pilot program authorized by Congress. The program includes 3/1, 5/1, 7/1, and 10/1 adjustables -- with 5.0% life caps (3/1 and 5/1) and 6.0% life caps (7/1 and 10/1). The 3/1 and 5/1 were originally restricted to 1.0% annual caps, however there was poor reception in the secondary market for 5/1 adjustables with such a limited annual cap after five years, so Congress authorized a change to 2.0% annual caps for the 5/1. These adjustables do not allow temporary buydowns.
- *Reverse mortgage program (255).* Home Equity Conversion Mortgages (HECM) provide equity-rich elderly homeowners with the opportunity to convert their equity into monthly income or a line of credit to help them meet living expenses while they remain in their homes (see Chapter 3). In September of 2003, FHA allowed the borrower to lock in rates at the beginning of the process rather than closing.
- *Energy Efficiency Improvements.* Under the FHA EEM Pilot Program, a borrower can finance into the mortgage 100% of the cost of eligible energy-efficient improvements. To be eligible for inclusion into the mortgage, the energy-efficient improvements must be "cost effective," i.e., the total cost of the improvements (including maintenance costs) must be less than the total present value of the energy saved over the useful life of the improvements. The mortgage includes the cost of the energy-efficient improvements in addition to the usual mortgage amount.

Costs to obtain an FHA mortgage

This section covers costs of obtaining an FHA mortgage that are unique to the FHA program.
- The downpayment requirement is described in the following table--

	FHA Maximum Loan-To-Value		
	$50,000 or less	$50,000 to $125,000	Over $125,000
Low Cost States	98.75%	97.65%	97.15%
High Cost States	98.75%	97.75%	97.75%
Required downpayment is 1.25% to 2.85%, depending upon the sales price.			
Borrower must invest at least 3.0% in the transaction (including downpayment according to maximum LTV above). The 3.0% cannot include discount points or prepaids. Seller can contribute up to 6.0% without affecting loan amount (3.0% must still be invested).			
Low Closing Cost States: Arizona, California, Colorado, Guam, Idaho, Illinois, Indiana, New Mexico, Nevada, Oregon, Utah, Virgin Islands, Washington, Wisconsin, Wyoming			

Chapter 2

- FHA mortgage insurance. FHA mortgage insurance, typically referred to as MIP, is the one closing cost that is unique to FHA mortgage programs. Every FHA mortgage must have mortgage insurance, regardless of the amount of the down payment. FHA collects mortgage insurance up-front and monthly, except for condominiums (Section 234C) and rehabilitation loans (Section 203K), which are only subject to monthly insurance costs. HUD proposed eliminating this exemption late in 2003. As of early in 2005 this change was not implemented.
  a. *Up-front premium.* Beginning January 1, 2001 the amount of the up-front mortgage insurance was lowered to 1.5% of the mortgage amount for 30 year and 15 year mortgages. The amount of FHA up-front mortgage insurance premium was 3.0% (2.0% for 15 year mortgages) for Federal Fiscal Years 1993 and 1994.[6] This premium dropped to 2.25% of the mortgage amount for FHA mortgages closed on or after April 17, 1994. The entire amount of this MIP can be financed into the loan amount. In other words:
     - If the FHA loan amount is $100,000 *(base mortgage amount)*;
     - The mortgage insurance premium would be *$1,500 ($100,000 x 1.5%)*;
     - The mortgage amount including MIP would be *$101,500 ($100,000 + $1,500) (mortgage amount including MIP)*.

  What really happens during an FHA mortgage transaction is that the borrower owes FHA a lump sum mortgage insurance premium. The lender making the FHA mortgage will actually lend the money for the premium to the borrower and send the money to FHA so that the mortgage will be insured. (FHA issues a *mortgage insurance certificate*, or *MIC*, to the lender that must be sent to Ginnie Mae as proof of insurance so the mortgage can be included with other mortgages in a *pooled mortgage security sale.*) If the mortgage is paid off before maturity, either through sale or through prepayment, FHA must refund the unused up-front MIP[7]. The amount of mortgage insurance to be refunded will decline each year (See Table 2-1). Effective with Mortgages endorsed for insurance after December 8, 2004, FHA will not refund unused up-front MIP except in cases in which the loan is refinanced into another FHA mortgage.

  b. *Monthly mortgage insurance.* There are two types of monthly mortgage insurance for FHA mortgages:
     - *Condominiums and 203K.* Since condominiums and 203K are not subject to up-front MIP, the monthly cost is stable at 0.5% over the life

Refunds of One Time FHA MIP

MIP Refunds: HUD will refund to the mortgagor unearned Mortgage Insurance Premium (MIP) if the contract of insurance is terminated before maturity of the mortgage.

Listed below are percentages of one-time Mortgage Insurance Premiums (MIP) refunded to FHA mortgagors when contract insurance is terminated (5-year schedule in effect for loans endorsed after January 1, 2001 and 3-year schedule in effect for loans endorsed after December 8, 2004).

Insurance Terminated at the End of Policy Year	7 Years	Percentage of MIP Refunded 5 Years	3 Years
1	90%	75%	58%
2	80%	55%	34%
3	60.2%	35%	10%
4	38.6%	17.5%	
5	21.8%	0%	
6	8.4%		
7	0%		

Table 2-1

---

[6] The Federal Fiscal Year runs from October 1 to September 30th. For example, the 1999 Federal Fiscal Year runs from October 1, 1998 to September 30, 1999.

[7] The refund of unused MIP must be differentiated from a refund of *distributive shares*. In the latter case, all FHA mortgages of a certain time period are put into *pools* by FHA. If there is residual money that remains at the end of the life of the pool, the money must be refunded to the borrowers. FHA discontinued the refund of distributive shares several years ago.

of the loan. HUD proposed changing this exemption in 2003.
- *All other properties.* The amount of monthly MIP and the length of the premium depend upon the amount of the down payment, or the loan-to-value. FHA loan-to-values are based on the mortgage amount divided by the acquisition cost. The acquisition cost is the sales price plus any allowable closing costs that are actually paid by the borrower. There is no current provision for removing the premium once the loan-to-value drops through prepayment except for loans closed after January 1, 2001. For 30-year mortgages closed after January 1, 2001, the premium is eliminated when the loan balance is 78% of the original purchase price, provided the premium has been paid for at least five years. Tables 2-3 and 2-4 summarize up-front and monthly MIP for FHA mortgages and give examples of how to calculate the monthly premiums.
- *FHA streamline refinances.* As discussed previously, FHA streamline refinances are simplified refinances that allow the borrower to lower the rate on current FHA mortgages with minimum documentation. Any refund of the MIP due from refinance of the old mortgage would be applied to the new MIP due. For example:
    - Original Base Mortgage Amount: *$100,000 ($102,000 with MIP)*;
    - New Base Mortgage Amount *$102,000* (rolling in closing costs);
    - MIP Refund From Previous Mortgage: *$1,000*;
    - New MIP: $102,000 x 1.5% = ($1,530 - $1,000 refund) *$530*.

FHA MORTGAGE INSURANCE CHART

| FISCAL YEARS | UPFRONT MIP | LOAN-TO-VALUES |||
		BELOW 90%	90% TO 95%	ABOVE 95%
1991 & 1992	3.8%	.50%-5 Yrs.	.50%-8 Yrs.	50%-10 Yrs.
FY 1993 UNTIL 4/17/94 – 30 yr	3.0%	.50%-7 Yrs.	.50%-12 Yrs.	.50%-30 Yrs.
FY 1993 UNTIL 4/17/94 – 15 yr	2.0%	None	.25%-4 Yrs.	.25%-8 Yrs.
4/17/94 and after – 30 yr	2.25%	.50%-7 Yrs.	.50%-12 Yrs.	50%-30 Yrs.
4/17/94 and after – 15 yr	2.0%	None	.25%-4 Yrs.	.25%-8 Yrs.
1/1/2001 and after – 30 yr	1.50%	.50%	.50%	.50%
1/1/2001 and after – 15 year	1.50%	None	.25%	.25%

NOTES:
* Monthly MIP is eliminated when loan balance is 78% of original purchase price effective with loans closed after 1/01/01 provided premium has been paid for at least five years.
* 1.75% up-front for first time homebuyers receiving housing counseling 9/22/97 to 12/31/00.
* 2.00% up-front for first time homebuyers receiving housing counseling as of 9/3/96 to 9/21/97.
* Up-front MIP is not applicable to condominiums and 203K. These loans are 50% monthly for 30 years.
* Federal Fiscal Year runs from October 1 to September 30. October 1992 started Fiscal Year 1993.
* *3.8% with no monthly MIP ended July 1, 1991.
* Lower upfront MIP for 15 year mortgages effective December 26, 1992.

Table 2-2

- *Additional Considerations.* While there are no other unusual costs associated with procuring an FHA mortgage, there are a few other rules that are interesting to note:
1. *Non-allowable FHA closing costs.* The borrower may not pay certain lender fees, e.g., tax service, underwriting fees, etc. If these fees are charged, the seller must pay these costs. The lender normally discloses these fees to the purchaser at loan application, therefore the seller may very well be surprised by his/her liability for these charges. The lender cannot charge these fees on an FHA refinance. **Continued on page 18**

Chapter 2

NATIONAL FHA MAXIMUM LOAN LIMITS

	1 Unit	2 Units	3 Units	4 Units	Percent of Conforming Limits
Base Loan Limits:	$172,632	$220,992	$267,120	$331,968	48%
Maximum High Cost:	$312,895	$400,548	$484,155	$601,692	87%

Northeast

Connecticut		New Hampshire		New York/NJ	
Bridgeport	$312,895	Manchester	290,319	SMSA	312,895
Hartford	254,600			Rochester	185,250
New Haven	290,319	New Jersey		Syracuse	172,632
New London	223,250	Atlantic City	$232,750		
Stamford	312,895	Atlantic/		Pennsylvania	
		Cape May	312,895	Allentown	$280,749
Delaware		Bergen	312,895	Harrisburg	172,632
Wilmington	$237,500	Camden	237,500	Philadelphia	237,500
		Newark	312,895	Pittsburgh	182,400
Maine		Trenton	289,750	Scranton/Wilkes	172,632
Portland	$248,900			York	182,400
		New York		Rhode Island	
Massachusetts		Albany	$172,632	Providence	$280,749
Boston	$312,895	Binghamton	172,632		
Cambridge	312,895	Buffalo	180,500		
Pittsfield	180,500	Dutchess	270,750	Vermont	
Springfield	180,500	Nassau-Suffolk	312,895	Burlington	$213,655

Southeast

Alabama		Kentucky		South Carolina	
Birmingham	$172,632	Lexington	$172,632	Charleston	$218,785
Mobile	172,632	Louisville	180,405	Columbia	172,632
Montgomery	172,632				
		Louisiana		Tennessee	
Arkansas		Baton Rouge	$172,632	Knoxville	$172,632
Little Rock	$172,632	New Orleans	172,632	Memphis	172,632
				Nashville	226,100
District of Columbia	$312,895	Maryland			
VA/MD/WVA MSA		Annapolis	$261,609	Texas	
Florida		Baltimore	261,609	Austin	$177,650
Ft Meyers	$189,050			Dallas	172,632
Ft. Lauderdale	280,000	Mississippi		Ft. Worth	172,632
Jacksonville	209,000	Jackson	$172,632	Galveston	172,632
Miami	280,000			Houston	172,632
Naples	299,250	North Carolina		Lubbock	172,632
Orlando	178,600	Asheville	$172,632	San Antonio	172,632
Sarasota	256,900	Charlotte	177,175		
Tampa	172,632	Greensboro	172,632	Virginia	
Tallahassee	172,632	Jacksonville	232,750	Norfolk/VA Beach	$285,093
West Palm Beach	280,000	Raleigh	175,600	Richmond	213,750
		Winston Salem	172,632		
Georgia				West Virginia	
Athens	$176,605	Puerto Rico		Morgantown	$173,375
Atlanta	227,905	San Juan	$247,000	Martinsburg	269,800
Brunswick	177,650			Charleston	172,632

Table 2-3

Sources of Mortgages

Midwest

Idaho		**Kansas**		**North Dakota**	
Boise City	$172,632	Topeka	$172,632	Fargo	$172,632
Blaine City	255,550	Wichita	172,632	Grand Forks	172,632
Illinois		**Michigan**		**Ohio**	
Chicago	$275,200	Ann Arbor	$226,100	Akron	$190,041
Springfield	172,632	Detroit	226,100	Cincinnati	179,091
		Flint	172,632	Cleveland	221,006
Indiana		Lansing	190,000	Columbus	208,801
Bloomington	$172,632			Dayton	181,695
Gary	275,200	**Minnesota**			
Indianapolis	175,750	Minneapolis/St. Paul	$232,750	**South Dakota**	
South Bend	172,632	Rochester	180,975	Rapid City	$172,632
				Sioux Falls	172,632
Iowa		**Missouri**			
Cedar Rapids	$172,632	Kansas City	$201,638	**Wisconsin**	
Des Moines	172,632	St. Louis	213,750	Green Bay	$172,632
Iowa City	172,632			Madison	203,200
		Nebraska		Milwaukee	194,800
		Lincoln	$172,632	Racine	184,300
		Omaha	172,632		

West

Alaska		**Colorado**		**Oregon**	
Anchorage	$228,950	Boulder	$290,319	Bend	$217,265
Juneau	219,900	Colorado Springs	206,798	Corvallis	222,205
		Denver	261,609	Eugene	172,900
Arizona		Ft Collins	212,800	Portland	213,750
Phoenix	$172,632			Medford	237,500
Tucson	172,632	**Hawaii**			
Flagstaff	204,250	Honolulu	$469,344	**Utah**	
		Kapaa	403,750	Provo	$175,750
California		Maui County	289,750	Salt Lake City	232,750
Bakersfield	$180,405			St George	180,405
Fresno	224,200	**Montana**			
Los Angeles	312,895	Billings	$172,632	**Washington**	
Long Beach	312,895	Missoula	182,250	Bremerton	$211,850
Modesto	275,500			Bellingham	202,113
Oakland	312,895	**Nevada**		Seattle	288,700
Orange County	312,895	Carson City	$253,650	Spokane	172,632
Sacramento	312,895	Las Vegas	269,000	Tacoma	288,700
Salinas	312,895	Reno	284,200	Olympia	185,155
Santa Barbara	312,895				
San Bernadino	196,100	**New Mexico**		**Wyoming**	
San Francisco	312,895	Albuquerque	$172,632	Cheyenne	172,632
San Diego	312,895	Los Alamos	242,250		
San Jose	312,895	Santa Fe	290,319		
San Luis	312,895				
Santa Cruz	312,895	**Oklahoma**			
Santa Rosa	312,895	Oklahoma City	$172,632		
Vallejo	312,895	Tulsa	172,632		
Ventura	312,895				

Note: This chart represents a sample of major metropolitan areas designated high cost areas and published by FHA Central office as of January of 2005. It does not represent all high cost areas designated by FHA at that time. Regional FHA offices may publish increased limits before the FHA Central office. Maximum limits are 1.5% higher in Alaska, Hawaii, Guam and the Virgin Islands ($464,344, $600,822; $726,232; $902,538).

Table 2-3 (Continued)

2. *Seller Contributions.* The seller is not allowed to *contribute* more than 6.0% of the sales price toward the borrower's closing costs. Allowable seller *contributions* include: discount points, prepaids, closing costs, and funds toward a temporary buydown. Any contribution over the 6% limit decreases the sales price as a basis for figuring the maximum FHA mortgage amount (in effect, this increases the down payment to the purchaser).
3. *Grant Programs.* FHA allows the downpayment to come from a grant from a non-profit agency. To fund the down payments on FHA mortgages, the non-profit typically allow contributions from the seller. It is the seller's "participation" that enables the non-profit agency to fund these grants, though the money may not be distributed directly from the seller to the purchaser.
4. *Lender paid closing costs.* The borrower may opt for a higher interest rate that will enable the lender to give a credit towards the borrower's closing costs. This does not affect the required FHA down payment in any way, unless the discount points to the seller are increased to accommodate this credit. For example:
   - Lender Interest Rate Quote: *6.00%* with one point
   - Closing Cost Credit Quote: *6.50%* with one point credit
   - If Mortgage is $100,000:   Credit *$1,000* towards closing costs
5. *FHA prepayments.* During the payoff of an FHA mortgage, the lender has the right to collect interest to the end of the month in which the payoff occurs. This differs from conventional mortgages in which interest collection stops the day the lender receives the payoff amount. This is important to note because a homeowner selling or refinancing a home with an FHA mortgage should schedule the closing towards the end of the month, but not the last day because this may not leave enough time for the closing agent to get the payoff to the present lender. If the payoff is received by the lender one day late (the first of the next month), the lender will be entitled to charge an extra month's interest.

FHA qualification requirements

The qualification requirements for FHA mortgages are less stringent than comparable conventional mortgages. The following differences highlight the extent of this leniency:

- *Qualification ratios.* While standard conventional qualification ratios are 28/36, FHA allows a housing ratio of 29% and a debt ratio of 41%. On January 27, 1995, FHA published Mortgage Letter 95-7 that stated its intention for these ratios to be guidelines only. In addition, FHA publishes specific *compensating factors* by which these ratios may be exceeded:
  - A conservative attitude towards the use of credit and demonstrated ability to accumulate reserves, resulting in a minimum of three months mortgage reserves after closing.
  - A minimum of 10% cash investment in the property.
  - A small (not more than 10%) increase in housing expense.
  - The borrower receives compensation not reflected in the effective income, but directly affecting the ability to pay the mortgage and other obligations.
  - A considerable amount of effective income comes from non-taxable sources.
  - Income of a temporary nature, while not considered effective, may be considered available to meet short-term non-recurring charges.
  - The term of the mortgage is less (by five years or more) than the maximum available.
  - Smaller families whose living needs permit them to live on less than larger families.
  - The ratios may be exceeded by 2% when the dwelling has been identified as energy efficient.

- A down payment of 25% or more decreases the importance of ratio calculations.

It should be noted that most FHA mortgages are now underwritten through automated underwriting systems and these systems may approve ratios significantly higher than 29/41 when positive factors such as high credit scores exist.

- *Cash requirements are less.* The cash requirements for an FHA transaction are less than those for a comparable conventional transaction:
  1. FHA requires less than the typical 5.0% down payment required on conventional mortgages. Conventional mortgages requiring less than 5.0% down typically require higher credit scores, a higher interest rate, and/or maximum income limits. FHA does not require minimum credit scores, though low credit scores will significantly affect the results of automated underwriting systems. In May of 2004, FHA required the use of its TOTAL Mortgage Scorecard as a tool to evaluate the results of automated underwriting systems.
  2. FHA does not require two months cash reserves. Three months reserves are required on 2-4 unit properties.[8] These reserves cannot come from a gift.
  3. All cash may come from a gift from an immediate family member, or someone with a *family-type* relationship. Many conventional mortgages require 5.0% of the cash to be from the purchaser's own funds. Gifts from a bridal registry or other legitimate occasion where substantial gifts are typically received are allowed, if deposited in a supervised account.
  4. The funds for down payment and closing costs can be borrowed, but the loan must be secured and the borrower must qualify for the additional monthly payments. Funds for the downpayment can be borrowed unsecured from an immediate family member or be provided by a non-profit or government agency.
  5. All mortgage insurance can be financed in the mortgage amount rather than paid in cash.
- *FHA co-borrower rules.* FHA allows co-borrowers to help qualify for the mortgage and these co-borrowers do not have to live in the property (one unit properties only).[9] The co-borrower must be an immediate family member or have a *family-type* relationship, and cannot contribute the vast majority of resources (cash and income) to the transaction. In other words, it must make sense that the occupant can make the payments and that the co-borrower is not an investor. The property must be one unit if the LTV is over 75% and a non-owner occupant co-borrower is being used.

FHA Monthly MIP Factors
Monthly MIP Payment per $1,000 of Loan Amount

Interest Rate	30 Year 0.50%	15 Year 0.25%
4.0%	0.4133	0.2036
4.5%	0.4136	0.2038
5.0%	0.4139	0.2040
5.5%	0.4141	0.2042
6.0%	0.4143	0.2043
6.5%	0.4146	0.2045
7.0%	0.4148	0.2046
7.5%	0.4149	0.2048
8.0%	0.4151	0.2049
8.5%	0.4152	0.2051
9.0%	0.4154	0.2052
9.5%	0.4155	0.2054
10.0%	0.4156	0.2055

To calculate monthly MIP, multiply the loan amount, in thousands, by the factor from the table. For example, a $100,000, 30 year loan at 7.5% would be 100 x 0.4149 = $41,49 monthly MIP.

Table 2-4

---

[8] 15 Days prepaid interest must be made a part of the required cash for qualification purposes. In other words, the lender must assume that the closing will take place in the middle part of the month.
[9] They are therefore referred to as non-owner occupant co-borrowers.

- *Non-citizens.* Borrowers do not have to have a *green card*[10] to receive an FHA mortgage. They must have a valid social security number and must be in the country legally. The social security number will be validated by FHA.
- *Second mortgages.* Governmental agencies may lend money for second mortgages to defray the purchase costs for qualified purchasers. Otherwise, FHA is more stringent than most mortgage programs with respect to the placing of the second mortgage behind an FHA mortgage during a purchase transaction. FHA does allow the placing of a second mortgage but:
  1. The combination of the first and second mortgage cannot lower the required down payment or raise the maximum mortgage amount. Therefore, the second mortgage will save the purchaser no cash at settlement.
  2. Regardless of the loan-to-value due to the existence of the second mortgage, the purchaser must still pay FHA mortgage insurance.
  3. The combined mortgage amount of the first and second trust cannot exceed FHA maximum mortgage limits set in the local jurisdiction.

  In other words, there is no advantage to placing a second mortgage behind an FHA first mortgage during a purchase transaction. There are no restrictions regarding placing a second mortgage behind an FHA mortgage when the FHA mortgage is being assumed by the purchaser of the property. This practice is quite common because it lessens the cash required for purchase assumption transactions.
- *Disadvantages.* No loan program comes without disadvantages. FHA mortgages are less advantageous than conventional alternatives when a larger down payment is made (or there is significant equity in a refinance) because mortgage insurance is always required. FHA also requires many forms in addition to forms required by conventional alternatives (see Chapter 7). One form, the Homebuyer Summary, essentially asks the appraiser to certify that many aspects of the home are working and/or in good condition. With this level of review, more conditions are expected on the FHA appraisals.

The Department of Veterans Affairs (VA)

The VA program was established in 1944 to provide for the veteran by guarantying against foreclosure a portion of mortgage loans procured through the program. The word "guaranty" is very important in this regard. Unlike FHA mortgages that are insured against default in a program paid for by the users of that program:

- The VA program is not an insurance program, but a benefit program for veterans. Throughout its history, VA losses are not offset by insurance premiums. It was only later in the program history that VA began collecting a *Funding Fee* to offset administrative expenses.
- The VA program guaranties only a *portion* of the mortgage against default while an FHA mortgage is 100% insured against default. If the loss in a foreclosure process exceeds the amount of the VA mortgage guaranty, the lender is at risk. Basically, when a VA mortgage goes into default, VA has the option of taking over the problem by auctioning the house and paying off the lender, or remitting to the lender the amount of guaranty in cash and letting the lender dispose of the property. The latter situation is called a *VA no-bid*. Congress sets the formula by which VA determines which defaults result in *no-bids*. VA lending has become more risky than FHA lending because the lender is giving *recourse*, or is at-risk for future losses beyond those

---

[10] A green card is a document that makes a non-citizen residing in the United States a resident alien, or one who can reside in the United States.

covered with the VA guaranty. Because of this extra risk, it is not unusual for lenders to charge higher points for VA mortgages as compared to FHA. Other lenders have added qualification standards that exceed VA minimums.
- The VA home loan program benefits a specific population group comprising veterans, active military and the members of the armed forces reserves. FHA is geared to benefit the population as a whole. Like FHA, VA does not provide funds for the mortgage—it just facilitates lending by providing assurance against default.

Who is eligible to obtain VA mortgages?

Any Veteran who served on continuous active duty for the number of days required during the time frames listed below and has received an honorable release or discharge is eligible for the program:

World War II	9/16/40 to 7/25/47	90 Days
Pre-Korean	7/26/47 to 6/26/50	181 Days
Korean Conflict	6/27/50 to 1/31/55	90 Days
Post Korean	2/01/55 to 8/04/64	181 Days
Vietnam Conflict	8/05/64 to 5/07/75	90 Days
Post Vietnam	5/08/75 to 9/07/80	181 Days (Enlisted)
	5/08/75 to 10/16/81	181 Days (Officers)
Enter After	9/07/80	24 Months (Enlisted)
	10/16/81	24 Months (Officers)
Persian Gulf	8/2/90 on	2 Years or Period called to active duty (not less than 90 days)

Note: If applicants are active military personnel, they need to have served 181 days to be eligible. If they are separated from service, they need to have had 24 months continuous duty to be eligible.

In addition, the following are also eligible:
- Commissioned Public Health Officers, National Oceanic and Atmospheric Administration Officers, Environmental Science Service Administration Officers, and Coast and Geodetic Survey Officers.
- A veteran discharged because of service related disability without minimum qualifying time may still be eligible.
- A surviving spouse (not remarried) of a veteran who died, either in service or after separation, as a result of a service connected injury or disease.
- Under the Veterans Home Loan Program Amendments of 1992, individuals who have completed a total of at least six years in the Reserves or National Guard.[11]

There is no limit to the number of VA mortgages a veteran can obtain as long as there is remaining *guaranty* or *eligibility* for each mortgage. Funding fee schedules indicate a higher cost for second time usage. There are some exceptions to the 24-month rule for reductions in force and other discharges for the convenience of the government.

---

[11] This eligibility was extended through September 30, 2007. Those eligible under this provision are subject to a higher funding fee.

Chapter 2

Types of transactions financed under VA

Owner-occupied purchase transactions. The vast majority of VA mortgages are owner-occupied purchase transactions. The purpose of the program is to assist the veteran in obtaining housing.

Owner-occupied refinance transactions. Veterans can refinance their present mortgages for the purpose of lowering the interest rate or taking equity out of the property. The maximum loan-to-value on these transactions is 90%. The veteran must have *guaranty* or *entitlement* that was not previously utilized in the procurement of a VA mortgage. The maximum mortgage amount for these loans is $144,000

Interest rate reduction refinances. A veteran can refinance his/her present VA mortgage to reduce the interest rate[12] under the *VA Interest Rate Reduction Loan (IRRL) Program*. The veteran need not still live in the home to effect an interest rate reduction refinance, and a new guaranty is not necessary. VA does not require the verification of income or a new appraisal on these *Interest Rate Reduction Loans* though lenders may require a new appraisal. All closing costs can be rolled into the new loan amount under this refinance program. VA issued a rule in early 1996 directing that lenders charge no more than two discount points on VA refinances. If the loan exceeds two discount points, a statement must be signed by the borrower and the amount exceeding two points must be paid in cash.

Assumptions. VA mortgages are freely assumable at the same rate and terms, with a credit check required for mortgages closed after March 1, 1988, but the veteran will not receive his/her eligibility back without a substitution of entitlement. For processing assumptions, the lender can charge $300, and 0.5% is charged by VA for a funding fee. The fee is $45 for loans closed before March 1, 1988. Owner occupants or investors can assume VA mortgages. The VA assumption fee was raised to 1.0% from 0.5% December 13, 2002 for one year to offset the cost of the hybrid ARM pilot program.

Types of properties eligible for VA

The types of properties eligible for VA financing mirror FHA programs for the most part:
- 1-4 unit single-family properties. Unlike FHA, the maximum mortgage amount is not increased for multiple unit properties.
- Properties located in planned unit developments (PUDs).
- Properties located in condominium developments.

Condominium developments have to be approved by VA and the guidelines are similar to those employed by FHA. The most pronounced exception is the fact that VA does not have a 51% owner-occupancy requirement for condominium projects and VA does not require environmental assessments for condominiums. In September of 2000, the VA lender handbook was updated to eliminate the requirement that planned unit developments need VA approval.

VA appraisals are called *Certificates of Reasonable Value*, or CRVs, and appraisals of new projects are called *Master Certificates of Reasonable Value*, or MCRVs. These appraisals are valid for a six-month period upon issuance. New homes must have plans and specifications approved directly by VA, however a small number of homes can be allowed on a *spot* basis with an approved homeowners warranty program. In these cases the appraisal would be ordered at what is called the

---

[12] A requires that the new payment be lower. The veteran can move to a 15-year mortgage which increases payments under this refinance program. A veteran may refinance out of an ARM even if the new payment is higher the lender must certify that the veteran is able to make the new payment in cases where the PITI is increased by 20% or more.

customer preference stage. At this stage the home is completely finished, except for items the purchaser chooses: carpet, tile, appliances, etc. After these items are installed, a final inspection is ordered and performed by VA. Exceptions to the warranty rule can be made on a spot basis if the builder is not more than occasionally involved with VA financing and certain acknowledgements are made by the veteran.

Unlike FHA, VA does not allow staff appraisers employed by the lender. Under a program called *LAPP (Lender Appraisal Processing Program)*, the appraiser sends the appraisal directly to the lender to process. Under normal VA procedures, all appraisals are sent to the Property Valuation Section of VA and VA issues the appraisal, or CRV. The lender can issue its approval after receiving the appraisal if the lender is a VA Automatic lender. In 2002, VA announced that 53% of eligible loans were processed using the LAPP appraisal procedures.

Mortgage types offered under VA

Fixed rates. By far the most prevalent VA mortgages are 30 year fixed rates. Until November of 1992, VA set an interest rate ceiling that could be charged to the veteran for all VA mortgages except for refinances. The veteran was also not allowed to pay any discount points charged in connection with the mortgage. Under the Veterans Home Loan Program Amendments of 1992, this interest rate ceiling was lifted and veterans were permitted to pay discount points directly.[13]

Temporary buydowns. Temporary buydowns of VA fixed rate mortgages have not been popular in the past few years. The reasons for this are:
- *Qualification.* VA does not allow qualification at the bought down rate unless it can be proven that the income will increase in the future. Cost of living increases are specifically excluded and the increase must be proven. VA will allow the lower payment to offset a debt payment that will be paid off in the near future.
- *Point premium.* Like FHA buydowns, Ginnie Mae treats buydowns differently for securitization purposes and this can result in a premium in addition to the actual cost of the buydown.

VA ARMs. Under the Veterans Home Loan Program Amendments of 1992, Congress authorized a test program to offer one-year adjustable rate mortgages that are identical to those offered under the FHA mortgage program (1% adjustment cap and 5% life cap with a "T" Bill index). The veteran is qualified at 1% over the initial interest rate. The authority expired in 1995 and was not renewed by Congress until December 2004. In December 2002 Congress authorized the creation a new pilot program to test hybrid ARMs (such as a 3/1) that were similar in characteristics to the new FHA hybrid ARMs.

Energy efficient mortgages. The 1992 Amendments also authorized the financing of improvements to properties to make the property energy efficient. From $3,000 to $6,000 (depending upon the degree of utility savings) can be added to the mortgage for these improvements for purchase and refinance transactions. This provision can be utilized even if the veteran is financing the maximum amount for which he/she is eligible.

Maximum VA mortgage amount

VA does not actually set a mortgage limit—it limits the amount of *guaranty* that can be extended for each mortgage. This guaranty allows for no-down-payment loans of up to the

---

[13] Under the rules implementing this legislation, veterans were not allowed to roll in the cost of discount points in VA refinance transactions. This rule has since been rescinded.

Chapter 2

conforming limit as of January of 2005. As the maximum conforming loan amount rises, so does the maximum VA mortgage amount. Conforming limits are 50% higher in Alaska, Hawaii, Guam and the U.S. Virgin Islands and these higher limits also apply to VA.

Costs to obtain a VA mortgage

Down payment. It is within the discussion of down payment that we must advance and define the concept of the words *guaranty*, *eligibility*, and *entitlement* that keep turning up within our exploration of VA mortgages. Basically, each veteran is *eligible* or *entitled* to have a certain portion of a VA mortgage *guarantied* against default. Usually, 25% of the mortgage amount is guarantied by VA. This guaranty serves as a substitute for cash equity in the eyes of the lender because the lender knows VA will send the equivalent in cash if the mortgage defaults. Therefore, the amount of guaranty will allow a maximum VA mortgage without a down payment by the Veteran.

Example:
If the Veteran has *eligibility* for a *$70,000 guaranty*, the maximum VA mortgage without a down payment would be:
$70,000 x 4 = *$280,000* (This means that VA will guaranty 25% of $280,000, or $70,000.)

How do we determine how much entitlement a veteran currently has? Basically, if the veteran never has used his/her VA eligibility in the past, the veteran would have a maximum entitlement of twenty-five percent of the conforming limit. If the veteran had a VA mortgage in the past and did not regain the used entitlement,[14] the veteran would have lost a certain amount of guaranty. Congress has periodically increased the guaranty throughout the history of the VA mortgage program. The amount of increase would give the veteran, who has already used all or most of his/her entitlement, what is called a *partial entitlement*.

For example:
- If a veteran purchased a home in 1979 for *$100,000*, the veteran would have used *$25,000* in entitlement.
- In 1988 the entitlement was increased to *$36,000*, giving the veteran a partial entitlement of *$11,000*.
- In 1989 the entitlement was increased to *$46,000* (1994 to *$50,750*, and in 2001 to $60,000, but only for the purpose of purchasing a home with a sales price greater than *$144,000*). Therefore, the partial remains at *$11,000* for a sales price below *$144,000* and *$35,000* for the purchase of a home over *$144,000*.
- In 2005 the entitlement was increased to 25.0% of the conforming limit.

The veteran can purchase a second home under the VA mortgage program without disposing of the first home as long as the next purchase is also for an owner-occupied home (the first home would have to be converted to a rental property), and as long as the new home has at least 25% in guaranty by VA or cash down payment by the veteran. In the above example, the veteran has only a partial of $35,000 and can only purchase four times that amount with no money down. Therefore, the veteran would have to make a 25% down payment for any portion of the sales price above $140,000.

---

[14] A veteran regains used entitlement in one of two ways. The most common method is reinstatement, which means that the property is sold and the mortgage is paid off (both events must occur). In October 1994 Public Law 103-446 was passed which allowed a one time only restoration for a veteran whose loan has been paid in full but had not disposed of the property. The second method is substitution of eligibility, which means that the home is sold and the VA mortgage is assumed by another veteran who substitutes his/her eligibility of an equal amount during the process of assuming the mortgage. In either case, if the veteran is selling his/her home and purchasing another, back-to-back settlements are not usually possible because the certificate of eligibility (COE) must be updated. In a back-to-back settlement, the home seller leaves one settlement table to go to the next settlement as the purchaser of another home on the same day.

The formula for figuring the maximum mortgage amount with partial entitlement would be:

Sales Price x 75% + Eligibility = Maximum Mortgage Amount

$160,000 x 75% = $120,000 + $35,000 = $155,000 ($5,000 down payment)

The amount of entitlement is designated on a VA form called a *Certificate of Eligibility*, or *COE*. This form is obtained through each Regional VA Office and can be updated every time there is a change in entitlement.

Funding fee. Though the VA mortgage program is not financed through user paid insurance, the veteran must pay a *funding fee* to reimburse the VA for the cost of administering the program. Effective October 1, 1993 veterans using their VA eligibility for a second time must pay a higher fee. The cost of the funding fee stated as a percent of the mortgage amount effective October 1, 2004 is as follows:

2.15% (2.40% Reservists) (3.30% Multiple Users)	-	For purchase mortgages with less than a 5% down payment. For all refinances except VA Interest Rate Reduction Refinance Mortgages.
1.50% (1.75% Reservists) (1.50% Multiple Users)	-	For purchase mortgages with at least 5% down, but less than a 10% down payment.
	-	1.75 for multiple use for reservists
1.25% (1.50% Reservists) (1.25% Multiple Users)	-	For purchase mortgages with at least a 10% down payment.
	-	1.50 for multiple use for reservists
.50%	-	For Interest Rate Reduction Refinance Mortgages including Reservists.
2.15%	-	Cash-out refinances first time use
(2.40% Reservists)	-	Cash-out refis are 3.3% for subsequent use for all users
1.00%	-	Manufactured homes
0.50%	-	Loan Assumptions

VA allows the funding fee to be financed into the mortgage amount without affecting the amount of eligibility.

Example:
Sales Price: *$100,000*
Mortgage Amount: *$100,000*
Amount of Funding Fee: *2.15%, or $2,150*
Mortgage Including Funding Fee: *$102,150*

Veterans receiving VA disability are eligible to have their funding fee waived by VA. The lender sends a *VA Indebtedness Letter* to VA to certify that the veteran does not have any outstanding obligations to the Department of Veterans Affairs. If evidence of VA disability is attached to this form, VA will indicate the exemption from the VA funding fee.

Non-allowable VA closing costs. Like FHA, VA does not allow the veteran to pay miscellaneous fees above and beyond the loan origination fee. Therefore, on purchase transactions the tax service, lender inspection, and other fees will typically be paid by the seller. These fees cannot be charged on refinances.

Chapter 2

The seller can pay all discount points, temporary buydown funds, closing costs, and prepaids associated with the transaction. With no down payment and the seller paying all closing costs, the veteran can literally move in with no cash utilized in the transaction. There is a limit of 4% of the sales price that the seller can *contribute* towards the borrower's costs in the transaction, however typical discount points and closing costs do not count towards the 4% limitation.

VA qualification requirements

VA makes home buying more affordable and achievable for veterans in several ways:
- *Residual method.* VA is the only major mortgage source that continues to use the *residual method* of qualification. The *residual method* figures qualification by subtracting all expected expenses from a veteran's income. If the *residual figure* is positive, the veteran qualifies. If the *residual figure* is negative, the veteran does not qualify. Generally, the residual method is an easier qualification standard than the widely utilized ratio method. A more in-depth discussion of this concept can be found in Chapter 4, *Qualifying For A Mortgage*.
- *Higher ratios.* VA also applies a second qualification standard: a *debt ratio* of 41%, that coincides with FHA's second ratio. Generally, if the second ratio exceeds 41% the lender must have compensating factors to approve the loan. This would include recalculation of the residual method to determine if the residual remains positive after 20% is added to the family support category. With most conventional standards employing a 36% debt ratio, the second standard of VA qualification remains more liberal than comparable conventional mortgages.
- *Cash requirements.* The cash requirement for a VA mortgage is less than any other major mortgage source:
  - No down payment is required.
  - The VA funding fee can always be financed.
  - The seller can pay for all closing costs and prepaids.
  - There is no requirement for cash reserves after closing.
  - The veteran can receive gift funds for any and all cash requirements.
  - The veteran can borrow on unsecured terms for any cash requirements, except to pay above the appraised value of the property if the sales price exceeds the appraised value.

Not all qualification requirements for VA mortgages are less stringent than conventional mortgages. There are some standards that are very strict:
- *Co-borrower requirements.* Since the VA mortgage program is a benefit program for veterans, it is quite understandable that the participation of *non-veterans* is restricted. Non-owner occupant co-borrowers are strictly forbidden in the VA mortgage program. There are basically only two classes of owner-occupant co-borrowers that are allowed:
  1. The spouse of the veteran is an eligible co-borrower. In addition, if the spouse of the veteran is also an eligible veteran, either entitlement can be utilized to acquire the VA mortgage.
  2. Another eligible veteran. Two non-related veterans can purchase a home together if they both are going to live in the house. In this case, a portion of the entitlement will be utilized by both veterans. These mortgages must be approved directly by VA, even if the lender has VA automatic authority.
  3. Non-veterans (not a spouse). Though VA may approve a loan purchased with a non-veteran, these loans are not likely to be guaranteed in full and therefore not eligible to be

purchased by Ginnie Mae. Because the loan cannot be sold, most lenders will not be able to make such a loan.
- *Secondary financing.* A second mortgage behind a VA first mortgage is not allowed to decrease the cash down payment required by the veteran (if there is one). For example, if the veteran has remaining eligibility of $15,000 and the sales price is $100,000:

    $100,000 x 75% = $75,000 + $15,000 = $90,000 maximum mortgage
    $100,000 - $90,000 = $10,000 minimum down payment

The VA mortgage is $90,000. The $10,000 must be in cash. A second trust is not allowed to "lower" the down payment:
The following configuration is not allowable:
$90,000 First Mortgage
5,000 Second Mortgage "90-5-5"
5,000 Down Payment

State and local bond issues

Financing for homes is provided by State and local governments through the Federal Bond Subsidy Act. This legislation authorizes these governments to issue tax-free bonds to the public. The purchasers of these bonds receive income at a specified interest rate, but the interest income earned is not taxable by state and federal governments. Because of the bonds' *tax-free* status, the interest rates paid by the governments can be less than what is paid by banks and other interest rate denominated investments. These lower interest rate bonds finance mortgages that also carry below market interest rates.

These below market rate mortgages are available to first-time homebuyers[15] whose income is not more than 100% of the median income for the area (moderate income), or 80% of the income for the area (low income). The local agency may offer lower interest rates to low income individuals.

The sales prices for the homes are limited to 90% of the average area purchase price[16] applicable for such homes. Typically, there may exist separate maximum sales prices for new homes and existing homes. There also is usually a limitation as to the allowable cash assets of the participants in the programs.

History of VA Entitlement	
$4,000	World War II
$7,500	Increase 7/12/50
$12,500	Increase 5/7/68
$25,000	Increase 10/2/78
$27,500	Increase 10/1/80
$36,000	Increase 2/1/88
$46,000	Increase 12/18/89*
$50,750	Increase 10/13/94*
$60,000	Increase 12/27/01*
$89,912	Increase 01/01/05**

VA will currently guaranty:
- 50% of mortgages up to $45,000
- $22,500 maximum for mortgages over $45,000 and up to $56,250
- The lesser of $36,000 or 40% of the mortgage for mortgages of $56,250 up to $144,000
- The lesser of $50,750 or 25% of the mortgage for mortgages over $144,000*
- The lesser of $60,000 or 25% of the mortgage for mortgages over $144,000*

*The increase is only for purchases over $144,000
**1/4 of the conforming limit of $359,650

Table 2-5

Continued on page 29

---

[15] By definition, a first time homebuyer is one who has not had an interest in real property for the previous three years.
[16] The term *acquisition cost* is utilized in the legislation to ensure that the maximum sales price is not exceeded by the purchase of an unfinished property. The *acquisition cost* is defined as the purchase price and the estimated cost to finish the property. This *acquisition cost* cannot exceed the maximum sales price.

Chapter 2

30 YEAR MORTGAGE RATE CHANGES – A 50+ YEAR HISTORY

Effective Date	Percent	Effective Date	Percent	Effective Date	Percent
April 24, 1950	4%	March 9, 1981	14%	June 2, 1989	10%
April 2, 1953	4 1/2%	April 13, 1981	14 1/2%	July 17, 1989	9 1/2%
December 3, 1956	5%	May 8, 1981	15 1/2%	February 23, 1990	10%
August 5, 1957	5 1/4%	August 17, 1981	16 1/2%	November 19, 1990	9 1/2%
September 23, 1959	5 3/4%	September 14, 1981	17 1/2%	February 5, 1991	9%
February 2, 1961	5 1/2%	October 12, 1981	16 1/2%	June 17, 1991	9 1/2%
May 29, 1961	5 1/4%	November 16, 1981	15 1/2%	August 12, 1991	9%
February 7, 1966	5 1/2%	January 25, 1982	16 1/2%	September 18, 1991	8 1/2%
April 11, 1966	5 3/4%	March 2, 1982	15 1/2%	December 20, 1991	8%
October 3, 1966	6%	August 9, 1982	15%	February 24, 1992	8 1/2%
May 7, 1968	6 3/4%	August 24, 1982	14%	July 6, 1992	8%
January 24, 1969	7 1/2%	September 24, 1982	13 1/2%	August 12, 1992	7 1/2%
January 5, 1970	8 1/2%	October 12, 1982	12 1/2%	October 28, 1992	VA Rate Deregulated
December 2, 1970	8%	November 15, 1982	12%	*November 1992	8.31%
January 13, 1971	7 1/2%	July 11, 1983	12 1/2%	January 1993	7.99%
January 18, 1971	7%	May 9, 1983	11 1/2%	July 1993	7.21%
August 10, 1973	7 3/4%	June 8, 1983	12%	January 1994	7.07%
August 25, 1973	8 1/2%	August 1, 1983	13 1/2%	July 1994	8.61%
January 22, 1974	8 1/4%	August 23, 1983	13%	January 1995	9.15%
April 15, 1974	8 1/2%	November 1, 1983	12 1/2%	July 1995	7.61%
May 13, 1974	8 3/4%	November 30, 1983	FHA Rate Deregulated	January 1996	7.03%
July 5, 1974	9%	March 21, 1984	13%	July 1996	8.25%
August 14, 1974	9 1/2%	May 8, 1984	13 1/2%	January 1997	7.82%
November 24, 1974	9%	June 8, 1984	14%	July 1997	7.50%
January 21, 1975	8 1/2%	August 13, 1984	13 1/2%	January 1998	6.99%
March 3, 1975	8%	October 22, 1984	13%	July 1998	6.95%
April 28, 1975	8 1/2%	November 21, 1984	12 1/2%	January 1999	6.79%
September 3, 1975	9%	March 25, 1985	13%	July 1999	7.63%
January 3, 1976	8 3/4%	April 19, 1985	12 1/2%	January 2000	8.21%
March 30, 1976	8 1/2%	May 21, 1985	12%	July 2000	8.15%
October 18, 1976	8%	June 5, 1985	11 1/2%	January 2001	7.03%
May 31, 1977	8 1/2%	November 20, 1985	11%	July 2001	7.13%
February 28, 1978	8 3/4%	December 13, 1985	10 1/2%	January 2002	7.00%
May 23, 1978	9%	March 3, 1986	9 1/2%	July 2002	6.49%
June 29, 1978	9 1/2%	November 24, 1986	9%	January 2003	5.92%
April 23, 1979	10%	January 19, 1987	8 1/2%	July 2003	5.63%
September 26, 1979	10 1/2%	April 10, 1987	9 1/2%	January 2004	5.71%
October 26, 1979	11 1/2%	May 5, 1987	10%	July 2004	6.06%
February 11, 1980	12%	September 4, 1987	10 1/2%	January 2005	5.71%
February 28, 1980	13%	October 5, 1987	11%		
April 4, 1980	14%	November 10, 1987	10 1/2%		
April 28, 1980	13%	February 1, 1988	9 1/2%		
May 15, 1980	11 1/2%	April 3, 1988	10%		
August 20, 1980	12%	May 20, 1988	10 1/2%		
September 22, 1980	13%	November 1, 1988	10%		
November 24, 1980	13 1/2%	December 19, 1988	10 1/2%		

Note: Following the VA maximum interest rate over the years provides a good insight to the movement of interest rates during the "modern era" of mortgage lending. *After deregulation of the maximum VA interest rate, the number provided from November 1992 forward is the Federal Home Loan Mortgage Corporation (Freddie Mac) Primary Mortgage Market Survey for 30-year fixed mortgages (does not include average points charged).

Table 2-6

Sources of Mortgages

There are *targeted areas* that are qualified census tracts, or areas of chronic economic distress in which 70% or more of the families have income 80% or less of the statewide median family level. In these areas the interest rate may be lower, or there may be leniency in one or more of the qualification rules or eligibility standards necessary to procure the mortgages. These include exceptions to the first time homebuyer requirement, and increased sales prices up to 110% of the average purchase price of the area. At least 20% of a particular bond issue must be available for lending within targeted areas.

Who is eligible for bond issues?

The eligibility standards may vary from program to program, but minimum standards include the principal residence of buyers who have not had an ownership interest in real property for the previous three years. The income of these buyers cannot exceed 100% of the median area income and there are maximum cash asset requirements. Later in this Chapter we present a chart of the medium income limits for major areas within the United States.

Types of transactions financed

Generally, lending is limited to owner-occupied purchase transactions. Refinances are prohibited. However, there are provisions for the agencies to issue loans for the rehabilitation of properties and home improvement loans.

Types of properties eligible

Generally, any types of properties that can be financed through FHA and VA can be financed through these programs, including condominium projects and planned unit developments. The home cannot be utilized for the generation of income. While the agencies may enforce this restriction differently, the regulations state that if over 15% of the home is utilized for business, the home would not qualify for financing. Two to four unit properties are not excluded, yet the maximum sales price is not increased for these properties. It is expected that the square footage dedicated to rental income would provide a problem concerning the aforementioned restriction regarding business use of the home.

Mortgage types offered

It would be unusual for anything other than a fixed rate mortgage and a temporary buydown of that fixed rate mortgage to be offered. Each bond issue would typically carry one or two rate and point options.

Some programs offer second mortgages that can lessen the cash requirements of a first mortgage program. The first mortgage might also be offered under a Bond Program, or the first mortgage may be an FHA, VA, or Conventional mortgage. Fannie Mae, Freddie Mac, and FHA have special provisions of their low-to-moderate income programs that allow the borrower to procure some portion of the necessary cash from a local or state jurisdiction—either as a loan, grant or a secured second mortgage.

Many of the mortgages offered under this program can be insured by FHA or guaranteed by VA. In effect, FHA or VA mortgages are offered, but a government agency is lowering the interest rate and providing the funds. In these cases, the borrower must meet the eligibility guidelines of the *Federal Bond Subsidy Act*, the local governmental entity, and the qualification guidelines of FHA or VA.

Chapter 2

Maximum mortgage amounts

The maximum mortgage amount will be governed by the sales price limitations in each jurisdiction. If the maximum sales price is $100,000 and the program requires a 5% down payment, then the maximum mortgage amount in this case will be $95,000, plus any mortgage insurance or funding fee that can be financed.

Costs to obtain a bond issue mortgage

The costs to obtain mortgages originated under the *Federal Bond Subsidy Act* will vary from program to program but the most common variations are as follows:

- *Down payments.* Required down payments vary from as much as five percent for those programs insured by conventional private mortgage insurance, to zero down payment for VA guaranteed mortgages and local entities that offer government sponsored mortgage insurance or second mortgages. If the mortgages are insured by FHA, the down payment will vary from 2.25% to 2.85%, depending upon the State.
- *Mortgage insurance.* If FHA or VA is the insuring or guaranteeing agency, then the costs will mirror those programs. The cost of programs with local and state government sponsored mortgage insurance varies from jurisdiction to jurisdiction. If private mortgage insurance is offered, the costs mirror those costs for a conventional mortgage with a similar down payment, unless a higher standard of coverage is required.
- *Recapture tax.* While the homebuyer will receive a significant advantage through a below market interest rate, the participation in these mortgage programs may carry costs further down the road. For loans closed after December 31, 1990, if the resale of the property occurs within ten years of the original purchase date, the homeowner may be subject to a *recapture tax* of up to 6.25% of the original loan amount. The amount of recapture tax will vary in accordance with various income levels, the amount of gain on the sale and the length of time between purchase and sale.

Bond issue qualification guidelines

Bond issue mortgages are generally more restrictive because of the eligibility requirements that include maximum income and liquid asset guidelines. Once the eligibility requirements are met, the qualification guidelines will be more lenient than conventional mortgages. These more lenient guidelines are typically in the form of higher acceptable ratios. If VA or FHA mortgage options are offered, the qualification guidelines of VA or FHA must be followed in addition to the bond requirements. Most jurisdictions do not allow non-owner occupant co-borrowers or non-citizens without green cards (non-resident aliens).

Rural Housing Service *(administered by the Farmers Home Administration)*

The Federal Government also guarantees mortgages for rural properties under a program administered by the rural development mission area of the U.S. Department of Agriculture. This program is called the Guaranteed Rural Housing (GRH) loan program. These mortgages can be purchased by Fannie Mae, Freddie Mac, and Ginnie Mae. The GRH program is limited to rural areas defined as a maximum of 10,000 population for areas within metropolitan statistical areas and 25,000 within other areas. The program only finances purchases of residential, owner-occupied properties, and does not provide mortgages for farms. The borrowers must have an income at or below 115% of the median income for the area. The GRH program provides 100% financing with no mortgage insurance and no loan limits. In addition, if the appraisal comes in higher than the sales price, the GRH program will cover closing costs.

There is a 2.0% guarantee fee that can be financed into the final loan amount and there is no required down payment. The government guarantees to 90% of any loss. The market share of these mortgages is growing. The mortgages are 30 year fixed with no seller contribution limit. The rate cannot exceed the lender's rate for VA mortgages. Applicants must be U.S. citizens or permanent resident aliens and the qualification ratios are 29/41

Conventional Conforming Mortgages

Conventional conforming mortgages are those that are eligible for purchase through the Federal National Mortgage Association (Fannie Mae) and the Federal Home Loan Mortgage Corporation (Freddie Mac) through authority granted by Congress. These agencies are chartered with governmental authority but are private enterprises known as *government sponsored enterprises (GSEs) or quasi-governmental institutions*. Wary of a future savings and loan-type bailout and concerned with progress the institutions have made in achieving public interests (such as providing financing for inner city housing and for minorities), Congress gave the Department of Housing and Urban Development the authority to regulate and oversee these institutions in 1992. Because of major accounting issues uncovered in the years 2003 and 2004, this oversight was expanded to the Office of Federal Housing Enterprise Oversight (OFHEO) in 2004.

Automated underwriting has enabled each agency to publish more liberal standards for loans that are more highly rated by these systems. It is important to note that as large banks have merged and the national mortgage industry leaders have increased their market share, the mega-giants have increased their leverage with these agencies. Each company is most likely to negotiate an individual commitment with one or both of the agencies; therefore, conforming products and qualification standards may vary, especially with regard to first-time homebuyer programs. Any standards given in this Section, including products offered, LTV limits, and underwriting guidelines will vary from lender to lender. The greatest variations will be apparent in the variety of conforming alternatives for low-to-moderate income borrowers. Every bank must have these alternatives to help meet the guidelines of the Community Reinvestment Act (CRA). To learn conforming guidelines, you must learn the standards of individual lenders.

Who is eligible for conforming mortgages?

There is no limitation on eligibility. Fannie Mae and Freddie Mac restrict loans to those who are lawfully residing in the U.S. as permanent or non-permanent resident aliens.
A living trust is an eligible borrower if the trustee is the occupant of the property.

Types of transactions financed

Many lenders negotiate specific commitments with Fannie Mae and Freddie Mac, and therefore the rules of conforming lending may vary slightly from lender to lender. Here we will attempt to outline the typical transactions financed:
- *Owner-occupied purchase and rate reduction refinance transactions.* Conforming programs normally offer an owner-occupied purchase and rate reduction refinance at a maximum 95% LTV, though programs are available with a lower down-payment for low-to-moderate income borrowers and borrowers with high credit scores. A larger down payment is typically required on 3-4 unit properties.

Chapter 2

- *Second home purchase and rate reduction refinance transactions.* A second home can be financed typically at the same LTV as primary purchases. In addition, the person applying for a mortgage on a second home must have no more than ten additional residential properties that are mortgaged.
- *Investor purchase and rate reduction refinance transactions.* Investor transactions typically require 10% equity in the property and carry higher interest rates as compared to owner-occupied transactions. The mortgage must be a fixed rate with no temporary buydown, and seller contributions are limited to 2% of the sales price. The limitation of ten additional financed properties applies to investor as well as second home mortgages. The borrower must have reserves equal to six months PITI after closing and must contract for rental-loss insurance.
- *Cash-out refinances.* The amount of cash out is usually limited to 90% of the value of the home for owner-occupied refinances, though once again, may lenders have negotiated more liberal limits especially for borrowers with high credit scores. Some mortgage instruments, such as balloon programs, may have more stringent cash-out refinance requirements as will investor properties, second homes, and those with lower credit scores. Early in 2003, both agencies raised their fees on cash-out transactions and Fannie Mae classified the paying off of any junior liens not used for the purchase of the home as a cash-out transaction.
- *Streamline refinance transactions.* If the purchaser approaches the present servicer to refinance an existing Fannie Mae and Freddie Mac mortgage solely to reduce the rate, streamline refinance programs are offered that may limit documentation, qualification, and valuation. For example:
  - If the lender will warrant that the property value has not diminished, a new appraisal may not be necessary;
  - Requalification may not be necessary if the payment of the new mortgage is no more than 15% higher than the qualification rate of the old mortgage, the income has not diminished, and the original mortgage process verified the income.
- *Rehabilitation and reverse mortgages.* Fannie Mae has programs to finance construction and home improvements (including FHA 203K mortgages) under their HomeStyle program and reverse mortgages (HECM) under their Home Keeper program.

Types of properties eligible

Generally, residential properties of one to four units are eligible for conventional mortgages. Properties of 2-4 units usually require higher down payments. In 2004, Fannie Mae lowered the required down payment requirement for manufactured homes to 5.0% of the purchase price. Planned unit developments and condominium projects have special requirements that can be quite complex. The following are examples of condominium classifications and requirements:

- Fannie Mae Limited Project Review
  - 80% maximum loan-to-value with no secondary financing
  - Must have minimum insurance standards
  - Lender can *warrant*[17] compliance
- Freddie Mac Class III
  - Project is complete and condominium association has been in control for at least one year
  - No additional phasing in the project

---

[17] When a lender warrants compliance, the agency does not have to approve the project. The lender signs a warranty form that attests to compliance with the standards.

- 60% of the units must be owner-occupied unless the LTV is 90% or less for purchase or a no-cash-out refinance or 75% or less for a cash-out refinance
- 90% of the units have been conveyed or under contract to different individuals
- Minimum insurance coverage must be maintained
- Lender can warrant compliance
- Fannie Mae Type A
  - Project complete, no additional phasing
  - Unit owners control association for one year
  - 90% of the units have been conveyed to different individuals
  - 60% of the project is comprised of owner-occupied or second homes (may be waived if LTV is 90% or below or 75% or below for a cash-out)
  - No more than 10% commercial usage in the project
  - Minimum insurance coverage must be maintained
  - Lender can warrant compliance

New condominium and planned unit development projects that are not complete will typically necessitate the direct approval of Fannie Mae or Freddie Mac. There are typically minimum owner-occupancy and presale requirements that can be met phase-by-phase as the project is built.

Fannie Mae also has a program to purchase mortgages secured by cooperative properties. These cooperatives must be located in areas that have demonstrated market acceptance for the cooperative form of ownership. *Type 1* coops are required to have 80% owner-occupancy. *Type 2* projects are directly approved by Fannie Mae and appear on the Fannie Mae approved list. Many of the requirements mirror those established by Fannie Mae for condominium projects (for example one entity cannot own more than 10% of the project).

Mortgage types offered

There is a wider variety of mortgages available through Fannie Mae and Freddie Mac than government mortgage sources. It should be noted that Fannie Mae and Freddie Mac also purchase second trust mortgages up to 50% of the limit for first trust mortgages. Generally, these second mortgages cannot be placed behind a conforming first mortgage in a purchase transaction to exceed the legislated conforming purchase limits. They may allow conforming seconds to lower the cash requirements for low-to-moderate income programs (for example Freddie Mac Affordable Seconds).

- *Fixed rate mortgages.* Fixed rate mortgages typically are available from a 10-year to 30-year term. Generally 15-year mortgages carry an interest rate approximately .25% to .50% less than 30-year mortgages. Fannie Mae has offered commitments to lenders specifically

Continued on page 37

A History of Conforming Mortgage Limits

	1 Unit	2 Units	3 Units	4 Units
1989	187,600	239,750	290,000	360,450
1990	187,450	239,750	289,750	360,150
1991	191,250	244,650	295,650	367,500
1992	202,300	258,800	312,800	388,800
1993	203,150	259,850	314,100	390,400
1994	203,150	259,850	314,100	390,400
1995	203,150	259,850	314,100	390,400
1996	207,000	264,750	320,050	397,800
1997	214,600	274,550	331,850	412,850
1998	227,150	290,650	351,300	436,600
1999	240,000	307,100	371,200	461,350
2000	252,700	323,400	390,900	485,800
2001	275,000	351,950	425,400	528,700
2002	300,700	384,900	465,200	578,150
2003	322,700	413,100	499,300	620,500
2004	333,700	427,150	516,300	641,650
2005	359,650	460,400	556,500	691,600

Table 2-7

Chapter 2

HUD Estimated Median Family Income Limits
Fiscal Year 2004 for MSAs

Note: Median income limits are utilized for a variety of purposes including several HUD housing/rental subsidy programs and also to determine benchmarks for Fannie Mae and Freddie Mac affordable lending program limits that may range from 100% to 170% of median family income limits.
Example: $31,700 x 115% = $36,455.

Northeast

Connecticut		**New Hampshire**		**Pennsylvania**	
Bridgeport	$75,800	Lawrence	$75,500	Allentown	$59,700
Danbury	96,500	Lowell	80,000	Altoona	46,400
Hartford	73,900	Manchester	69,800	Erie	51,400
New Haven	71,600	Nashua	78,900	Harrisburg	60,500
New London	66,700	Portsmouth	69,600	Johnstown	43,600
Norwalk	111,600			Lancaster	61,600
Stamford	111,600	**New Jersey**		Philadelphia	68,800
Waterbury	64,900	Atlantic/Cape May	61,700	Pittsburgh	55,100
		Bergen-Passaic	83,500	Reading	61,700
Delaware		Jersey City	53,800	Scranton/Wilkes	51,300
Dover	$51,800	Middlesex	92,000	Sharon	347,900
Wilmington	71,000	Monmouth	78,200	State College	59,100
		Newark	80,300	Williamsport	47,800
Maine		Trenton	83,800	York	61,300
Bangor	$52,600	Vineland	53,200		
Lewiston	49,500			**Rhode Island**	
Portland	62,700	**New York**		Newport County	$67,500
Portsmouth	69,600	Albany	$62,600	Providence/	60,000
		Binghamton	50,700	Warwick	
Massachusetts		Buffalo	53,600		
Boston	$82,600	Duchess Co.	72,900	**Vermont**	
Brockton	72,900	Elmira	49,100	Burlington	$68,800
Fitchburg	62,200	Glens Falls	49,900		
Lawrence	75,500	Jamestown	44,500		
Lowell	80,000	Nassau-Suffolk	85,300		
New Bedford	55,000	New York	54,400		
Pittsfield	56,900	Rochester	58,800		
Springfield	59,400	Syracuse	54,100		
Worcester	69,300	Utica-Rome	49,200		
		Westchester	93,400		

Southeast

Alabama		**Arkansas**		**Florida**	
Anniston	$45,800	Fayetteville	$52,000	Daytona Beach	48,600
Birmingham	55,200	Fort Smith	45,200	Ft. Lauderdale	57,700
Columbus	47,900	Little Rock	55,100	Ft. Myers	54,100
Decatur	50,100	Pine Bluff	45,600	Ft. Pierce	50,800
Dothan	47,200	Texarkana	44,700	Ft. Walton Beach	54,700
Florence	44,700			Gainesville	52,200
Gadsden	42,900	**District of Columbia**		Jacksonville	56,600
Huntsville	60,300	VA/MD/DC	$85,400	Lakeland	46,700
Mobile	47,800			Melbourne	54,700
Montgomery	52,100				
Tuscaloosa	51,200				

Table 2-8

34

Sources of Mortgages

Southeast (Continued)

Miami	45,400	Maryland		Brownsville	31,400
Naples	63,300	Annapolis	$68,600	Bryan	54,000
Ocala	42,400	Baltimore	68,600	Corpus Christi	47,000
Orlando	54,700	Hagerstown	54,400	Dallas	65,100
Panama City	49,200	Suburban D.C.	85,400	El Paso	37,700
Pensacola	50,700			Ft. Worth	62,700
Sarasota	54,300	Mississippi		Galveston	59,800
Tallahasee	56,500	Biloxi	$46,900	Houston	61,000
Tampa/		Jackson	50,600	Killeen	47,500
St. Petersburg	51,200			Laredo	33,100
West Palm Beach	62,100	North Carolina		Longview	47,500
		Asheville	$49,700	Lubbock	46,700
Georgia		Charlotte	61,800	McAllen	29,100
Albany	$47,000	Fayetteville	46,900	Odessa	48,500
Athens	53,000	Greensboro	55,500	San Angelo	44,400
Atlanta	69,000	Hickory	49,800	San Antonio	51,500
Augusta	51,600	Jacksonville	41,300	Sherman	51,400
Columbus	47,900	Raleigh-Durham	69,800	Texarkana	44,700
Macon	53,500	Wilmington	54,200	Tyler	50,400
Savannah	53,200	Winston Salem	55,500	Victoria	53,000
				Waco	46,800
		South Carolina		Wichita Falls	47,200
		Charleston	55,900		
Kentucky		Columbia	60,600	Virginia	
Clarksville	$46,200	Florence	49,000	Charlottesville	$63,700
Evansville	56,400	Greenville	54,900	Danville	43,000
Gallatin	49,200	Myrtle Beach	51,500	Lynchburg	49,400
Lexington	58,300			Norfolk/	
Louisville	58,200	Tennessee		VA Beach	55,900
Owensboro	53,600	Chattanooga	$50,900	Richmond	63,800
		Clarksville	46,200	Roanoke	54,400
Louisiana		Jackson	49,600	Suburban D.C.	85,400
Alexandria	$44,000	Knoxville	51,800	Warren County	57,400
Baton Rouge	54,900	Memphis	54,100		
Houma	49,400	Nashville	60,700	West Virginia	
Lafayette	47,200			Berkeley	$53,600
Lake Charles	49,300	Texas		Charleston	53,900
Monroe	46,700	Abilene	$47,200	Huntington	44,600
New Orleans	49,900	Amarillo	49,400	Jefferson	62,600
Shreveport	47,600	Austin	66,900	Parkersburg	48,200
St. James Parish	47,600	Beaumont	47,900	Wheeling	46,600
		Brazoria	62,900		

Midwest

Idaho		Peoria	58,200	Kokomo	60,000
Boise City	$55,000	Rockford	57,900	Lafayette	59,300
		Springfield	60,100	Muncie	52,200
Illinois		St. Louis	65,900	South Bend	57,400
Champaign	60,400			Terre Haute	47,700
Chicago	69,600	Indiana			
Davenport	56,200	Bloomington	59,100	Iowa	
Decatur	52,000	Cincinnati	64,000	Cedar Rapids	$65,700
DeKalb Co.	64,200	Elkhart	56,600	Davenport	56,200
Grundy Co.	67,900	Evansville	56,400	Des Moines	65,300
Kankakee	55,000	Fort Wayne	58,600	Dubuque	56,500
Kendall Co.	75,400	Gary-Hammond	60,300	Iowa City	72,100
		Indianapolis	63,800	Sioux City	52,600
				Waterloo	56,300

Table 2-8 (Continued)

Midwest (Continued)

Kansas		Missouri		Hamilton	64,500
Kansas City	$68,400	Columbia	$62,000	Lima	52,500
Lawrence	62,200	Joplin	46,900	Mansfield	50,700
Topeka	58,200	Kansas City	68,400	Steubenville	46,300
Wichita	58,500	Springfield	51,400	Toledo	56,800
		St. Joseph	51,900	Youngstown	49,600
Michigan		St. Louis	65,900		
Ann Arbor	$77,700			South Dakota	
Battle Creek	57,400	Nebraska		Rapid City	$51,800
Benton Harbor	52,100	Lincoln	$63,600	Sioux Falls	60,100
Detroit	66,800	Omaha	64,000		
Flint	55,200	Sioux City	52,600	Wisconsin	
Grand Rapids	61,200			Appleton	$62,700
Jackson	58,000	North Dakota		Eu Claire	56,200
Kalamazoo	57,400	Bismarck	$60,600	Green Bay	63,000
Lansing	64,600	Fargo	60,700	Janesville	58,200
Muskegon	61,200	Grand Forks	54,300	Kenosha	62,800
Saginaw	55,200			La Crosse	56,200
		Ohio		Madison	73,200
Minnesota		Akron	$60,300	Milwaukee	63,800
Duluth	$53,200	Canton	53,200	Racine	60,500
Minneapolis/		Cincinnati	64,000	Sheboygan	59,400
St. Paul	76,400	Cleveland	59,900	Wausau	58,500
Rochester	71,000	Columbus	63,800		
St. Cloud	58,900	Dayton	57,700		

West

Alaska		Ft Collins	66,500	Oregon	
Anchorage	$78,700	Greeley	55,400	Eugene	$54,300
		Pueblo	45,000	Medford	52,100
Arizona				Portland	67,900
Phoenix	$58,600	Hawaii		Salem	55,400
Tucson	50,400	Honolulu	$65,700		
Yuma	39,800			Utah	
		Montana		Provo-Orem	$56,100
California		Billings	$53,600	Salt Lake City/	
Fresno	$45,900	Great Falls	45,300	Ogden	61,100
Los Angeles	53,500				
Oakland	82,200	Nevada		Washington	
Orange County	74,200	Las Vegas	$54,700	Bellingham	$57,900
Sacramento	64,100	Reno	63,200	Bremerton	63,500
San Diego	63,400			Olympia	66,100
San Francisco	95,000	New Mexico		Richland	61,900
San Jose	105,500	Albuquerque	$54,200	Seattle	71,900
Santa Barbara	64,700	Las Cruces	38,800	Spokane	54,600
Santa Cruz	75,300	Santa Fe	66,000	Tacoma	62,100
Santa Rosa	74,600			Vancouver	67,900
Vallejo	73,900	Oklahoma		Yakima	46,600
Ventura	77,400	Enid	$46,800		
		Fort Smith	45,200	Wyoming	
Colorado		Lawton	45,300	Casper	$55,900
Boulder	$81,900	Oklahoma City	52,100	Cheyenne	55,700
Colorado Springs	62,100	Tulsa	54,500		
Denver	69,500				

Note: Source FHA. Does not include non-metropolitan counties. Some local areas may have community lending income limits higher than the standard 100% to 170% of median incomes.

Table 2-8 (Continued)

on 20-year and 10-year terms. At times Fannie Mae has also offered 40-year terms on a test basis. The rates on 20-year mortgages are typically below 30-year rates and 10-year mortgages are typically below 15-year rates, depending on prevailing interest rate spreads.

- *Balloon mortgages.* Fannie Mae and Freddie Mac offer balloon mortgages, with the 7/23 and 5/25 programs being the most popular. Usually, these require a greater down payment (typically 10%). Those with higher automated underwriting scores may be allowed a smaller down payment. These products include a conditional refinancing or "reset" option allowing the borrower to change to a fixed rate mortgage at maturity. Balloon mortgages have been very popular in the past because their interest rates are lower than fixed rate/fixed payment mortgages. The popularity of these mortgages has decreased as the availability of hybrid adjustables such as the 5/1 and 7/1 have increased. Hybrids typically carry higher LTV alternatives and a larger rate spread from fixed rates because the investor can adjust the rate annually after the fixed period.
- *Adjustable rate mortgages.* Both Fannie Mae and Freddie Mac offer a wide variety of adjustable rate mortgages. The more common adjustment periods range from six months to seven years and they are typically based upon Treasury or Libor indices. Most adjustable programs require a minimum 10% down payment and are not available for investor transactions. As with balloon mortgages, the down payment requirement may be less for individuals with less risk according to automated underwriting systems (AUS). Qualification standards for adjustable programs are more stringent than their fixed rate counterparts. If the ARM has an adjustment period of one year or less and an annual cap of more than 2%, qualification may typically be the start rate plus 2% or at the Fully Indexed Accrual Rate (FIAR). In 2004, Freddie Mac began purchasing interest-only adjustables as well as interest-only products fixed for ten and fifteen years.
- *Temporary buydowns.* Most fixed rate and balloon mortgages can be offered with temporary buydowns as long as it is not an investor transaction. Buydowns on cash-out refinances may also be restricted. Qualification may not be at the initial rate if the LTV is over 95% and/or the buydown is not of a fixed rate. If a *compressed buydown* is offered (allows adjustments semi-annually instead of once per year), the qualification rate is usually 1% below the note rate.
- *Growing equity mortgages.* The most popular growing equity mortgage (GEM) was offered for years by Freddie Mac and was called the *Equal* program. In 1991 Freddie Mac eliminated this 15-year program and another has yet to become as popular during the past decade.
- *Reverse mortgages.* Under Fannie Mae's Home Keeper program.
- *Rehabilitation mortgages.* Under Fannie Mae's HomeStyle Program. There is an option for refinances under the Homestyle Program unlike FHA 203k mortgages.

Maximum conforming mortgage amount

The maximum mortgage that Fannie Mae and Freddie Mac can purchase is indexed yearly, in tandem with the median sales price financed with a conventional mortgage in October of each year.

The new conforming mortgage amount is announced in November of each year and is effective January 1, of the following year. The current (2003) mortgage limits are as follows[18]:

1 Unit Properties:	$359,650	3 Unit Properties:	$556,500
2 Unit Properties:	$460,400	4 Unit Properties:	$691,600

---

[18] The limits are 50.0% higher in Alaska, Guam and Hawaii

Chapter 2

The costs to obtain conforming mortgages

Down payment. For owner-occupied transactions, a minimum 5% down payment is required. Some programs exist that require a 0%-3% down payment for low-to-moderate income borrowers and for those with higher credit scores. In 2000, both Fannie Mae and Freddie Mac both introduced zero down mortgage programs.

Conventional mortgage insurance. Fannie Mae and Freddie Mac both require coverage from a private mortgage insurance company if less than a 20% down payment is made. This insurance protects the lender against default and coverage is required that will protect the lender against any risk typically beyond a 75% LTV. In the private mortgage insurance example, the mortgage insurance would cover the first $28,500 of the loan amount. If the mortgage defaults, the lender would have to absorb losses if less than $66,500 is recovered in a foreclosure transaction.

Generally, the cost of this insurance (MI) will vary according to the loan-to-value of the mortgage and the mortgage product. The highest cost would be for 100% LTV mortgages. Costs can also vary from one private mortgage insurance company to the next[19] and for different regions of the country. In most states, the State agency regulating the insurance industry must approve rate schedules. Monthly costs will vary from .32% to 1.30% of the mortgage.

The option exists to finance the mortgage insurance premium rolling the cost into the mortgage amount[20] in a program that simulates the FHA mortgage insurance program. The advantage of this is saving cash up-front and having the entire premium financed so that it can be deducted from taxes as interest.

Two new options were introduced to the mortgage insurance scene in 1993. One requires no up-front premium, but carries a higher monthly insurance payment.[21] This option is being offered by almost all major mortgage insurance carriers and is called the monthly premium option. By far, this program is the most popular in the mortgage industry. The second option is offered by many lenders. This program is called lender paid mortgage insurance and it eliminates up-front mortgage insurance cost through a higher interest rate rather than increased monthly insurance or mortgage amounts. The advantage of this program is as follows:

- No mortgage loan approval is required from a mortgage insurance company. It should be noted that many lenders do have delegated underwriting authority from mortgage insurance companies and therefore do not have to send their mortgages to these companies for approval.
- No up-front cash is required, even with as little as five percent down payment.

Private Mortgage Insurance Example

Sale Price	$100,000
Mortgage amount	$95,000
Coverage required	x 30%
Covered amount	$28,500
Lender risk	$66,500
Lender risk	67%
Mortgage amount	$95,000
Up-front rate	x 1.00
Up-front cost	$950
Mortgage amount	$95,000
Annual renewal rate	x 0.49
Annual renewal cost	$465.50
	÷ 12
Monthly renewal cost	$38.79

Monthly Private Mortgage Insurance Example

Sale price	$100,000
Loan-to-value	x 95%
Mortgage amount	$95,000
Insurance rate	x .67%
Annual insurance	$637
Monthly payment	$53.04

---

[19] Examples of private mortgage insurance companies: General Electric Insurance (GEIMCO), PMI Mortgage Insurance (PMI), United Guaranty Insurance (UGIC), Mortgage Guaranty Insurance (MGIC), Radian Guaranty, Republic Mortgage Insurance (RMIC).
[20] Note that the loan-to-value including the mortgage insurance may be restricted to 95%. If the mortgage insurance causes the loan-to-value to rise over 90% LTV, the qualification standards of a 95% mortgage will be utilized.
[21] For example, a 95% LTV mortgage with the 1.00% up-front premium eliminated may have the monthly premium increased from .49% to .67%.

Sources of Mortgages

- There is no loss in equity due to increased mortgage amounts.
- The total payment is tax deductible.

The main disadvantage of lender paid insurance is the fact that the higher rate can never be eliminated from the mortgage payment even if the LTV of the mortgage eventually drops below 80%. Some lenders have introduced lender-paid insurance options that can be cancelled in the future in accordance with conforming guidelines.

Cancellation of private mortgage insurance. Under the Homeowner's Protection Act of 1998, homeowners have the right to request cancellation of private mortgage insurance when their equity reaches 20% of the present value of the home if more than five years have elapsed since the origination date (or 75% if more than two years have elapsed). When equity is scheduled to reach 22% based on the original value, the lender must cancel the insurance automatically. For mortgages existing before July 29, 1999, lenders must send an annual notice as to how the homeowner may apply for cancellation. For these existing mortgages, the rules for dropping mortgage insurance will vary by lender and program. The following represent typical guidelines for the elimination of mortgage insurance.

Elimination of private mortgage insurance. Other than making a down payment of 20% or more, to eliminate the need for private mortgage insurance a second mortgage can be placed behind a first mortgage, as long as the LTV of the first mortgage is no more than 80% and the combined loan-to-value of the first and second mortgages (CLTV) is no more than 95% (80-15-10). Rules and maximum CLTVs for these "piggyback" mortgages vary from lender to lender and some lenders may have negotiated exceptions to conforming requirements, though these may require a higher rate.

Second Mortgage (80-10-10 Mortgage)	
Sale price	$100,000
1st trust (80%)	-$80,000
2nd trust (10%)	-$10,000
Down payment (10%)	$10,000

Why would a borrower want to eliminate mortgage insurance in favor of paying a higher rate or procuring a second mortgage?

- Mortgage insurance premiums are not tax deductible as is monthly mortgage interest.
- Each private mortgage insurance company may have underwriting guidelines that may differ from Fannie Mae and Freddie Mac. For example, perhaps the agency does not require a non-citizen to possess a green card when he/she has a particular loan-to-value; while some mortgage insurance companies have such a requirement. Or the agency might permit lending within a condominium complex while the mortgage insurance company does not.
- Though second mortgage rates are higher than first mortgage rates, the borrower would be paying the higher rate on a smaller portion of the loan as opposed to the entire balance, which is the case with mortgage insurance. This must be weighed against the one disadvantage -- that mortgage insurance can be eliminated in 2-5 years.

Other costs associated with conforming mortgages. Unlike FHA and VA, lender fees are completely negotiable on conforming mortgages, and it does not matter whether the purchaser or seller pays points or lender fees as long as general seller contribution limits are not violated.

Continued on page 41

Chapter 2

Private Mortgage Insurance—Typical Rates

Monthly Only Premium Schedule

LTV	30 Year Fixed Coverage	At Closing	Monthly	1% ARMs At Closing	Monthly	2% ARMs At Closing	Monthly	15 Year Fixed Coverage	At Closing	Monthly
95 plus	35%	0	.96%	0	1.26%	0	1.30%	35%	0	.85%
91 to 95	30%	0	.78%	0	.88%	0	.92%	25%	0	.56%
86 to 90	25%	0	.52%	0	.61%	0	.65%	12%	0	.23%
81 to 85	12%	0	.32%	0	.33%	0	.37%	6%	0	.18%

Alt A (A-) Monthly Only Premium Schedule

LTV	30 Year Fixed Coverage	At Closing	Monthly	1% ARMs At Closing	Monthly	2% ARMs At Closing	Monthly
95 plus	35%	0	2.57%	—	2.89%	—	—
91 to 95	30%	0	1.80%	0	2.00%	0	2.24%
86 to 90	25%	0	1.22%	0	1.37%	0	1.51%
81 to 85	12%	0	.72%	0	.80%	0	.89%

Financed Mortgage Insurance

LTV	30 Year Fixed Coverage	Refund	1% ARMs Refund	2%-ARMs Refund
95 to 100	35%	4.65	5.60	6.35
91 to 95	30%	3.05	3.40	3.60
86 to 90	25%	2.10	2.25	2.40
81 to 85	12%	1.25	1.30	1.45

Lender Paid Mortgage Insurance

LTV	30 Year Fixed Coverage	Rate Add-On	Buydown Rate Add-On	ARMs Rate Add-On	15 Year Fixed Coverage	Rate Add On
91 to 95	30%	.68%	.78%	.82%	30%	.59%
86 to 90	25%	.44%	.53%	.57%	25%	.35%
81 to 85	12%	.26%	.18%	.31%	12%	.17%

Notes:
- Coverage is the percentage of loan amount that will be covered against default. The coverage shown will reduce the lender's exposure to a minimum of 75% of the sales price. The above costs and coverages are typical and will vary by company, product, and jurisdiction. Temporary buydowns may be priced on a 1% ARM schedule, fixed rate schedule, or a separate buydown schedule depending upon the company. Some example coverages (such as agency reduced coverages of 25% for 95 LTV 30 year fixed) may require minimum automated underwriting score.
- Financed Mortgage Insurance entails a one-time premium that is added to the mortgage amount. The total mortgage amount including insurance may be limited to 95% LTV depending upon the program. Example: 2.00% premium with a mortgage amount of $100,000. Total mortgage amount would be $102,000.
- Monthly Mortgage Insurance entails a monthly premium without any up-front costs. If the monthly premium is .62% on a $100,000 mortgage, the cost would be $620 annually or $51.67 monthly.
- Lender Paid Mortgage Insurance entails a higher interest rate paid without an increase in the mortgage amount. For example, if the premium is .90% and the interest rate is 7.00%, then the borrower would pay 7.90% for the life of the mortgage. These rate add-ons vary depending on credit score.
- Partial Self-Insured Option. (after notes to Lend Paid Mortgage) This option was introduced by Fannie Mae and Freddie Mac in 1999 for conforming mortgages-- 95% LTV 18% Coverage, .75%* Price Adjustment (monthly premium @.50%)
  90% LTV 12% Coverage, .375%* Price Adjustment (monthly premium @ .34%)
  * point adjustment can be converted to note rate adjustment- .75% would add approximately .15% to note rate.
- Coverage required may be higher for certain types of transactions such as cash-out refinances and investor properties.

Table 2-9

Qualification Guidelines

Income Qualification. The ratio method is employed on conventional mortgages with the most common ratios being 28/36. Fannie Mae will typically use 28/36 ratios on mortgages with a 95% loan-to-value. The use of automated underwriting system has greatly reduced reliance on qualification ratios.

Community Home Buyer/Affordable Programs. Congress has directed Fannie Mae and Freddie Mac to focus on programs that help first time home buyers and other home buyers with low to moderate incomes. These programs are restricted to borrowers whose incomes typically do not exceed 100% of the median income of the particular region with a higher limit in designated areas. Qualification standards for these programs are generally more liberal than standard Fannie Mae and Freddie Mac underwriting. Standards may be relaxed for down payments, minimum cash invested, reserves required, and more. One option for low-to-moderate income buyers includes "community seconds" that may be offered by non-profits or government agencies. These second mortgages may be at below-market interest rates and/or have deferred payments. They are also designed to lessen the cash requirements for purchase.

Cash requirements. Most conventional conforming mortgage programs require that the borrower invest at least 5% of their own cash in any purchase transaction and have the equivalent of two months mortgage payment in reserve after closing. This 5% can be borrowed as long as the purchaser can qualify for the additional debt and an owned asset secures the loan. Beyond the 5% cash requirement, total cash outlays can be lowered as follows:

- *Gift.* A gift from an immediate family member for closing costs. If the down payment is a minimum of 20%, a borrower may be able to procure a gift for all cash requirements.
- *Contributions.* The seller can pay closing costs (not including prepaids) within the following limitations of total seller contributions:

95% LTV	3% Maximum Seller Contribution
90% LTV or below	6% Maximum Seller Contribution
75% LTV or below	9% Maximum Seller Contribution
Investor Transactions	2% Maximum Seller Contribution

    Seller's contribution maximum is based upon the sales price, not the mortgage amount.
- *Reduced closing cost programs.* Since the fees and rates are negotiable, lenders may offer programs with no points or reduced closing costs coupled with a higher interest rate. These programs do not increase the necessary down payment, thereby reducing the cash necessary for closing.
- *Low-to-moderate income programs.* The aforementioned low-to-moderate income programs require only 3% or less from the purchaser's own funds and may require no cash reserves after closing. Programs have also been introduced with a 3% down payment and more recently (latter half of 2000), Fannie Mae and Freddie Mac introduced programs that require no down payment and may not have maximum income limits. Depending on the option selected, affordable programs may also allow second mortgages to lower the down-payment requirements. *Co-borrowers.* At a 95% LTV, co-borrowers may be required to live in the property under Fannie Mae guidelines. In addition, at lower LTVs there may be a minimum debt ratio requirement of 43% for the owner-occupant when there is a co-borrower who does not live in the property. The occupant must make the first 5% down payment from his/her own funds. Certain exceptions can

be obtained for parents purchasing homes for adult children who are physically handicapped or developmentally disabled. Freddie Mac has published more liberal guidelines for mortgages rated as "Accept" under LP automated underwriting.
- *Secondary financing.* Second mortgages are permitted but the first mortgage may be limited to 80% LTV and a minimum 10.0% down payment may be required (see mortgage insurance section). Secondary financing is not allowed under most balloon first mortgage programs. In addition, there may be requirements for the type of second mortgagee allowable, including:
    * The second mortgage must not balloon in less than five years.
    * There must be regular payments required.
    * There must be no deferred interest.
    * For an *open* equity line, the amount of available credit will be used to calculate maximum CLTV or combined loan-to-value of the first and second trust.
    * Open lines of credit may not be allowed with low-to-moderate income conforming programs.

A second mortgage that meets these requirements and therefore is acceptable for placement behind a conforming first trust mortgage is called a *conforming second mortgage*. In the past few years, programs have proliferated that allow more liberal secondary financing. The most popular of these is an "80-15-5" that requires only a 5% down payment. Many lenders obtain exceptions from Fannie and Freddie to offer these options--but overall requirements and costs may vary.

Conventional Non-Conforming

If we consider conventional non-conforming mortgages to be those that are not insured by FHA, guaranteed by VA, issued under the authority of the Federal Bond Subsidy Act, or purchased by Fannie Mae or Freddie Mac, then this category is the whole universe of mortgages that do not fit into the most common categories. Since we are talking about a whole universe of mortgages, it is quite impossible to summarize their common characteristics. What we will attempt to accomplish in this section is to list the most common types of non-conforming mortgages and demonstrate how they differ from their conforming counterparts:
- *Jumbo mortgages.* Mortgages that exceed Fannie Mae/Freddie Mac conforming loan limits are usually referred to as *jumbo* mortgages. The vast majority of these mortgages are underwritten to Fannie Mae and Freddie Mac guidelines and would require private mortgage insurance coverage commensurate with conforming mortgages. Interest rates for jumbo mortgages may typically be anywhere from .125% to .50% above conforming alternatives--though adjustable programs may require no rate premium. A typical example of down payments required under a jumbo program:

    5% to 450,000   15% to 650,000
    10% to 550,000   20% to 850,000

    It should be noted that many jumbo investors have programs that require no down payment as an option with a higher interest rate and/or with mortgage insurance.
- *Non "A" credit mortgages (subprime).* Fannie Mae, Freddie Mac and most jumbo mortgage investors purchase mortgages made to borrowers who have relatively good credit histories, stable income and reasonable income qualification. Those who do not meet these criteria may be classified as *B, C* and *D* credit borrowers. There are sources which focus on the purchase of these mortgages, usually at a much higher interest rate and requiring a larger down payment than A credit mortgages. As the non-conforming (B&C Lending) market has grown it has

become easier to classify borrowers in accordance within their category of credit. For example, the following might represent sample categories for a non-conforming lender:

Mortgage Level	Credit Score	LTV Maximum	Mortgage Delinquency
A Credit	620	95%	0 x 30
A- Credit	580	90%	1 x 30
B Credit	520	85%	3 x 30
C Credit	520	80%	60 day late allowed
D Credit	N/A	75%	120 days past due maximum

Note: For each level of credit, the non-conforming rates would increase (B rates are higher than A-). Mortgage delinquencies may be measured during the past 12 or 24 months. "Rolling 30s" may count as one delinquency. A "rolling 30" is more than one month which is late due to one payment not being on time and the borrower not catching up. In other words, one payment skipped may result in nine months of late payments, but only one "rolling 30."

Non "A" credit mortgages are not limited to those with poor credit payment histories. They may include borrowers who do not meet normal eligibility guidelines such as being self-employed for a short period of time, non-resident aliens, investors with many investment properties and more. In addition, in recent years Freddie Mac has moved into lending for A- level borrowers by offering programs for lower credit scores at a higher "conforming" rate.

- *Non-conforming properties.* Non-conforming properties include those located in condominium projects not approved by major agencies, partial commercial usage, excess acreage, a high "land-to-value" ratio, cooperatives, etc. Many local banks provide funding for non-conforming properties for customers of those institutions.
- *Self-insured/portfolio mortgages.* In the past, many savings and loan institutions offered mortgages that were not insured through conventional mortgage insurance companies. A higher interest rate was charged to absorb the risk of insuring the mortgages through the savings institution. The savings and loan crisis of the late 1980's greatly minimized the sources of mortgages that are self-insured or otherwise originated to be held (for *portfolio*), though some sources still exist. The regulatory agencies watch savings institutions carefully for the origination of non-conforming mortgage products that could not be sold on the secondary markets if the need for liquidation of assets arises. These portfolios are also subject to extreme risk, as increases in market interest rates would make the assets less valuable.
- *Non-conforming mortgage products.* There are many mortgage products offered by mortgage sources, but are not salable to Fannie Mae and Freddie Mac. Examples might include *cost of funds index (COFI)* based adjustables with potential negative amortization and 30 year amortized mortgages with 15-year balloons. Other examples might include conforming first trusts that have non-conforming seconds: for example, conforming standards might require an "80-15-5." Non-conforming mortgages may allow a "80-20." Non-conforming seconds have become a very popular tool utilized to decrease down payments or eliminate mortgage insurance. The qualification standards may or may not follow conforming guidelines. Generally, following these guidelines may help in the eventual sale of these non-conforming mortgages in the secondary market after the mortgages are *seasoned*.

Major Mortgage Source Comparisons

	FHA	VA	CONFORMING
Eligibility	One FHA loan per Borrower	Veterans and active military	Unlimited
Types of Transactions	Owner occupied purchase and refinance Rate reduction refinance for investors	Owner occupied purchase and refinance Rate reduction refinance for investors	Owner occupied, second homes, investor purchase and refinance
Types of Properties	Single family, PUDs, condos	Single family, PUDs, condos	Single family, PUDs, condos, coops
Mortgage Types	Fixed rates, buydowns, ARMs, reverse, rehab	Fixed rates, buydowns, ARMs	Fixed rates, buydowns, ARMs, balloons, reverse, rehab, seconds
Maximum Mortgage Amount	$172,632-331,968 (base) $312,895-601,692 (max) Regional Variation	$359,650 (1-4 Units) No Regional Valuation	$359,650 (1) $556,500 (3) $460,400 (2) $691,600 (4) Regional Variation Only For Alaska, Hawaii, Guam
Costs: Insurance	30 yr: 1.5% up-front/ .50% monthly 15yr: .25% monthly	Funding Fee: 2.15% up-front (100% LTV) (more for 2nd time usage and reservists)	Insurance Example-- .78% monthly (95% LTV/30 yr fixed) Rates will vary
Costs: Down Payment	Minimum 1.25% to 2.85%	No down payment with full eligibility	5% Principal residence 3% Low-to-mod income 0% Programs available
Qualification	29/41 Ratios	41 Back ratio/ Positive residual	25-33 Front ratio 33-38 Back ratio
Assumptions	Owner occupants only with credit approval[22]	With credit approval[23]	Not typically. Some ARMs are assumable with credit approval
Misc.	→ 100% gift allowed → No green card req. → Max seller contribution 6%[24] → No required reserves → 85% LTV cash-out refis	→ 100% gift allowed → Max seller contribution 4%[25] → No required reserves → 90% LTV cash-out refis	→ 3% of buyer's own cash required[26] → Max seller contribution 3% at 95% LTV → 1-2 months PITI reserves[27] → 90% LTV cash out refis

Table 2-10

---

[22] After 12/15/89. Loans closed before that date require no credit approval except if a release of liability for the original mortgage holder is desired. If the mortgage was closed after 12/1/86 and before 12/15/89, an investor may assume only if the LTV is paid down to 75%. Before 12/1/86 there were no limits on investor assumptions.

[23] If the commitment was issued before 3/1/88 there is no credit approval required. There is always credit approval required for a substitution of eligibility.

[24] Buyer must invest 3% cash in the transaction.

[25] Seller can pay typical closing costs and discount points for the purchaser in addition to the 4% limitation.

[26] Low-to-moderate income programs can require less from borrower.

[27] Low-to-moderate income homebuyer programs may not require reserves.

3

Types of Mortgages

As the secondary market for mortgages has grown, so have the varieties of mortgages available to the average consumer. Twenty years ago, the only choices would have been a 30-year fixed rate, a 15-year fixed rate, and an adjustable rate mortgage. Today an applicant can walk into a mortgage company and choose from five, ten, or even interest-only mortgage products. This chapter will try to give some basis for comparing and selecting among these products.

This discussion is organized by categorizing all mortgages within three major groups--

- Fixed rate and fixed payment mortgages;
- Fixed rate hybrids: non-fixed payments and balloons;
- Adjustable rate mortgages.

Fixed rate/fixed payment mortgages

A fixed rate mortgage, occasionally abbreviated as FRM, is the simplest and the most common of all mortgage instruments. During the past 10 years, fixed rate mortgages have ranged from a low of 30% to a high of 80% of the total residential first trust mortgages originated in the United States. The volume of fixed rate activity tends to increase as market rates decrease, which makes the higher payments of fixed rates more affordable. The only variation among fixed rate mortgages is in the mortgage *term*. The *term* is the life of a mortgage: the period of time over which the money is lent. To be considered fixed rate, the mortgage must have two major characteristics:

- The interest rate and payments must be fixed over the term of the mortgage.
- At the end of the mortgage it must be paid off completely.

A mortgage that is paid off completely by the end of its term is said to be *fully amortized*. To *amortize* is simply to decrease the principal balance on the mortgage on a monthly basis, or to *pay down* the mortgage balance. An *amortization schedule* may be produced for any mortgage, laying out the payments over the life of the mortgage. In this section we have illustrations of annual amortization schedules for the most common fixed rate mortgage terms: 30, 20, and 15 years. Annual amortization schedules show the principal reduction each year.

The example amortization schedules are based on a $100,000 mortgage because it provides an easy basis for extrapolating to other mortgage amounts. If you are seeking a mortgage of $50,000, you can simply divide all amounts shown in the chart by two. If you are seeking a mortgage of $150,000, then multiply the amounts in the chart by one and one-half.

Chapter 3

Many applicants receive amortization schedules when they apply for a mortgage. It is an important document that enables you to follow the progress in paying down the mortgage. It is also important to know how an amortization schedule is calculated. Too many borrowers merely look at the schedule, but have no idea how the interest is actually calculated. To illustrate how a monthly amortization schedule is calculated, we will manually compute the first three months of a schedule.

Computation of an amortization schedule

We will use a $100,000 mortgage with a 30-year term, at a 7% interest rate. First, we need to know the monthly payment for this loan. Calculating monthly payments is quite complex, requiring either a special table or a financial calculator. Using such a method, we find that the monthly payment for this loan is $665.30.[28] Next, we need to find the monthly interest rate by dividing the annual rate by 12 (7% ÷ 12 = *0.583%*). Since this is a fixed rate mortgage, neither of these numbers will change at all during the life of the loan.

To perform the amortization calculation for the first month, we take the loan amount and multiply it by the monthly interest rate ($100,000 x 0.583% = *$583.33*). Thus, $583.33 of the first month's payment goes to pay interest. Subtracting this amount from the payment reveals the portion that goes toward payment of the principal ($665.30 − 583.33 = *$81.97*). We now subtract this amount from the original loan amount to find how much principal remains as of the end of the first month ($100,000 − 81.97 = *$99,918.03*).

We repeat this procedure for the second month. The interest paid this month is calculated from the new principal balance and the monthly

Annual Amortization Table
20 Year Term
$100,000 Loan Amount
7% Fixed Rate Loan

Year	Monthly Payment	Total Annual Principal	Total Annual Interest	Remaining Balance
1	$775.30	$2,378.96	$6,924.64	$97,621.04
2	$775.30	$2,550.93	$6,752.67	$95,070.11
3	$775.30	$2,735.35	$6568.25	$92,334.76
4	$775.30	$2,933.09	$6,370.51	$89,401.67
5	$775.30	$3,145.12	$6,158.48	$86,256.55
6	$775.30	$3,372.48	$5,931.12	$82,884.07
7	$775.30	$3,616.28	$5,687.32	$79,267.79
8	$775.30	$3,877.70	$5,425.90	$75,390.09
9	$775.30	$4,158.02	$5,145.58	$71,232.07
10	$775.30	$4,458.61	$4,844.99	$66,773.46
11	$775.30	$4,780.91	$4,522.69	$61,992.55
12	$775.30	$5,126.53	$4,177.07	$56,866.02
13	$775.30	$5,497.12	$3,806.48	$51,368.90
14	$775.30	$5,894.48	$3,409.12	$45,474.42
15	$775.30	$6,320.63	$2,982.97	$39,153.79
16	$775.30	$6,777.54	$2,526.06	$32,376.25
17	$775.30	$7,267.49	$2,036.11	$25,108.76
18	$775.30	$7,792.84	$1,510.76	$17,315.92
19	$775.30	$8,356.20	$947.40	$8,959.72
20	$775.30	$8,959.72	$343.35	$0.00

Table 3-1

Annual Amortization Table
15 Year Term
$100,000 Loan Amount
7% Fixed Rate Loan

Year	Monthly Payment	Total Annual Principal	Total Annual Interest	Remaining Balance
1	$898.83	$3,909.82	$6,876.14	$92,090.18
2	$898.83	$4,192.47	$6,593.49	$91,897.71
3	$898.83	$4,495.54	$6,290.42	$87,402.17
4	$898.83	$4,820.51	$5,965.45	$82,581.66
5	$898.83	$5,168.99	$5,616.97	$77,412.67
6	$898.83	$5,542.66	$5,243.30	$71,870.01
7	$898.83	$5,943.35	$4,842.61	$65,926.66
8	$898.83	$6,372.99	$4,412.97	$59,553.67
9	$898.83	$6,833.70	$3,952.26	$52,719.97
10	$898.83	$7,327.72	$3,458.24	$45,392.25
11	$898.83	$7,857.41	$2,928.55	$37,534.84
12	$898.83	$8,425.42	$2,360.54	$29,109.42
13	$898.83	$9,034.53	$1,751.43	$20,074.89
14	$898.83	$9,687.62	$1,098.34	$10,387.27
15	$898.83	$10,387.27	$398.02	$0.00

Table 3-2

---

[28] Note: This book contains a table of interest rate factors which will enable you to quickly calculate a payment for 30, 20, 0r 15 year mortgages.

interest rate ($99,918.03 x 0.583% = *$582.86*). Subtracting the interest from the payment gives the principal paid in the second month ($665.30 – 582.86 = *$82.44*). Subtracting this from the principal gives the principal remaining as of the end of the second month ($99,918.03 – 82.44 = *$99,835.59*).

And the third month—

Interest paid $99,835.59 x 0.583% =*$582.37*
Principal paid $665.30 – 582.37 = *$82.93*
Principal remaining $99,835.59 – 82.93   =*$99,752.66*

Now that we understand how amortization schedules are derived, we can appreciate how computers and sample amortization schedules eliminate the tedium of having to go through the above process for each month of a 360-month (30-year) loan!

Fixed loan alternatives

We previously mentioned that fixed rate loans are most commonly available in 15, 20, and 30-year terms. Of these three, which is the most popular and what advantages does one have over the other? The 30-year mortgage is easily the most popular fixed rate mortgage, averaging the lion's share of the fixed rate market even in times of low market rates that have made 15-year mortgages more affordable. The source of this popularity is simple: the 30-year fixed rate mortgage requires the lowest payment of the three. More of the payment goes to interest (and less to principal), maximizing the tax deduction. In comparison, the 15-year mortgage would have a higher payment, a lower interest deduction, and faster payoff of the principal. Thus, the purpose of a 15-year mortgage is early payoff and interest savings over the mortgage term.

Annual Amortization Table
30 Year Term
$100,000 Loan Amount
7% Fixed Rate Loan

Year	Monthly Payment	Total Annual Principal	Total Annual Interest	Remaining Balance
1	$665.30	$1,015.79	$6,967.81	$98,984.21
2	$665.30	$1,089.21	$6,894.39	$97,895.00
3	$665.30	$1,167.94	$6,815.66	$96,727.06
4	$665.30	$1,252.39	$6,731.21	$95,474.67
5	$665.30	$1,342.91	$6,640.69	$94,131.76
6	$665.30	$1,440.00	$6,543.60	$92,691.76
7	$665.30	$1,544.08	$6,439.52	$91,147.68
8	$665.30	$1,655.73	$6,327.87	$89,491.95
9	$665.30	$1,775.41	$6,208.19	$87,716.54
10	$665.30	$1,903.76	$6,079.84	$85,812.78
11	$665.30	$2,041.39	$5,942.21	$83,771.39
12	$665.30	$2,188.94	$5,794.66	$81,582.45
13	$665.30	$2,347.19	$5,636.41	$79,235.26
14	$665.30	$2,516.86	$5,466.74	$76,718.40
15	$665.30	$2,698.81	$5,248.79	$74,019.59
16	$665.30	$2,893.90	$5,089.70	$71,125.69
17	$665.30	$3,103.11	$4,880.49	$68,022.58
18	$665.30	$3,327.42	$4,656.18	$64,695.16
19	$665.30	$3,567.97	$4,415.63	$61,127.19
20	$665.30	$3,825.89	$4,157.71	$57,301.30
21	$665.30	$4,102.46	$3,881.14	$53,198.84
22	$665.30	$4,399.03	$3,584.57	$48,799.81
23	$665.30	$4,717.02	$3,266.58	$44,082.79
24	$665.30	$5,058.04	$2,925.56	$39,024.75
25	$665.30	$5,423.70	$2,559.90	$33,601.05
26	$665.30	$5,815.75	$2,167.85	$27,785.30
27	$665.30	$6,236.19	$1,747.41	$21,549.11
28	$665.30	$6,687.00	$1,296.60	$14,862.11
29	$665.30	$7,170.32	$813.21	$7,691.40
30	$665.30	$7,691.72	$294.86	0

Table 3-3

Fixed Rate Monthly Payments
7.0% Interest/$100,000 Mortgage

Term Years	Total Payment	Principal Payment	Interest Payment
15	$898.83	$318.83	$580.00
20	$775.30	$195.30	$580.00
30	$665.30	$85.30	$580.00

Table 3-4

Table 3-4 compares the breakdown of the first month's payment for each of the three terms. This chart clearly illustrates the immediate differences between the various fixed rate mortgages. Each has the same initial monthly interest but the 15-year mortgage has an extra payment of $233.53 that goes entirely to pay off the principal. While the interest payment is the same for the first month under each mortgage, the interest paid monthly will reduce much more slowly under the 30-year instrument.

Chapter 3

Table 3-5 illustrates interest savings and payment comparisons for each of these mortgages. Note we have made payment and savings comparisons from more than one angle. One can solely look at the interest savings and payment savings over the life of the mortgage—this is a perfectly legitimate comparison. In this instance, we can see that the 15-year mortgage saves over $77,000 in interest over its 15-year term (compared to the 30 year alternative). Also note that the 20-year mortgage saves over $53,000 over its 20-year term (again, compared to the 30-year mortgage).

Comparison of Fixed Rate Mortgages

5% Investment Interest
$100,000 Loan Amount
7% Fixed Rate Loan

	Mortgage Term in Years		
	30	20	15
Monthly Payment	$665	$775	$899
Extra Payment	$0	$110	$234
Total Payment	$239,511	$186,071	161,789
Extra Pmt. Over Term	$0	$26,400	$42,120
Interest Savings	$0	$53,440	$77,722
Total Savings	$0	$27,040	$35,602
Investment Savings	$0	$38,332	$55,447
Adjusted Savings	$0	$15,108	$22,275

Table 3-5
Note: Adjusted Savings does not take into account being able to invest the payment savings at the end of the mortgage until the end of the original term.

The 20-year mortgage achieves two-thirds of the prepayment of a 15-year mortgage, using a 30-year mortgage as a basis of comparison. Yet the additional payments required for a 20-year mortgage are only 47% of the additional payments for a 15-year mortgage ($110 extra vs. $234). How can this be? It is because the prepayment is more difficult for each extra year of prepayment. As you shorten the mortgage, it gets harder and harder (requires greater extra payments) to shorten the life. For example, a 10-year payoff would require an extra payment of $495.78 per month as compared to the 30-year payment of $665.30. In other words, it takes an extra $234 per month to reduce the term from 30 to 15 years, but another $262 each month to reduce the term from 15 to 10 years.

The monthly prepayment chart (Table 3-6) illustrates this concept quite vividly and could be very helpful if you are considering prepaying an existing mortgage. It shows that $20 of extra payment on a $100,000 mortgage saves nearly three years off the term of the mortgage. It takes $50 to achieve the next three years of savings. Each level of extra payment achieves less result. In comparing a 20-year mortgage to a 15-year mortgage, we achieve almost 70% of the result for 45% of the extra payment, making the 20-year mortgage a more efficient prepayment instrument.

However, these numbers change somewhat when we factor in the effect of interest *income* that could be earned by not paying the extra payment of a 20 or 15-year mortgage. If one chose to make the lower payments of a 30-year mortgage, theoretically one could place the extra payment in an investment account on a regular basis and earn investment income on that money. Tables 3-5 and 3-6 impute a rate of investment income of 5%, which is reasonable for the long-term. We then subtract the interest income from the interest savings.

Types of Mortgages

Effect of Monthly Payment
$100,000 Loan at 7%, 30-year Amortization, 5% Investment Interest

Extra Payment	Principal & Interest	Months to Payoff	Years to Payoff	Total of Payments	Pmt. Savings Over Term	Extra Pmt. Over Term	Invest. Interest	Adjusted Savings
0	$665	360	30.00	$239,511	$0	$0	$0	$0
20	$685	328	27.33	$224,477	$15,034	$6,559	$10,831	$4,203
50	$715	291	24.25	$207,856	$31,655	$14,550	$22,646	$9,009
75	$740	267	22.25	$197,412	$42,099	$20,025	$29,913	$12,186
100	$765	247	20.58	$189,003	$50,508	$24,696	$37,321	$13,187
150	$815	217	18.08	$176,192	$63,319	$32,544	$49,689	$13,630
200	$865	193	16.08	$166,814	$72,697	$38,592	$55,858	$16,839

Table 3-6

Note: Calculations do not take into account investing the payment savings over the term for the remainder of the term of the mortgage (from 15 to 30 years or from 20 to 30 years).

We do not project the investment income beyond the term of each mortgage—conceptually we could show extra savings by investing funds in years 16 through 30 on the 15-year mortgage, because payments are no longer being made. Our calculation solely shows the savings while the mortgage instrument is in existence—and in effect cuts the advantage of the 15 and 20 year mortgages by over half.

Before leaving our comparison of fixed rate, fixed payment instruments, we must cover three additional points:

- *Interest rates*. Though our comparison chart compares the fixed rate instruments at the same interest rate of 7.0%, 15-year mortgages are generally at a rate that is approximately 0.25% below 30-year mortgages. In other words, we could have just as easily compared a 6.75%, 15-year mortgage to a 7.0%, 30-year mortgage. This difference in interest rates will actually decrease the extra payment of a 15-year mortgage by approximately $15 each month.

- *Prepayment penalties*. Many mortgage applicants ask whether they can prepay their mortgage without incurring some form of prepayment penalty. This penalty is a sum of money that must be paid if the mortgage is paid off before the term is up or even paid down faster than the amortization schedule requires. Prepayment penalties are no longer common in the mortgage industry--although they have made somewhat of a comeback in recent years, especially with regard to adjustable rate mortgages that tend to prepay more quickly. Mortgages sold to VA and FHA generally cannot carry these penalties.

  Mortgage factors example
  The 30-year factor for an 8% mortgage is 7.34. Therefore, the monthly mortgage payment is $734.00 for a $100,000 mortgage (7.34 x 100).

- *Mortgage payments*. With our chart examples comparing the payment characteristics of a mortgage, we would do well to spend a few minutes giving our readers the ability to figure the payment. Within this book, there is a payment factor chart that gives the payment factors for 30, 20, and 15-year mortgages at a variety of interest rates. These factors are the payment factors per $1,000; one need only multiply by the mortgage amount.

Actually, the factors shown are *short factors* that are abbreviations of factors, which are many decimal places long. This means the payments calculated with the short factors may be as much as one dollar per month off from the exact number. This is a level of inaccuracy that we are willing to accept in the interest of simplifying the calculations.

Chapter 3

The bi-weekly mortgage

A relatively new phenomenon in the world of mortgage finance is the bi-weekly mortgage. The *bi-weekly mortgage* was imported from Canada and takes advantage of new pay patterns of the American population. Many years ago workers were paid either weekly or monthly. Now more and more people are paid every two weeks. The concept is to make one-half of what would otherwise be your monthly mortgage payment every two weeks.

When one makes one-half of a monthly mortgage payment every two weeks, one actually makes an extra monthly mortgage payment each year:

- There are 52 *weeks* in *one year*.
- Therefore, *every other week* would be 26 *mortgage payments* (one-half of one month each).
- There are *12 months in one year*.
- If one were to make *one-half of each* mortgage payment, one would then make *24 payments in one year*. Therefore, you are making *two extra one-half* mortgage payments, or *one month extra* each year.

The Bi-Weekly Advantage

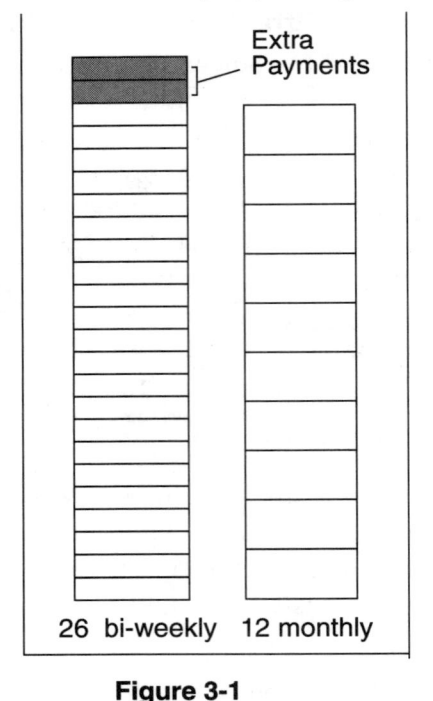

[Figure: bar chart comparing 26 bi-weekly vs 12 monthly payments, with Extra Payments labeled at top]

Figure 3-1

Bi-Weekly Mortgage Example

- $100,000 mortgage
- 9% interest rate

Monthly pmt. $804.62
Bi-weekly pmt. $402.31
Extra yearly pmt. $804.62

Payoff in:
  569 bi-weekly pmts.
  285 months
  23 years

Increased monthly payment to achieve same payoff:
  $54.65 per month for
  $859.27 total payment

What is the result of this extra mortgage payment each year? The bi-weekly is a fixed rate/fixed payment mortgage that pays off in approximately 23 years.

The bi-weekly mortgage is simply a convenient way to match your personal pay method with an early payoff of your mortgage. There are a few disadvantages of bi-weekly mortgages:

1. The secondary market for bi-weekly mortgages has not really developed. Therefore, one is not likely to receive the benefit of a lower interest rate for the shorter term of this mortgage. In other words, bi-weekly mortgages are more likely to be priced as 30-year instruments rather than 20-year mortgages.

2. The 26 payments each year will cause more work for a *mortgage servicer*. The mortgage servicer actually receives the mortgages payments each month, applies the principal, pays real estate tax bills when they are due, etc. Most mortgage companies offering a bi-weekly option will require that the mortgage payment be transferred directly from the bank of the borrower. This is called *direct payment* and is similar to having your paycheck *direct deposited* in your bank account. Though many people prefer this option for paying their mortgage because of the convenience, others prefer to have the flexibility of making the payment during the 15-day *grace* period after which a mortgage is due. This period is called a grace period because the mortgage servicer will

not charge a late payment until the mortgage is actually 16 days late. With the bi-weekly option, you lose payment flexibility.

Finally, companies have developed programs that will offer to convert your present mortgage to a bi-weekly option. These companies are not making new mortgages—they are simply arranging for a different payment schedule on your present mortgage. Before paying a fee for such a service, bear in mind that you can just as easily add an amount to each monthly payment yourself to achieve the same prepayment effect as the bi-weekly mortgage. If the charge is $500, then you could have funded several months of extra payments in the above bi-weekly example.

Interest-Only Programs

In recent years, interest-only programs have become more popular. These programs would be offered at similar interest rates advertised for fully amortized mortgages. The major advantage of these programs is obviously a lower payment --

$100,000	Mortgage
6.0%	Rate
$599.55	Payment
$500.00	Interest-only payment
20%	Payment decrease

Earlier versions of these programs typically included a balloon payment at the end of a particular term (and this still exists for many commercial mortgages). New versions are more likely to have a fixed rate period followed by annual adjustments that are fully amortized for the remainder of the 30-year term (for example, a 5/1 ARM). Another alternative is a longer fixed rate period (10 or 15 years), with one adjustment and full amortization for the remaining 30-year term (10/15 or 15/15).

Fixed rate hybrids

The category of fixed rate hybrids includes all fixed rate mortgages that either do not have a fixed payment or do not pay off completely at the term of the mortgage (are not fully amortized). We will further divide this classification into subcategories:

- *Balloon mortgages*
- *Graduated payment mortgages (GPMs)*

Annual Amortization Table
30Year Amortization, 5 Year Term
$100,000 Loan Amount
7% Fixed Rate Loan

Year	Monthly Payment	Total Annual Principal	Total Annual Interest	Remaining Balance
1	$665.30	$1,015.79	$6,967.81	$98,984.21
2	$665.30	$1,089.21	$6,894.39	$97,895.00
3	$665.30	$1,167.94	$6,815.66	$96,727.06
4	$665.30	$1,252.39	$6,731.21	$95,474.67
5	$665.30	$96,858.07	$6,640.69	$94,797.06

Table 3-7

Balloon mortgages

Balloon mortgages are usually fixed rate and fixed payment mortgages that do not amortize completely. Regular monthly payments are made during a certain specified time interval, and at the end of that interval a lump sum payment of all remaining principal is due. Balloons are also called *bullets* or *calls*, referring to the one time payment.

Chapter 3

For example, a *30 due in 5, 30/5 or 5/25*, mortgage would have payments that are amortized over 30 years, but with a balloon payment at the end of the fifth year. That balloon payment would include any principal due at the end of the fifth year. Table 3-7 gives an example of this type of mortgage instrument. Note that this loan is identical to a 30-year fixed rate loan for the first four years. The fifth year is also the same, up until the very last payment (the 60th payment). That payment is the sum of the normal $665.30, plus the entire remaining principal of $94,131.76, for a *total of $94,797.06*!

Why would anyone choose such a financing instrument? Since the lender need only guarantee the interest rate for five years, there is less risk if rates should later increase. That lower risk means that the lender can offer the balloon loan at a lower interest rate and payment.

By opting for the shorter-term instrument, the lower payment helps one qualify for a larger mortgage. Even if qualification is not an issue, the mortgage payment becomes more affordable. Those opting for this mortgage instrument would be gambling on either moving or refinancing before the five-year term is complete. But what if there is a recession that prevents resale of the property (moving) and the owner loses his/her job and cannot refinance? The balloon instrument also carries a risk that comes with the reward of lower rates and payments.

Freddie Mac and Fannie Mae have addressed this risk in an effort to make balloon products more popular financing instruments. Each carries a *conditional right to refinance* option. This conditional right to refinance enables the applicant to refinance the mortgage to a fixed rate for the remaining term of the mortgage after the balloon occurs (maturity). The rate is fixed according to a formula that is set against whatever that agency's fixed rates are at the time of conversion.[29] The right to refinance is called conditional because certain conditions must be met to give the borrower a right to convert to a fixed rate:

- No payments can be more than 30 days late during the past year;
- There are restrictions as to the types of liens that can be placed against the property (for example, a second mortgage);
- The rate of conversion can be no more than 5.0% over the current note rate or the lender can refuse conversion[30];
- A written request must be made to the mortgage holder within 60 days of the maturity date.

Graduated payment mortgages

A graduated payment mortgage, also known as a GPM, is a class of fixed rate mortgages that has a fixed rate, but also a payment that can vary during the term of the mortgage. As opposed to an adjustable rate mortgage that typically has a rate and payment that varies over the term of the mortgage, a graduated payment mortgage has payment variations that are known at the inception of the mortgage term, i.e., the borrower will know what his/her payments will be over the life of the

---

[29] The typical formula for conversion to fixed rate offered in the Fannie Mae 7-Year Balloon Product is the Fannie Mae's required net yield for 30 year fixed rate mortgages subject to a 60-day mandatory delivery commitment, plus .5%, rounded to the nearest .125%. Freddie Mac uses an identical formula.

[30] Many borrowers feel that this cap is protecting the borrower such as a life cap would on an adjustable rate mortgage. Actually, the option not to convert under high market rate conditions may be at the lender's discretion.

Types of Mortgages

mortgage even though the payments are changing. Payment changes on an adjustable rate mortgage will typically vary in accordance with future changes in interest rates and therefore are unknown.

There are two distinct types of graduated payment mortgages that we will address in this section:

- *Growing equity mortgages (GEMs)*
- *Temporary buydown mortgages*

Growing equity mortgages

Growing equity mortgages, or *GEMs*, increase their rate of mortgage payoff with each increase in payment. Therefore, with a GEM one might start with 30-year amortization but wind up paying off the mortgage in less than 30 years. Or, the loan may start with a 15-year amortization but at a payment that is much lower than attributed to prevailing 15-year market rates. In the past Freddie Mac offered the Equal Program. The Equal Program carried 15-year amortization at a below market rate and payment increases equal to 7.5% of the previous year's payment.

With GEMs, you start with the equivalent 30-year fixed rate payment and end with a payment higher than the initial 15-year payment would have been. The theory here is simply:

Delay of pain

Many would like to have the equity build-up of a 15-year mortgage, but almost no one wants to deal with the higher payments. Growing equity mortgages allow one to start at 30-year amortization and graduate to 15-year amortization, delaying the pain of higher payments for future years. Even a 4% cost of living income increase would be almost double the effect of a 7.5% increase in mortgage payment. Thus, the mortgage is increasing more slowly than even conservative income growth. GEMs are obviously not a mortgage for those with incomes that are likely to remain fixed in future years.

Despite the advantage of GEMs, their popularity seems to have peaked during the 1980s when many builders offered the Freddie Mac Equal Program.

Temporary buydown mortgages

To buy down a mortgage is to lower the interest rate. A temporary buydown lowers the interest rate during a certain period of the mortgage's term, usually the first few years. The purpose of a temporary buydown is to make the payments affordable during the early years of the mortgage, allowing the borrower's income to grow into the higher payment of later years. Unlike a growing equity mortgage, the purpose of a temporary buydown is

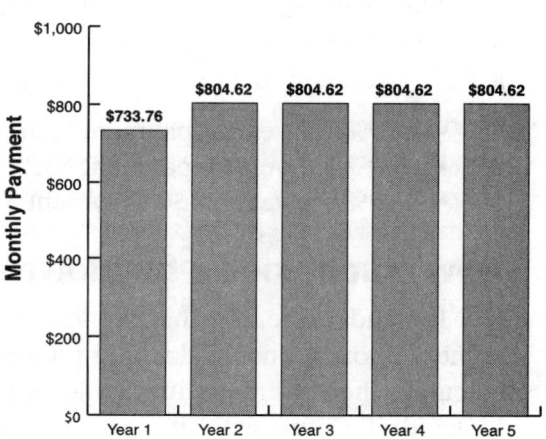

1-0 Buydown

Year 1: $733.76
Year 2: $804.62
Year 3: $804.62
Year 4: $804.62
Year 5: $804.62

2-1 Buydown

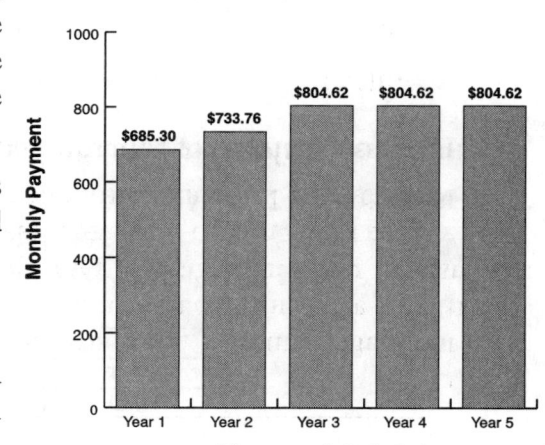

Year 1: $685.30
Year 2: $733.76
Year 3: $804.62
Year 4: $804.62
Year 5: $804.62

Figures 3-2 & 3-3

Chapter 3

not necessarily to delay the pain of a quicker payoff of the mortgage balance, though temporary buydowns can be used on 15-year instruments to accomplish a similar purpose as a GEM. The temporary buydown is typically used to help a purchaser qualify for a larger mortgage amount—similar to the use of an adjustable rate or balloon mortgage. The advantage of a temporary buydown over an adjustable rate mortgage is that the long-term interest rate and payment of a temporary buydown is fixed which adds security. In short, a temporary buydown of a fixed rate mortgage gives many of the short-term advantages of an adjustable with the long-term security of a fixed rate.

A temporary buydown is quite simple:

- *7.0% 30-year fixed rate $100,000 mortgage*
- *A 1.0% buydown would have a 6.00% rate for one year.*

Therefore, the mortgage would be:

- *6.0% for year 1 (payment $599.55 for the first 12 months)*
- *7.0% for years 2-30 (payment $665.30 for the last 348 months)*

This example is called a 1-0 annual buydown. The interest rate is bought down 1.0% for one year. The buydown is typically named after the extent of the buydown: a *2-1* buydown would lower a 7.0% fixed rate to 5.0% in the first year and 6.0% in year two:

- *5.0% for year 1 (payment $536.82 for the first 12 months)*
- *6.0% for year 2 (payment $599.55 for the second 12 months)*
- *7.0% for years 3-30 (payment $665.30 for the last 336 months)*

How much does a buydown cost?

It stands to reason that the lower payments and interest rate of a temporary buydown does not come without a cost. Calculating the actual cost of a temporary buydown is also very easy. Simply calculate the difference in payments over the period of the mortgage in which the interest rate is lowered. To illustrate, let's return to the examples already brought forth, using the $100,000 loan amount at a 7% rate with a 30-year term. First, the 1-0 buydown:

Year	Monthly Payment at 7%	Payment at Buydown Rate	Difference times 12
1	$665.30	$599.55 (6%)	$789.00

Expressed in terms of points, the cost would be: *$789.00 ÷ $100,000, or 0.78 points*.[31]

Now, for the 2-1 buydown:

Year	Monthly Payment at 7%	Payment at Buydown Rate	Difference times 12
1	$665.30	$536.82 (5%)	$1,541.76
2	$665.30	599.55 (6%)	$789.00
Total			2,330.76

Expressed in terms of points, the cost would be *$2,330.76 ÷ $100,000, or 2.33 points.*

---

[31] A point is a cost equal to 1% of the loan amount.

Types of Mortgages

It should be noted that the lower payments might not be the only costs associated with a temporary buydown. These are merely the cost of *subsidizing* the payment over the period of time of the buydown. These *extra* points are placed into an escrow account so that the actual payments can be supplemented during the term of the buydown. For this reason, a temporary buydown is sometimes called a *subsidy*. The cost of this subsidy may not cover the full cost of the buydown because the loan may carry a premium in the secondary market. The investor purchasing the mortgage knows that the borrower is not making the full-required payment in the early years of the mortgage and may have been qualified at the lower payment. This increases the risk of default over a fixed rate-fixed payment mortgage and makes the mortgage worth less in the secondary market (or increases its costs in terms of points).

A second factor decreases the loan's value in the secondary market. The eventual fixed rate on a temporary buydown is likely to be higher than market fixed rates. Therefore, the borrower is more likely to refinance out of the instrument after the fixed rate is achieved. We say that this type of mortgage instrument is more likely to *prepay* and therefore carries less *servicing value*.

Fortunately, temporary buydowns are now widely acceptable on mortgage markets, making these secondary premiums less common. The one exception is for FHA and VA mortgages because of Ginnie Mae securitization requirements. The effect upon the cost of FHA and VA buydowns? FHA and VA mortgages that carry temporary buydowns can cost up to one point more than their fixed rate/fixed payment counterparts. This extra cost is in addition to the actual cost of the buydown.

There are several other variations of temporary buydowns in addition to the popular *1-0* and *2-1* examples already brought forth:

- *3-2-1*—A mortgage that is bought down 3.0% the first year, 2.0% the second year and 1.0% the third year is certainly going to be comparatively expensive. Such a deep buydown will cost over five points and is typically offered only by sellers and builders endeavoring deep concessions to dispose of a property. In addition, many programs will not qualify the borrower at a first-year payment rate that is in excess of 2.0% below the fixed rate[32] of the mortgage. FHA and VA mortgages are even more restrictive in this regard.[33]

    Example of an "Odd" Buydown

Note Rate:	7%
Buydown Type:	1.5%-0.5%
Rate Year 1:	5.5%
Year 2:	6.5%

- *Odd buydowns*—The buydowns we have described up to this point involve buying down the note rate a full percentage point each year. It is possible to buy the note rate down less than a full percentage point. There is no rule that precludes such odd buydowns as long as one basic rule is followed: each year the rate of the mortgage cannot increase more than 1.0%. The advantage of odd buydowns is the ability to customize a mortgage to the needs of an individual borrower. If the purpose of the temporary buydown is to help a home purchaser qualify for a larger sales

---

[32] The fixed rate of a mortgage bought down is referred to as the *note rate*, or the rate that is contained on the legal document (note), which sets out the terms of the loan. Anytime there is a mortgage that is a non-fixed payment, we refer to the *note rate* as the eventual rate of the mortgage or the rate upon which the mortgage is based.

[33] Current VA rules preclude using a temporarily bought down rate to qualify any borrower unless there is clear evidence that the income will increase. The lower payment can be used to offset a borrower's debt payment that will expire before the mortgage reaches the note rate. FHA ceased allowing qualification on the bought down rate in 2004.

Chapter 3

price, yet a full buydown of 2% below the note rate is not needed, then a 1.5% buydown the first year will be less costly.

- *Compressed buydowns*—The buydowns we have introduced have rate increases each year of the mortgage. *Annual* buydowns are overwhelmingly the most common class of temporary buydowns. In the past, temporary buydowns have been introduced that allow rate increases every six months. These are called *compressed buydowns*. Because the period of the buydown is cut in half, so is the cost of the buydown. For example, a *2-1* buydown would cost approximately 1.25 points instead of approximately 2.5 points. Of course the borrower would be subjected to much more rapid payment increases. Knowing this, many lenders and agencies will not qualify the borrower at the bought down rate because the mortgage can increase more than 1.0% each year. Compressed buydowns are currently not a popular mortgage alternative.

Lender subsidized buydowns

To fully explain the concept of a lender-subsidized buydown we would have to delve into the world of mortgage costs and the secondary market. We will briefly explore the purchaser's view of the lender-subsidized buydown here.

The advantages of a temporary buydown are quite clear:

1. Starting at a lower rate and payment than prevailing fixed rate mortgages;
2. Increasing payments are limited to the early years of the mortgage; and
3. Long term fixed rate and payment security.

The one disadvantage is also quite clear: the cost of the buydown. As seen earlier, a typical 2–1 buydown on a 30 year fixed rate mortgage can cost approximately 2.5 points. The cost of these extra points can be borne by the seller or the purchaser in a real estate transaction. Because a fixed rate mortgage already may have points associated with obtaining the mortgage, the total cost can be quite high. If one were opting for a temporary buydown, it would be an advantage to buy the rate down from a rate that carries fewer points:

2-1

Starting Rate (percent)	Fixed-Rate Quote (percent & points)		Buy-down Cost (points)		Total Cost (points)
4.75%	6.75% & 3	+	2.5	=	5.5
5.00%	7.00% & 1	+	2.5	=	3.5
5.25%	7.25% & 0	+	2.5	=	2.5
5.50%	7.50% & -1	+	2.5	=	1.5

In this example, if the seller were paying two points as a *sales concession* to persuade the purchaser to buy the home, the purchaser might opt for a 30 year fixed rate at 6.75%. If one were looking for a 2–1 buydown, the likely choice would be a 7.0% fixed rate. What if the seller was not paying *any points* and the purchaser was very short on cash and could not afford to pay points as well? In most cases, we can then continue to *buy up* the fixed rate to lower the total points of the buydown. As we increase the note rate, the points actually are reduced to zero. Increasing the rate further above prevailing interest rates (up to 7.5% in this example) actually reduces the points to a negative number. Creating a significant "yield-spread" premium. These points are credited to the purchaser, reducing the points required for the buydown.

Continued on Page 59

Types of Mortgages

HISTORY OF MAJOR ARM INDICES

One-Year Treasury

	1995	1996	1997	1998	1999	2000	2001	2002	2003	2004
JAN	7.05	5.09	5.61	5.24	4.51	6.12	4.81	2.16	1.36	1.24
FEB	6.70	4.94	5.53	5.31	4.70	6.22	4.68	2.23	1.30	1.24
MAR	6.43	5.34	5.80	5.39	4.78	6.22	4.30	2.57	1.24	1.19
APR	6.27	5.54	5.99	5.38	4.69	6.15	3.98	3.48	1.27	1.43
MAY	6.00	5.64	5.87	5.44	4.85	6.33	3.78	2.35	1.18	1.78
JUN	5.84	5.81	5.69	5.41	5.10	6.17	3.58	2.20	1.01	2.12
JUL	5.59	5.85	5.54	5.36	5.03	6.08	3.62	1.96	1.12	2.10
AUG	5.75	5.85	5.56	5.21	5.20	6.18	3.47	1.76	1.31	2.02
SEP	6.62	5.83	5.52	4.71	5.25	6.13	2.82	1.72	1.24	2.12
OCT	5.59	5.55	5.46	4.12	5.43	6.01	2.33	1.65	1.25	2.23
NOV	5.43	5.42	5.46	4.53	5.55	6.09	2.18	1.49	1.34	2.50
DEC	5.31	5.47	5.53	4.52	5.84	5.60	2.22	1.45	1.31	2.67

Three-Year Treasury

	1995	1996	1997	1998	1999	2000	2001	2002	2003	2004
JAN	7.66	5.20	6.16	5.38	4.61	6.49	4.77	3.56	2.18	2.27
FEB	7.25	5.14	6.03	5.43	4.90	6.65	4.71	3.55	2.05	2.25
MAR	6.89	5.79	6.38	5.57	5.11	6.53	4.43	4.14	1.98	2.00
APR	6.66	6.11	6.61	5.58	5.03	6.36	4.42	4.01	2.06	2.57
MAY	6.27	6.27	6.42	5.61	5.33	6.77	4.51	3.80	1.75	3.10
JUN	5.80	6.49	6.24	5.52	5.70	6.43	4.35	3.49	1.51	3.26
JUL	5.89	6.45	6.00	5.47	5.62	6.28	4.31	3.01	1.93	3.05
AUG	6.10	6.45	6.06	5.24	5.77	6.17	4.04	2.52	2.44	2.88
SEP	5.89	6.41	5.98	4.62	5.75	6.02	3.45	2.32	2.23	2.83
OCT	5.77	6.08	5.84	4.18	5.94	5.85	3.14	2.25	2.26	2.85
NOV	5.57	5.82	5.76	4.57	5.92	5.79	3.22	2.32	2.45	3.09
DEC	5.39	5.91	5.74	4.48	6.14	5.26	3.62	2.23	2.44	3.21

Five-Year Treasury

	1995	1996	1997	1998	1999	2000	2001	2002	2003	2004
JAN	7.76	5.36	6.33	5.42	4.60	6.58	4.86	4.34	3.05	3.12
FEB	7.37	5.38	6.20	5.49	4.91	6.68	4.89	4.30	2.90	3.07
MAR	7.05	5.97	6.54	5.61	5.14	6.50	4.64	4.74	2.78	2.79
APR	6.86	6.30	6.76	5.61	5.08	6.26	4.76	4.65	2.93	3.39
MAY	6.41	6.48	6.57	5.63	5.44	6.69	4.93	4.49	2.52	3.85
JUN	5.93	6.69	6.38	5.52	5.81	6.30	4.81	4.19	2.27	3.93
JUL	6.01	6.64	6.12	5.46	5.68	6.18	4.76	3.81	2.87	3.69
AUG	6.24	6.64	6.16	5.27	5.84	6.06	4.57	3.29	3.37	3.47
SEP	6.00	6.60	6.11	4.62	5.80	5.93	4.12	2.94	3.18	3.36
OCT	5.86	6.27	5.93	4.18	6.03	5.78	3.91	2.95	3.19	3.35
NOV	5.69	5.97	5.80	4.54	5.97	5.70	3.97	3.05	3.29	3.53
DEC	5.51	6.07	5.77	4.45	6.19	5.17	4.39	3.03	3.37	3.60

11th District Cost of Funds (COFI)

	1995	1996	1997	1998	1999	2000	2001	2002	2003	2004
JAN	4.75	5.03	4.82	4.99	4.61	4.90	5.51	2.82	2.31	1.81
FEB	4.93	4.98	4.76	4.97	4.56	4.97	5.43	2.74	2.26	1.84
MAR	5.01	4.87	4.78	4.92	4.52	5.00	5.20	2.65	2.21	1.81
APR	5.06	4.84	4.82	4.90	4.49	5.08	4.95	2.72	2.21	1.80
MAY	5.14	4.82	4.86	4.88	4.48	5.20	4.75	2.77	2.13	1.71
JUN	5.18	4.81	4.85	4.88	4.50	5.36	4.50	2.85	2.11	1.76
JUL	5.14	4.82	4.89	4.91	4.50	5.46	4.27	2.82	2.02	1.82
AUG	5.13	4.84	4.90	4.90	4.56	5.51	4.11	2.76	1.95	1.88
SEP	5.11	4.83	4.94	4.88	4.61	5.55	3.97	2.76	1.92	1.93
OCT	5.12	4.84	4.96	4.76	4.67	5.59	3.63	2.71	1.91	1.96
NOV	5.12	4.84	4.95	4.69	4.77	5.61	3.37	2.54	1.82	2.03
DEC	5.06	4.84	4.96	4.66	4.85	5.62	3.07	2.38	1.90	2.12

Table 3-8

HISTORY OF MAJOR ARM INDICES

Six-Month Libor

	1995	1996	1997	1998	1999	2000	2001	2002	2003	2004
JAN	6.75	5.25	5.63	5.84	5.07	6.13	5.20	1.99	1.35	1.21
FEB	6.31	5.23	5.72	5.63	4.97	6.29	4.85	2.07	1.34	1.20
MAR	6.50	5.44	5.69	5.70	5.13	6.33	4.65	2.33	1.26	1.16
APR	6.38	5.50	6.00	5.75	5.06	6.53	4.24	2.10	1.29	1.37
MAY	6.00	5.57	6.00	5.81	5.04	6.73	3.92	2.09	1.22	1.58
JUN	5.81	5.73	5.31	5.75	5.25	7.11	3.91	1.95	1.12	1.94
JUL	5.88	5.82	5.94	5.78	5.65	7.00	3.69	1.86	1.15	1.99
AUG	5.94	5.71	5.81	5.75	5.71	6.89	3.45	1.82	1.21	1.99
SEP	5.94	5.67	5.84	5.63	5.92	6.83	2.52	1.75	1.78	2.17
OCT	5.88	5.50	5.84	5.25	5.96	6.76	2.15	1.62	1.22	2.30
NOV	5.75	5.48	5.81	4.98	6.12	6.72	2.03	1.47	1.23	2.62
DEC	5.66	5.54	5.91	5.15	6.06	6.64	1.98	1.38	1.22	2.78

Moving Treasury Average (12-MTA)

	1995	1996	1997	1998	1999	2000	2001	2002	2003	2004
JAN	5.60	5.79	5.56	5.60	4.99	5.21	6.00	3.26	1.94	1.23
FEB	5.84	5.64	5.61	5.58	4.94	5.34	5.87	3.06	1.86	1.23
MAR	6.01	5.55	5.64	5.55	4.89	5.46	5.71	2.91	1.75	1.23
APR	6.14	5.49	5.68	5.50	4.83	5.58	5.53	2.79	1.65	1.24
MAY	6.19	5.46	5.70	5.46	4.78	5.70	5.32	2.67	1.55	1.29
JUN	6.22	5.47	5.69	5.43	4.76	5.79	5.10	2.55	1.45	1.38
JUL	6.23	5.49	5.66	5.42	4.73	5.88	4.90	2.41	1.38	1.46
AUG	6.25	5.49	5.66	5.39	4.73	5.96	4.67	2.27	1.34	1.52
SEP	6.24	5.51	5.63	5.33	4.77	6.04	4.40	2.18	1.30	1.60
OCT	6.19	5.50	5.62	5.21	4.88	6.08	4.09	2.12	1.27	1.68
NOV	6.10	5.50	5.63	5.14	4.97	6.13	3.76	2.07	1.26	1.77
DEC	5.95	5.51	5.63	5.05	5.08	6.11	3.48	2.00	1.24	1.89

Certificate of Deposit Index (CODI)

	1995	1996	1997	1998	1999	2000	2001	2002	2003	2004
JAN	4.63	5.92	5.39	5.62	5.47	5.33	6.47	3.69	1.69	1.13
FEB	4.89	5.85	5.39	5.63	5.41	5.42	6.43	3.63	1.64	1.11
MAR	5.11	5.76	5.41	5.64	5.36	5.51	6.37	3.08	1.59	1.10
APR	5.31	5.69	5.43	5.64	5.30	5.61	6.26	2.83	1.53	1.09
MAY	5.49	5.63	5.46	5.63	5.25	5.73	6.12	2.83	1.48	1.08
JUN	5.61	5.57	5.49	5.62	5.19	5.88	5.89	2.42	1.42	1.12
JUL	5.73	5.54	5.51	5.62	5.15	6.01	5.64	2.26	1.36	1.16
AUG	5.82	5.52	5.51	5.62	5.12	6.13	5.39	2.11	1.30	1.21
SEP	5.90	5.49	5.53	5.62	5.11	6.23	4.82	1.96	1.25	1.28
OCT	5.95	5.47	5.54	5.60	5.11	6.32	4.82	1.87	1.19	1.36
NOV	5.98	5.44	5.56	5.56	5.19	6.37	4.46	1.82	1.17	1.45
DEC	5.97	5.41	5.59	5.52	5.25	6.42	4.07	1.77	1.15	1.56

Prime Rate

	1995	1996
JAN	8.50	8.25
FEB	9.00	8.25
MAR	9.00	8.25
APR	9.00	8.25
MAY	9.00	8.25
JUN	9.00	8.25
JUL	8.75	8.25
AUG	8.75	8.25
SEP	8.75	8.25
OCT	8.75	8.25
NOV	8.75	8.25
DEC	8.50	8.25

	1997	1998
JAN	8.25	8.50
FEB	8.25	8.50
MAR	8.50	8.50
APR	8.50	8.50
MAY	8.50	8.50
JUN	8.50	8.50
JUL	8.50	8.50
AUG	8.50	8.50
SEP	8.50	8.25
OCT	8.50	8.00
NOV	8.50	7.75
DEC	8.50	7.75

	1999	2000
JAN	7.75	8.50
FEB	7.75	8.75
MAR	7.75	9.00
APR	7.75	9.00
MAY	7.75	9.50
JUN	7.75	9.50
JUL	8.00	9.50
AUG	8.25	9.50
SEP	8.25	9.50
OCT	8.25	9.50
NOV	8.50	9.50
DEC	8.50	9.50

	2001	2002
JAN	9.00	4.75
FEB	8.50	4.75
MAR	8.00	4.75
APR	7.50	4.75
MAY	7.00	4.75
JUN	6.75	4.75
JUL	6.75	4.75
AUG	6.50	4.75
SEP	6.00	4.75
OCT	5.50	4.75
NOV	5.00	4.25
DEC	4.75	4.25

	2003	2004
JAN	4.25	4.00
FEB	4.25	4.00
MAR	4.25	4.00
APR	4.25	4.00
MAY	4.25	4.00
JUN	4.00	4.00
JUL	4.00	4.25
AUG	4.00	4.50
SEP	4.00	4.75
OCT	4.00	4.75
NOV	4.00	5.00
DEC	4.00	5.25

Table 3-8 (Continued)

Types of Mortgages

The example at 7.5% illustrates the concept of the *lender-subsidized buydown*. The total cost of the mortgage in terms of points is less than the cost of the buydown. The 5.5%–6.5%–7.5% buydown has a total cost of 1.50 points, or one point less than the total cost of the buydown. When the total cost of the mortgage is actually less than the cost of the buydown, the mortgage is called a *lender-subsidized buydown* because the lender is actually supplying some of the points necessary for the *escrow* of the buydown funds. The lender will be reimbursed for these funds when the loan is sold in the secondary market at a premium (known as a yield spread premium). It should be noted that there is a point of diminishing returns as one moves the rate above market. There will be less credit at higher rates on a proportional basis because the servicing value of the loan will diminish. Why pay to own a loan that is more likely to refinance because of higher-than-market rates?

Adjustable rate mortgages

The last classification of mortgage types involves mortgages that have interest rate changes over time. These are called *adjustable rate mortgages, adjustables, ARMs, or AMLs. Adjustable rate mortgages* are more complex than their fixed rate/fixed payment counterparts because of these rate changes. We will first discuss these complexities before introducing the many types of adjustables that are available as mortgage instruments in today's marketplace.

Determining adjustable rates—the index

Adjustables must contain mechanisms to determine future rate changes. Every adjustable rate mortgage has an *index* that determines the rate of the mortgage in future years.

An *index* is an indicator or reference of particular interest rates that are being measured by that indicator. As this indicator or measure of rate increases, so will the rate on the adjustable mortgage in the future. One could devise an index for any interest rate. For example:

If we wanted to use the *prime* lending rates of major banks:

Bank A -- Prime is presently *8.00%*
Bank B -- Prime is presently *9.00%*
Bank C -- Prime is presently *8.50%*

Our index would simply create an average:

8.00% + 9.00% + 8.50% = 25.5%
25.5% ÷ 3 = 8.50%

If we took this measurement over time (say, every six months) we could track our *Prime Lending Rate Index* over the years:

January, 1990	*8.5%*	July, 1990	*8.0%*
January, 1991	*7.5%*	July, 1991	*7.5%*
January, 1992	*9.0%*	July, 1992	*8.5%*

An adjustable rate mortgage based upon this index might be called a *prime rate adjustable*.

There seems to be no limit on the different type of indices that may rule the future rate changes of adjustable rate mortgages. The following presents an introduction to many of the more common indices.

Chapter 3

Common adjustable rate indices

- *Prime Lending Rate.* The prime-lending rate is the lowest rate charged to the *best customers* of the bank for short-term lending. A bank may lend using its own prime rate as the index upon which future adjustments of the rate will be based. It is more likely that banks will lend based upon an average of prime rates for major banks. Since each bank determines its own prime rate it would seem that the average would provide more protection for the borrower. However, typically the major banks move their prime lending rates in tandem and there is little variation in this measure within the industry.

- *Treasury Constant Maturity Indices.* Also know as the "T" Bill and TCM indices, these indices were actually the most common offered for first trust mortgages in the past. Treasury Securities are issued by the Federal Government to raise capital. These securities are offered in various denominations or lengths: 3-month, 6-month, 1-year, 2-year,....all the way up to 30 year. Short-term securities (for example, 3-month) are known as *"T"Bills*. Medium-term securities (for example, 3-year) are known as *"T" Notes*. Long-term securities (30-year) are known as *"T" Bonds*. A particular *TCM* index actually averages all outstanding securities with the term of the index left until maturity. For example, a 6-month index would be an average of all outstanding treasury securities with six months left in their term. This is what the term *averaged for a constant maturity* denotes. Typically, a one-year adjustable rate mortgage carries a *1 Yr TCM*, or *1 Yr "T" Bill* index. This matches the length of the adjustment term of the mortgage to the TCM index.

- *11th District Cost of Funds Index.* The State of California has long been the home of very large savings and loan institutions. These institutions created adjustable rate mortgage instruments tailored to the booming California real estate market during the 1980s. This market was characterized by rapidly escalating prices and an extreme amount of mobility among purchasers. The borrowers in California and other escalating markets were not interested in long-term security. They were interested in qualifying for the largest mortgage possible so that they could take advantage of rising prices.

  The *11th District* refers to the 11th Federal Home Loan Bank District that includes the State of California. The *Cost of Funds (COFI)* index is a measure of the expense these institutions incur to attract funds, or deposits. It makes sense that they would try to match the interest they charge on mortgages to their actual cost of doing business. These adjustable rate mortgages became quite popular in the 1980s and were offered by many institutions outside of the 11th District.

  Another version of the Cost of Funds Index is the Monthly Median Cost of Funds of all FSLIC-insured institutions. Though it would seem that a national index of the cost of funds for all savings institutions would become a standard, this index has not been utilized as often as the 11th District Index in the formulation of mortgage products.

- *Certificate of Deposits Index (CODI).* Similar to the COFI is the *Certificate of Deposits Index (CODI)*. The COFI and CODI programs are calculated in a similar fashion. The CODI responds more quickly to changes in the market and the index is published mid-month. The CODI index is the average of the most recently published monthly yields on 3-month certificates of deposits for the 12 most recent calendar months as published by the Federal Reserve Board.

- *LIBOR Index.* The *LIBOR* Index is a relative newcomer to the mortgage scene but the instrument has become very important in the development of foreign sources of funds for mortgages. *LIBOR* is short for London Interbank Offered Rates. It is the average rate of interest that major international banks are willing to pay each other in the London Interbank Market for US dollar-denominated deposits for various terms. Fannie Mae and Freddie Mac have actually developed indices of these rates and these are often used as the index for LIBOR based adjustable rate mortgages. It makes sense that if we were to attract foreign dollars to finance our mortgage markets, we would have to integrate the measurements employed by overseas financial institutions.

- *The Consumer Price Index.* Since the inflation rate is the major determinant of the future of interest rates, it is not surprising that there has been some interest in making the Consumer Price Index an index for adjustable rate mortgages. The Consumer Price Index is the government's main gauge for measuring the current inflation rate. In the past, FHA authorized a pilot program for PLAMs, or *Price Level Adjustment Mortgages*. The *PLAM* would have adjustments partially based on changes in the inflation rate and partially based on a more common index such as the 1-year TCM. Thus far, inflation based adjustables have not had an impact on the adjustable rate mortgage market.

- *Moving Treasury Average (also called Monthly Treasury Average) (MTA).* The Monthly Treasury Average is a relatively new ARM index. This index is the 12-month average of the monthly average yields of U.S. Treasury securities adjusted to a constant maturity of one year. It is calculated by averaging the previous 12 monthly values of the 1-Year TCM. Because this index is an annual average, it is steadier than the 1-Year TCM indices. The MTA index generally fluctuates slightly more than the 11th District COFI, although its movements track each other very closely. Its typical use is for adjustables with similar characteristics as those that are tied to the COFI index. The index is sometimes referred to as the 12-month moving average treasury or 12-MAT for short.

Determining adjustable rates—the margin

While the adjustable rate mortgage's rate movements are determined by the index, each adjustable also has a *margin* to determine exactly where the rate will be fixed after each rate change. It makes sense that financial institutions would not lend money exactly at the yield of treasury securities, because they could receive that yield from the federal government. In the case of the Cost of Funds Index, the savings institutions cannot afford to lend money out at the same rate they are paying depositors. Therefore, you can think of the *margin* as a *profit margin* over the index for an adjustable rate mortgage.

What are common margins for adjustable rate mortgages? The most common adjustable rate mortgage for first trust mortgages is a 1-year adjustable that has a rate change every year. A common index for the *1-year adjustable* is the *1-Year "T"Bill* or *TCM* index. The most common margin used with this mortgage instrument is 2.75% over the value of the index.

Index and Margin—Determining the Rate of an ARM

At each rate change, the new rate is determined by the index plus the margin. For example:

	Index	=	5.00%
+	Margin	=	2.75%
	New rate	=	7.75%

Over time, the rates might change as follows:

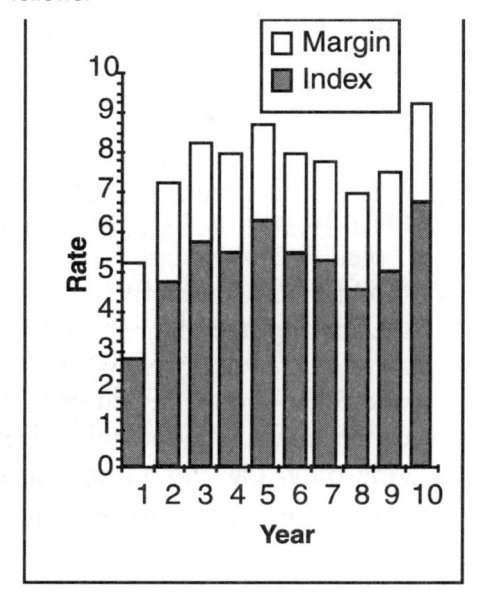

Chapter 3

Adjustable rate mortgage 3margins will typically range from 2.0% for an FHA adjustable to 3.0% for mortgages on properties that are not owner-occupied (investor). Even higher margins would be prevalent in the subprime market.

Once we know the index and the margin, the formula is simple: *the index + the margin = the new rate* each time the ARM is adjusted. However, since most indices can have any value (for example, the one year TCM can be at 4.05) and mortgages are commonly limited to "increments of one-eighth percent" (4.000%, 4.125%, or 4.250%), there is some question as to how the rate is actually figured at adjustment. There are actually four possibilities:

1. Round the rate to the *nearest* one-eighth of a percent;
2. Round the rate *up* to the next one-eighth of a percent;
3. Round the rate *down* to the next one eighth of a percent;
4. No rounding (more likely with a rate that is set monthly.

Let's take an example to illustrate the first three:

Index	One Year TCM
Value at Adjustment	3.95
Margin	2.75
Index plus Margin	6.70
1. *Nearest* one-eighth of a percent	6.75%
2. Round *up*	6.75%
3. Round *down*	6.625%

The most common form of adjustment calculation is the second example, rounding *up* to the next one-eighth of one percent.

Determining adjustable rates—the starting rate

The initial rate for an adjustable will be chosen from one of two options:

- *Fully indexed accrual rate (FIAR)*. The *fully indexed accrual rate* is simply the present value of the index plus the margin. Therefore, if the index is presently at 4.0% and the margin is set at 2.75%, the *FIAR* will be 6.75%. It should be noted that the FIAR based on the present index would be used to calculate the annual percentage rate as required by the Truth In Lending Act.

- *Teaser rate*. The FIAR would seem to be the logical starting rate for an adjustable rate mortgage. Unfortunately, the FIAR typically causes starting rates for ARMs to be at a level that is too high to be attractive to consumers. Basically, the FIAR puts the starting rate of an adjustable too close to the starting rates of fixed rate mortgages. Without a *spread*, or a guaranteed lower rate for a certain period of time, consumers generally will not chose adjustable rate mortgages over fixed rate alternatives. Adjustables are therefore marketed with what are called *teaser rates*, or starting rates that are below market or the FIAR.

Adjustables are Named After Their Adjustment Periods:

One Year ARM—
 rate changes every year

Three Year ARM—
 rate changes every 3 years

Three/One ARM
 fixed for 3 years, then rate changes annually

Types of Mortgages

In the previous example with a FIAR at 6.75%, the starting rate of the adjustable might be 4.5%. Of course, these teaser rates more or less guarantee future increases in rates for the adjustable, even if market rates (the index values) stay the same in the future.

Determining adjustable rates—time periods

There are literally hundreds of adjustable rate mortgages on the market today and the most significant variable among these mortgages is the *adjustment period*. The *adjustment period* is simply the frequency of the rate changes.

The most popular adjustable rate mortgage is the *1 Year ARM* which has rate changes annually. There are adjustables that change monthly, every six months, every three years, and even once in ten years. Adjustables that have more frequent rate changes will carry lower starting rates than long-term *adjustables* that have rate changes only every three or more years. To balance out these lower starting rates, the *short-term* adjustables will have a greater risk of rate increases because of the more frequent rate changes.

It is also possible that the period of rate change may not be fixed on an adjustable. For example, a *prime plus* home equity second mortgage may have a rate change every time the prime rate changes. This means that the rate may not change for two years or it may change every month, depending upon how often the banks change their prime-lending rate.

The period of rate change on an adjustable may also change during the term of the mortgage. The most common example of these are the *3/1, 5/1, 7/1,* and *10/1*, also known as *hybrid ARMs*. These adjustables have fixed rates for a certain period of time and then change into one-year adjustables after that period. For example, a *3/1 ARM* will have a fixed rate for three years and then will adjust annually every year thereafter. This may be compared with a *3/3 ARM* that has rate changes every three years over the term of the mortgage. A *3/3 ARM* is also known as a *true three-year adjustable*. Another variation, a *"2-28"* can have a fixed rate for two years and then change every six months over the remaining term.

Determining adjustable rates—protection against unlimited rate changes

The risk would be unpalatable for any borrower or mortgage purchaser if an adjustable rate mortgage's interest rate could increase without limits with each adjustment. For this reason, the vast majority of ARMs marketed today offer limits on future rate adjustments. These limits are called *caps*. There are two types of rate caps usually offered:

1. *Adjustment period caps limit each rate change*. A one-year adjustable would have an annual cap and a three year adjustable would have a cap every three years. By far the most common cap is 2.0% during each rate change with some notable exceptions:

   - A six-month adjustable is likely to have a 1.0% cap each six months, which is the equivalent of 2.0% each year.

   - Some *5/1, 7/1,* and *10/1* adjustables allow maximum (life cap) adjustments after the fixed rate term expires and before the annual changes begin. Once the annual changes are in effect, there is typically a 2.0% annual cap in place.

     For example, a 5/1 ARM that starts at 7.0% may have a rate fixed at 7.0% for five years. If there is a life cap of 5.0%, the adjustable can move to 12.0% after the fifth year. Every year

Chapter 3

thereafter, there is an annual cap on rate adjustments of 2.0%. This example would be quoted as *"5/2/5"* caps.

- Some one-year adjustables have a 1.0% annual adjustment cap, including ARMs offered by FHA. The added protection of a lower adjustment cap is normally accompanied by a higher starting rate on that particular adjustable, as opposed to one-year adjustables with 2.0% adjustment caps.

It is important to note that adjustment period caps limit increases and decreases each adjustment term. A 2.0% annual cap on a one-year adjustable dictates that the adjustable cannot decrease more than 2.0% in any year as well as limiting the increase to 2.0%.

2. *Life caps* give rate protection over the term of the mortgage. If a one-year adjustable has a starting rate of 5.0% and a life cap of 6.0%, then the interest rate can never exceed 11.0% at any time during the mortgage term. Six percent is the most common life cap among adjustables though there are once again some common exceptions, including FHA one-year adjustables, which have a 5.0% life cap.

Determining adjustable rates—the floor

Many who opt for adjustable rate mortgages assume the starting rate may go down from the initial *teaser rate* of the adjustable. This is typically not the case. The starting, or *teaser* rate of the adjustable may actually also be the *floor* of the adjustable. A *floor* is the lowest rate that an adjustable rate mortgage can achieve. Because the starting rates of most adjustables are below market, the concept of a floor is typically not very disturbing. Using the example, we can see there is a teaser rate on this loan because the starting rate is 2.25% below the Fully Indexed Accrual Rate, or FIAR. Since the *floor* is also the starting rate, or 4.5%, the question is--

Adjustable Rate Floor Example

At each rate change, the new rate is determined by the index plus the margin. For example:

Index	=	4.00%
Margin	=	2.75%
FIAR	=	6.75%
Start rate	=	4.50%
Floor	=	4.50%
− Margin	=	2.75%
Index at floor		
	=	1.75%

"How low would the index have to go for the adjustable to drop below that 4.50% starting rate?"

As shown in the example, the index would have to be less than *1.75%* for the floor to take effect, which is a very large move on the downside. Also note that the index would have to drop to 1.75% in order for the rate not to adjust upward at the next adjustment period. This is why teaser rates virtually assure rate increases in future years for ARMs.

Which is more important—the margin or the caps?

Many borrowers tend to think that adjustables will increase as fast as the caps will allow them to increase. The reasons for this happening are two fold:

1. Teaser rates have made future increases much more likely. As our discussion of adjustable rate mortgage *floors* has illustrated, most ARMs start below market and therefore make increases in the early years very likely. When the mortgage rate is increasing, it is more likely that the caps will be a factor.

Types of Mortgages

2. We tend to think of the *worst-case scenario* when we think of ARM products. The *worst-case scenario* simply means that the adjustable will increase as fast as it is allowed to increase—the only constraint being the caps. In this scenario there is no involvement by the margin-plus-index rate setting mechanism.

In a *real world* scenario, sometimes the caps will constrain future movements of the adjustable rate mortgage and at other times the index and the margin will determine the rate. We can think of the index and the margin as telling us where the rate ***should*** go, with the caps telling us how far we ***can*** go. Think of the caps as a fence around the playground constraining how far a child can wander. The adjustment period cap is an inner fence that moves with the child and the life cap is an outer fence that remains in place forever. Because of teaser rates, the early years will usually test the involvement of caps. After a few adjustments, the margin and index will become more important.

Let's take an example:

Type	One year ARM
Index	One year TCM
Margin	2.75
Starting Rate	4.25
Index at Start	4.00
FIAR	6.75
Annual Cap	2.00
Life Cap	6.00

Index History:

Year	Rate
1	4.25
2	5.00
3	5.50
4	9.00
5	9.50
6	7.00

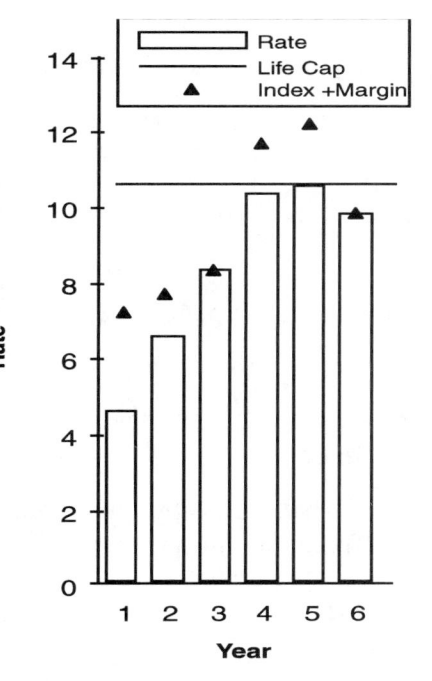

The graph at the right shows the resulting rates over the first years of the loan. Here is how the rates are determined during the first six years.

Year 1. The first year's rate is the start rate of *4.25%*. The index and margin do not directly affect this rate.

Year 2. The index plus the margin equals *7.75%*, which is more than *2.0%* above the starting rate of *4.25%*. The adjustment cap of *2.0%* is the limit. The new rate is *6.25%*.

Year 3. Index plus margin equals *8.25%*, which is the same as the *2.0%* allowable adjustment cap. The new rate is *8.25%*.

Year 4. Index plus margin equals *11.75%*, which is more than *2.0%* above the previous year's rate and the life cap. Therefore, the caps will rule. The new rate is *10.25%*.

Year 5. Index plus margin is *12.25%*. Last year's rate plus *2.0%* is *12.25%*. However, both of these rates are above the life cap. The rate stays at *10.25%*, the life cap.

Year 6. Index plus margin has dropped to *9.75%*. This is below the life caps and within the annual cap limits (which are up or down), so the ARM rate drops to *9.75%*.

One year ARM

Starting Rate 5.00%

Caps
　　Annual 2.00%
　　Life 6.00%

Worst Case:

Year	Rate
1	5.00%
2	7.00%
3	9.00%
4	11.00%
5-30	11.00%

Three Year ARM

Starting Rate 7.00%

Caps
　　3-Year 2.00%
　　Life 6.00%

Worst Case:

Year	Rate
1-3	7.00%
4-6	9.00%
7-9	11.00%
9-30	13.00%

Chapter 3

The worst case scenario

When a mortgage applicant opts for an adjustable rate mortgage the applicant often asks, *"What is the worst that can happen to me?"* This is a reasonable question to ask. If the adjustable rate mortgage goes up as fast as it can—yet is still palatable to the consumer—they are a good candidate for this type of mortgage. We call this the *worst-case scenario* for the adjustable. On the previous page you will find illustrations of a few *worst-case scenarios* for particular ARM products.

It can be seen from these examples that the *worst-case scenario* is not affected by the margin or the index. The only factors are the starting rate and caps, as the ARM will increase as fast as the caps will allow. It does not matter if the index increases 2.0% each year or goes up to 50.0%

Why would someone opt for an adjustable knowing that the worst case could happen? There are many reasons for this:

- Perhaps the applicant will only own the home for a few years.

- Perhaps the applicant's income will be increasing dramatically in the future.

- Perhaps the applicant cannot qualify for the higher payments of a fixed rate mortgage.

Potential negative amortization

Thus far, all adjustables we have examined are examples of *positively amortized* mortgages. That is, every payment applied to the mortgage actually decreases the amount of principal that is outstanding until the mortgage is completely paid off at the end of the mortgage term. Most adjustable rate mortgages are fully amortized 30-year adjustables. Earlier in our discussion of graduated payment mortgages, we introduced the concept of *scheduled negative amortization*. In the case of scheduled negative, the mortgage's principal balance actually increased during the early term of the mortgage and the increasing payments caused accelerated prepayments later in the mortgage term after the period of scheduled negative. The term *scheduled* refers to the fact that any increase in principal balance is known from the beginning of the mortgage term.

Potential Negative Amortization

Type	1 year ARM
Term	30 year
Amount	$100,000
Start Rate	5.00%
Caps	
Annual	2.00%
Life	6.00%
Payment[34]	7.50%
Year 1:	
Rate	5.00%
Payment	$536.82
Neg. Am.	$0.00 per mo.
Year 2a:	
Rate	7.00%
Int. Cap.	$665.30
Pmt. Cap.	$577.08
Payment	$577.08
Neg. Am.	$88.22 per mo.
Year 2b:	
Rate	5.50%
Int. Cap	$567.79
Pmt. Cap	$577.08
Payment	$567.79
Neg. Am.	$0.00 per mo.

Adjustable rate mortgages can also allow for negative amortization. In the case of an adjustable the future rate of the mortgage is not known and therefore the amount of negative amortization in the future is also not known at the mortgage's inception. This is why we say that the adjustable has only a *potential for negative amortization*.

The feature of negative amortization in an adjustable rate mortgage is brought into play with the introduction of a *payment cap*. Quite simply, a payment cap will limit the amount that the payment

---

[34] Note that the payment cap is 7.5% of the payment, not the interest rate. For example, a $1,000 monthly payment with a 7.5% payment cap would have a cap of $75 for the next payment increase. This 7.5% figure is typical for ARMs with potential negative amortization and is roughly the amount of payment increase that would take place if the interest rate increases by 1% to 1.25%.

Types of Mortgages

can increase—usually each year. In a typical ARM, the payments are adjusted to fully amortize the mortgage each time there is a rate adjustment. In the case of an adjustable with potential negative, one can limit payment increases, perhaps to less than is required by the new interest rate to fully amortize the mortgage. The example on the previous page illustrates the concept of a payment cap and negative amortization.

The first year payment is the same as with any other adjustable rate mortgage—it is at the start rate and does not involve any negative amortization. In example 2a, the interest rate caps would allow the payment to rise to *$665.30* each month, but the payment cap is *$88.22* less, or *$577.08*. Therefore, *$88.22* will be added to the loan balance each month, increasing the principal amount of the loan *$1,058.64* at the end of year one. In example *2b*, the payment cap is actually higher than the required payment. Therefore, the required payment of *$567.79* will be made and the loan will be fully amortized in the second year. This is why we say that the loan has *potential negative amortization*. We cannot predict whether the loan will have negative amortization because we do not know whether future rate increases will make the payments rise faster than the payment cap. After analyzing this example, we should take into consideration the following:

- There is usually a limit by which the loan balance can increase over the life of the loan. This limit typically ranges from 110% to 125% of the loan balance. For example, if the original mortgage balance was $100,000 and the limit of increase was 110%, then the loan balance can never exceed $110,000.

- Adjustable rate mortgages with potential negative amortization will typically require higher down payments than other adjustables because of the potential increase in mortgage balance.

- It should be noted that the payment cap is an option, not a requirement. Because there may be no prepayment penalties associated with this feature, one can always opt to make the full-required payment in any one year and the mortgage will not be subject to increase.

- When one compares adjustable rate mortgages with negative features to others that do not have these features, one should simply remove the payment cap option before making the comparison of start rates, indices, margins and interest rate caps. Now how do the loans compare?

Conversion features

Many adjustable rate mortgages have *conversion features*, which is the ability to convert the mortgage from an adjustable to a fixed rate at some juncture during the loan term. Similar to negative amortization, a conversion feature is an option that does not have to be utilized. When shopping for a conversion feature on an adjustable rate mortgage, one should consider:

- *What is the front-end cost of the conversion feature?* Unlike potential negative amortization, the major components of the mortgage are not likely to change because of this feature. The caps, margin, and index are all likely to stay the same, but many adjustables with conversion options may cost more than comparable instruments without these options, usually in terms of a higher starting rate and/or points. One must compare these costs to the potential benefit of a conversion option to determine if the option of converting to a fixed rate makes sense in terms of the extra cost.

- *What is the back end cost of converting?* Though most conversions do not require the typical costs of refinancing, there is usually a flat fee at the time of conversion. This fee can range from

Chapter 3

$250 to $1,000. Because you do not have to utilize the option to convert to a fixed rate, you will not incur this fee unless you actually utilize the conversion feature. Since the back-end fee is not certain, it may not be as significant as a front- end cost that definitely will be incurred at the inception of the mortgage.

- *What is the window of conversion?* Most convertible adjustable rate mortgages do not allow one to convert at any time. Most allow conversion at the time of rate adjustment (annually on a one-year adjustable) and may also limit the years in which conversion may be effected. For example, a typical conversion feature may allow conversion on the second through fifth *anniversary* dates. In this case the term anniversary date is utilized to describe the first day of the month each full year after the mortgage inception.

- *What is the fixed rate of conversion?* The mortgage will convert to the market for fixed rates at the time of conversion. This is likely to be higher than the adjustable's interest rate at that particular juncture. How is the rate of conversion figured? There is actually an index and margin within the conversion feature that will be specified in the initial program disclosure at loan application. Usually the index will be one that measures conventional fixed rates purchased by Fannie Mae or Freddie Mac. To this index is typically added a margin of approximately 0.625% on conforming loan limits and 0.875% on jumbo loan limits. There may be no cap on the conversion. This means that if market fixed rates are 20%, then the loan will convert at that rate.

- *Can the lender keep you from converting?* The answer is yes! If the mortgage payment history shows late payments or the loan is not current at the time of conversion, the note usually provides for removal of the option to convert. There may be other restrictions, so it pays to read loan disclosures carefully.

- *Is converting better than refinancing?* Though refinancing may actually cost more than converting, one should check the market for available interest rates through refinancing before one converts. The minimal amount of costs for conversion and the associated interest rate should be compared to the heavier cost of refinancing and interest rates associated with refinancing.

Reverse Mortgages

The formal name for FHA reverse mortgages is The Home Equity Conversion Mortgage, or HECM. A reverse mortgage lends on the basis of a homeowner's equity in a home. The homeowner does not need monthly income to qualify for the mortgage program nor do they make payments on the loan until the home is sold, the borrower becomes deceased, or permanently moves away.

If one were to borrow $50,000 under a traditional mortgage program, the homeowner could need an annual income of $20,000 or more. Over 70% of seniors own their home outright, but many do not have the income stream to support themselves. This presents a *catch 22:* sitting on a pot of gold that they need desperately but cannot touch. A reverse mortgage makes this pot of gold achievable. Selling the home is an option, but this can mean relocating from a long-term residence, which is traumatic for many seniors.

Reverse mortgages present three major opportunities for homeowners:

- They can receive a lump sum of cash. This is identical to receiving cash from a first or second mortgage refinance—except that there are no monthly payments required.

Types of Mortgages

- They can opt for an open line of credit. Home equity lines of credit (HELOCs) are very popular in America today. Once again, the major difference with regard to reverse mortgages is that a monthly payment is not required.
- They can opt for a monthly income. This monthly payment from the lender would continue until the borrower become deceased, the home is sold or the homeowner permanently moves away.

Combinations of the three are also possible. For example, under the FHA sponsored program the homeowner may opt for a lump sum of cash and a monthly payment.

More lenders are providing this option for their applicants in recent years. Resources for learning more about reverse mortgages include, The National Reverse Mortgage Lenders Association (NRMLA), *Your New Retirement Nest Egg: A Consumer Guide to the New Reverse Mortgages* (NCHEC Press) by Ken Sholen and *The Reverse Mortgage Handbook* by T.E. Ballman (Jawbone Publishing Corp.)

The costs associated with setting up a reverse mortgage can make the loan a very expensive option if a small amount of money is utilized and/or the homeowner uses the money for a very short period of time. The issue of disclosing costs has been debated for some time and is partially solved by a law that requires lenders to provide a Truth-in-Lending disclosure, or TALOC (Total Annual Loan Cost). Higher overall borrowing costs for small loan amounts or a shorter term is germane to all lending but is especially complex when dealing with the added complexity of a reverse mortgage. Because of this factor, a home equity line of credit may be a better alternative for many seniors.

There are strict limitations on the amount of the home's equity that can be utilized. For example, FHA allows a cash-out refinance of up to 85% of the home's value. Under HUD's reverse program the homeowner may be able to tap only 40% or less of the value—depending on factors that include the expected life of the homeowner. There is no free lunch—if no mortgage payments are being made the lender needs an extra margin of security. FHA also requires HECM counseling.

With the graying of America already underway, reverse mortgages promise to continue growing in popularity. In 1995, Fannie Mae released its reverse mortgage program called the Home Keeper. This action promised to help make reverse mortgages available to more homeowners across the nation. To be eligible for the Home Keeper one must be at least 62 years of age, own the home free and clear, and occupy the property as his/her primary residence. The program requires consumer education sessions on reverse mortgages and the program includes three payment options. The mortgages are priced as adjustable rate loans. Fannie Mae also purchases reverse mortgages insured by FHA and has become the nation's largest investor in reverse mortgages with the addition of their Home Keeper product.

Chapter 3

4

Qualifying For a Mortgage: Ratios and Residuals

There are a multitude of variables that factor into the consideration of one's qualifications for a mortgage loan: credit, amount of down payment, cash reserves, job stability, the property, etc. Many of these factors can move into the realm of subjectivity. Overriding the whole process are mathematical calculations that actually dictate the major portion of the decision making process: ratios and residuals. All of the other factors are actually minimum standards: for example minimum cash reserves. In other words, if the mathematics meets program standards, as long as the applicant meets other minimum standards the mortgage will be approved. It should be noted that increased reliance on automated underwriting systems (AUS) has decreased the industry's reliance upon these calculations and increased the industry's reliance upon credit scoring (discussed later in this Chapter).

Mortgage math

Residual	Ratios
• VA mortgages	• All conventional mortgages
• Some jumbo mortgages	• FHA mortgages
	• Partial standard for VA mortgages

If the ratios do not meet standards, there must be other overriding considerations, for example, a very large down payment or a high credit score. These additional overriding considerations are called *compensating factors*. A compensating factor is actually a positive that outweighs a negative factor in the application.

In this chapter, we deal with the calculation of ratios and residuals, which are the mathematical standards of qualification for almost all mortgages.

The ratio method of qualification

The philosophy of the ratio method of qualification is simple: a certain percentage of income is allowed to be allotted to housing expense and other monthly liabilities, or debts. Almost everyone who has rented an apartment has been informed by the leasing agent that one qualifies for a rent payment of *one weekly paycheck out of the month*. The leasing agent was crudely calculating a ratio of 25%: one quarter of the monthly income can be attributed to the housing expense.

In calculating mortgage ratios, we use the *gross monthly income*, or *GMI*, which represents the income before all deductions are taken out.

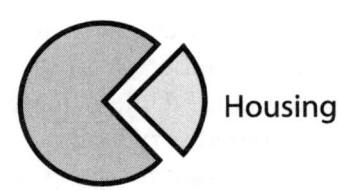

Simply put:

$60,000 annual salary equals *$5,000* gross monthly income ($60,000 divided by 12)

It is the gross monthly income that serves as the denominator for the calculation of all mortgage ratio calculations.

There are actually two ratios calculated with the gross monthly income as the denominator for most mortgage programs:

- Housing, first, front, or inside ratio
- Debt, second, back, or outside ratio

$$\frac{XYZ}{\text{Gross Monthly Income (GMI)}}$$

The housing ratio

The numerator of the housing ratio will be the monthly mortgage payment and any association dues required if the property is located in a condominium or planned unit development project. Let us review the components of a monthly mortgage payment:

The monthly mortgage payment (PITI + HOA)

- **PI**- Monthly principal and interest payment
- **T**- Monthly real estate property taxes
- **I**- Monthly insurance payments:
- Monthly homeowners (and flood) insurance for all properties except condominiums
- Monthly mortgage insurance for all FHA mortgages and conventional mortgages with less than a 20% down payment
- **HOA**- Monthly condominium or homeowners association dues (and any special assessments)

Now that we have the ability to calculate the numerator and the denominator of the housing ratio, we can calculate the ratio.

In the example to the right, we say that the applicant's housing ratio is *17.4%*. The next question is, is that ratio acceptable? Unless there is another very negative factor, in most cases the applicant would be considered very well qualified.

It should be noted that the calculation of housing ratios may be adjusted at times in the case of the purchase or refinance of a property located within a condominium. The monthly condominium association fees commonly include part or all of the utilities of the unit. If one were purchasing a single-family home, we would not include utilities in the housing ratio. If we included the total condominium fee in the housing ratio, there would be utility expense included in the calculation. In the example on the following page, we would actually reduce the amount of the fee by the percentage of the fee that is dedicated to utilities.

The monthly mortgage payment

$95,000	Conventional mortgage
$100,000	Sales price
7.0%	Interest rate
$1800	Annual real estate property taxes
$240	Annual homeowners insurance
$30	Monthly homeowners association dues

PI = $632.50
T = $150.00
I = $20.00 (Homeowners Insurance)
     $38.79 (Mortgage Insurance)
HOA = $30.00
PITI = $871.29 (incl. HOA)

Maximum acceptable housing ratios

- 25% for some adjustable rate programs
- 28% for conforming
- 29% for FHA
- 33% to 38% for low-to-moderate income programs
- 33% for some jumbo and conforming programs with minimum 10% down payment

$$\frac{\$871.29}{\$5,000} = 17.4\%$$

The debt ratio

The debt ratio is also known as the *back, outside, or second* ratio. This ratio calculation adds monthly liabilities, with more than ten months remaining, to the housing expense to calculate the total monthly indebtedness of the applicant. It should be noted that car leases and credit card payments would always be counted regardless of the length of time left on the loan. These debts would be monthly liabilities, not normal living expenses:

- Monthly expenses for medical, life, and auto insurance are not considered liabilities included in the debt ratio;
- Installment loans and the monthly payments on credit cards are considered liabilities included in the debt ratio. In each of these cases, the applicant is *paying on a debt.*

The one monthly expense that can sometimes fall into the *debt* column is child-care. Generally, child-care is not counted as a monthly debt for conventional mortgages (this may vary for different programs). Child-care is more likely to be counted as a debt under VA qualification calculations.

Monthly child support, separate maintenance, or alimony pursuant to a legal separation agreement and/or divorce decree would be considered a monthly debt in all qualification calculations.

One type of monthly debt that can sometimes become part of the income calculation is *rental negative* on a rental property owned by the applicant. To calculate the rental negative, one would take the income on the rental property from the rental lease and subtract the monthly mortgage payment including taxes, insurance and any homeowners association fees. In most cases, the rental income would be reduced by 25%, which is referred to a *vacancy and/or maintenance factor*. If the rental negative became a positive, the income would be added to the gross monthly income. Most lenders will consider taking the rental negative (or income) directly from the Schedule E of the applicant's tax returns.

The debt ratio calculation

Monthly Debt Breakdown:
$300 Monthly Car Payment
$100 Personal Loan
$100 Monthly Credit Card Payments (if not taken from the credit report—we use 5.0% of the outstanding balance as an estimation)

Reducing a condo fee

PITI	$1,000
Monthly condo fee	$250
PITI + condo fee	$1,250
Monthly income	$3,000
Housing ratio	41.66
Condo fee	$250
Monthly association budget	$10,000
Utilities portion of budget[35]	$5,000
Percentage	50%
Condo fee after reduction	$125
PITI + reduced fee	$1,125
New housing ratio	37.50

Rental negative

Monthly income: $1,000
Vacancy factor: (-) 25%
Net income: $750
Monthly PITI: (-) $800
Rental negative: ($50)
(to be included as a debt)

$$\frac{PITI + HOA + Debts}{Gross\ Monthly\ Income} = Debt\ Ratio$$

$$\frac{\$938.26 + 30.00 + 500}{\$5,000} = 29.38\%$$

Maximum acceptable debt ratios

- 33% for some adjustable rate mortgages with 5% down payment
- 36% for conforming mortgage programs
- 38% to 40% for low to moderate income programs and many jumbo mortgages with minimum 10% down payment
- 41% for FHA and VA

---

[35] The utilities portion of the budget might as a loose interpretation include garbage collection, water, electricity, gas or any other expense that a single family homeowner would have to pay out of pocket but we would not normally include in the housing expense in our calculation of the housing ratio.

Chapter 4

Pre-qualification using ratios

Thus far we have simply been attempting to answer the question:

Does the applicant qualify for the proposed mortgage payment?

This question assumes that the house, mortgage amount and interest rate are known. Suppose these become unknown variables?

Housing and debt ratios

Together we express common housing and debt ratios as follows:
- 25/33 for some adjustable rate mortgages with 5% down payment
- 28/33 for some temporary buydowns
- 28/36 for conventional mortgage programs
- 33/38 for some jumbo programs
- 29/41 for FHA mortgages
- 41 debt ratio only for VA mortgages

Suppose someone wants to know how large a mortgage or home purchase for which they qualify—before the home or loan program is identified? This is typically the process one would follow in a visit to a real estate office—the process of pre-qualification. Pre-qualification refers to the process of qualifying for a hypothetical purchase or refinance transaction before the transaction actually takes place. It is the answer to the questions:

How large a mortgage will I qualify for? and How large a house can I afford?

The mathematical process of pre-qualification actually involves working through the ratio calculations backwards. We know the income level, but we want to determine the maximum mortgage payment and maximum mortgage amount for which the potential borrower qualifies.

Here are the ratios:

$$\text{Housing Ratio:} \quad \frac{\text{PITI} + \text{HOA}}{\text{GMI}}$$

$$\text{Debt Ratio:} \quad \frac{\text{PITI} + \text{HOA} + \text{Debt}}{\text{GMI}}$$

Now let's work backwards:

Housing Ratio: GMI x 28% = PITI + HOA
Debt Ratio: GMI x 36% = PITI + HOA + Debts

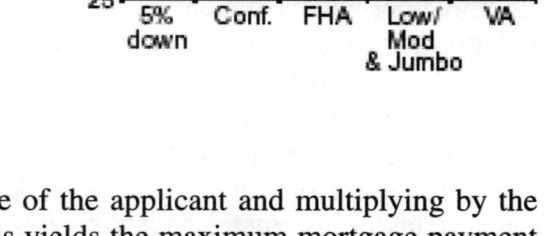

Explanation: We are taking the gross monthly income of the applicant and multiplying by the maximum housing and debt ratios (in this case 28/36). This yields the maximum mortgage payment and the maximum mortgage payment with debts. Let us take an example:

Income: $5,000 Monthly
Debts: $500 Monthly
How large a mortgage payment will the above scenario support?
Housing Ratio: $5,000 x 28% = $1,400 = Maximum PITI + HOA
Debt Ratio: $5,000 x 36% = $1,800 - $500* = $1,300 = Maximum PITI + HOA

*Since the monthly debts are $500, we subtract $500 from $1,800 to arrive at the maximum mortgage payment as dictated by the second, or debt, ratio. The maximum mortgage payment

Qualifying for a Mortgage: Ratios and Residuals

is actually the lower of these two figures: in this case $1,300. If we used the $1,400 figure, the second ratio would be too high:

$$\text{Debt Ratio} = \frac{\$1,400 + \$500}{\$5,000} = 38.00\% \text{ (exceeds 36\%)}$$

The debt ratio will always be the controlling ratio if the debt exceeds the maximum allowed, which in this case is 8.0% (36.0% minus 26.0%). If the total debts are less than 8.0% of the income, then the housing ratio will be the lower of the two.

The maximum mortgage payment by itself does not yield information that is very useful. What most potential home purchasers want to know is:

How large a mortgage can I qualify for?

We need to convert the maximum mortgage payment to a maximum mortgage amount. Of course, there are some very important variables:

- What is the interest rate of the mortgage?
- What is the term of the mortgage?
- What are the monthly taxes, insurance, and homeowners association dues?

Here are the assumptions:

- A market rate of interest for a fixed rate, which is the most common mortgage (In this case we will use 8.0%).
- Thirty year amortization because this will yield the largest mortgage and is the most common mortgage choice.
- Taxes, insurance and HOA dues represent 20% of the total mortgage payment.

Calculation Example:
1. Maximum mortgage payment: $1,300
2. Maximum mortgage payment minus taxes, insurance, and HOA dues: $1,040 ($1,300 x 80%)
3. Maximum mortgage at 8%: $141,690 ($1,040 divided by 7.34 multiplied by 1,000, (7.34 is the interest rate factor for a 8.00%, 30-year mortgage)

Interest Rate Factors
Monthly P&I Payment per $1,000 of Loan Amount

Int. Rate	30 Year	20 Year	15 Year
4.0%	4.77	6.06	7.40
4.5%	5.07	6.33	7.65
5.0%	5.37	6.60	7.91
5.5%	5.68	6.88	8.17
6.0%	6.00	7.16	8.44
6.5%	6.32	7.46	8.71
7.0%	6.65	7.75	8.99
7.5%	6.99	8.06	9.27
8.0%	7.34	8.36	9.56
8.5%	7.69	8.68	9.85
9.0%	8.05	9.00	10.14
9.5%	8.41	9.32	10.44
10.0%	8.78	9.65	10.75
10.5%	9.15	9.98	11.05
11.0%	9.52	10.32	11.37
11.5%	9.90	10.66	11.68
12.0%	10.29	11.01	12.00
12.5%	10.67	11.36	12.33
13.0%	11.06	11.72	12.65
13.5%	11.45	12.07	12.98
14.0%	11.85	12.44	13.32
14.5%	12.25	12.80	13.66
15.0%	12.64	13.17	14.00

Multiply the loan amount divided by $1,000 to obtain principal and interest payment.

Table 4-1

Our pre-qualification efforts should include an extra calculation designed to answer a second question: *If the maximum mortgage amount is not enough to qualify me to purchase the house I want, by how much does the interest rate have to be reduced in order to qualify?*

In the above case, we have pre-qualified someone for a mortgage amount of $141,690. Let's assume that the applicant needs a mortgage amount of $165,000 and does not have the *compensating factors* to exceed the ratios and still achieve loan approval. In this case:

Maximum Mortgage Payment: $1,040
Mortgage Amount Needed: $165,000   1,040 divided by 165 = 6.30

Chapter 4

If we look on the payment factor chart located in Table 4-1, 6.30 is the payment factor on a 30-year mortgage at 6.50%. Therefore, the interest rate would have to be reduced from 8% to approximately 6.50% (either through an adjustable rate mortgage or a temporary buydown) in order for the purchaser to qualify.

If one finds these calculations cumbersome, the following tables simplify this process. First, Table 4-2 allows you to take a maximum mortgage payment and convert it to a mortgage amount at different interest rates. It assumes that taxes, insurance, and homeowners association dues will be 20% of the total mortgage payment.

Table 4-3 actually qualifies typical incomes. It starts with an income, multiplies by the standard housing ratio of 28% and gives maximum mortgage payments, maximum mortgage amounts and maximum monthly debts allowed at that payment (assumed to be 8% of income, or the difference between 28% and 36%). To use this table, find the column with your approximate income, and the row with your approximate interest rate, and find the cell where these two intersect. This cell contains three values. The top value in that cell is the maximum mortgage amount, the middle value is the maximum monthly mortgage payment amount, and the bottom value is the maximum monthly debts allowed at the given payment amount.

Mortgage Amounts for Given Payments
Assuming 80% of total payment is for Principal and Interest (P&I) and a 30-year fixed-rate loan

Interest Rate	$500	$800	$1,000	$1,200	$1,500	$2,000	$2,500	$3,000
5.0%	74,513	119,220	149,025	178,830	223,538	298,051	372,563	447,076
5.5%	70,449	112,718	140,897	169,077	211,346	281,795	352,244	422,692
6.0%	66,717	106,747	133,433	160,120	200,150	266,867	333,583	400,300
6.5%	63,284	101,255	126,569	151,882	189,853	253,137	316,422	379,706
7.0%	60,123	96,197	120,246	144,295	180,369	240,492	300,615	360,738
7.5%	57,207	91,531	114,414	137,297	171,621	228,828	286,035	343,242
8.0%	54,513	87,221	109,027	130,832	163,540	218,054	272,567	327,080
8.5%	52,021	83,234	104,043	124,851	156,064	208,086	260,107	312,129
9.0%	49,713	79,540	99,425	119,311	149,138	198,851	248,564	298,276
9.5%	47,571	76,113	95,141	114,170	142,712	190,283	237,853	285,424
10.0%	45,580	72,929	91,161	109,393	136,741	182,321	227,902	273,482
10.5%	43,728	69,965	87,457	104,948	131,185	174,913	218,642	262,370
11.0%	42,003	67,204	84,005	100,806	126,608	168,010	210,013	252,015
11.5%	40,392	64,627	80,784	96,941	121,176	161,569	201,961	242,353
12.0%	38,887	62,220	77,775	93,330	116,662	155,549	194,437	233,324
12.5%	37,479	59,967	74,958	89,950	112,438	149,917	187,396	224,875
13.0%	36,160	57,856	72,320	86,784	108,480	144,639	180,799	216,959
13.5%	34,922	55,875	69,844	83,813	104,766	139,688	174,610	209,532
14.0%	33,759	54,014	67,518	81,021	101,277	135,036	168,795	202,554

Table 4-2

Credit Scores and Automated Underwriting Systems

In the past few years, lenders have been using automated credit scores to determine whether a borrower's credit history meets loan approval. Though credit scores alone do not constitute the only decision-making factor, they can be an overriding factor within the overall approval process. Basically, automated systems are able to look at the facets of a credit history from a standpoint of predicting whether a particular consumer represents an unreasonable risk of defaulting on the loan. The analysis of the performance of thousands of mortgage payment histories matched to their owner's credit histories enabled Fair, Isaac and Co. (FICO scores) to develop what are called *credit scores*. The FICO scores can also be referred to as Beacon (Equifax), Empirica (Trans Union), and The TRW/Fair, Isaac Model (TRW) depending on which national credit data repositories report these scores. The good news is that evaluating a credit history is no longer as subjective a process. If a borrower has a low FICO score (below 620), they are considered a high credit risk. If they have a high FICO score (over 660), they are considered a below average risk.

What does this mean for the consumer? The information that determines credit scores is compiled by credit bureaus that have been scrutinized for not being accurate at all times. Therefore, it is incumbent upon all consumers to review their credit information and correct all inaccuracies. Remember the automated adage always applies: *garbage in, garbage out*. If you are buying a home you should also realize that many loan programs exist for those with lower scores, but these may require higher rates or larger down payments. In an effort to "demystify" the process, in June of 2000, Fair, Isaac and Company made public a list of the factors used in determining credit scores as well as introducing a web-based service to explain individual credit scores (www.myfico.com). This explanation indicates that the most important factors determining credit scores are payment histories and amounts owed on credit accounts.

The Fair and Accurate Credit Transactions Act modified the Fair Credit Reporting Act in 2003 to require for the first time that financial institutions notify the consumer if negative credit is being reported from their institution. This Act also entitled each consumer to a free credit report annually. Regulations implementing these provisions were published in late 2004.

Fannie Mae and Freddie Mac have incorporated credit scoring into their credit evaluation process. For example, on 1-unit properties, Freddie Mac has instructed lenders to perform different levels of review for different credit scores. For 1-unit properties that are manually underwritten, FICO score of over 660 would require a basic review. A FICO score of 620 to 660 would require a more comprehensive review of the file. A FICO score of less than 620 indicates that a lender should be cautious. Freddie Mac has indicated to lenders that these are not approval levels. A FICO score below 620 can be approved—but the file is to be looked at very closely.

FICO scores below 620 that cannot be approved with compensating factors through the agencies often will fall within the categories of A- to D credit non-conforming lending. There is more information regarding non-conforming mortgages in Chapter 2. Freddie Mac has released a program for lending to borrowers with an A- credit rating as well.

In recent years, Fannie Mae and Freddie Mac have developed technologies that further their review of automated credit scores in the form of sophisticated automated underwriting systems. The Freddie Mac system is known as *Loan Prospector (LP)* and the Fannie Mae system is called *Desktop Underwriter (DU)* or *Desktop Originator (DO)* for mortgage brokers. These systems utilize credit scores and other factors to rate loans and make underwriting decisions. *Automated Underwriting Systems (AUS)* are changing the loan process significantly. A high rating might allow less underwriting documentation, a smaller down payment or higher underwriting ratios than normally would be required. A lower rating might require a rate premium. *Automated Underwriting Systems* are also being developed for non-conforming alternatives—including B/C credit loans. Through these systems, underwriting decisions are becoming more rapid and uniform throughout the industry.

Chapter 4

Mortgage Qualification by Income and Interest Rate
Assuming 28% of income for house payment, 8% for debts, and a 30 year fixed-rate loan

Interest Rate	\$1,500	\$2,000	\$2,500	\$3,000	\$4,000	\$5,000	\$7,500	\$10,000
5.0%	78,238[1] / \$420[2] / \$120[3]	104,318 / \$560 / \$160	130,397 / \$700 / \$200	156,477 / \$840 / \$240	208,635 / \$1,120 / \$320	260,794 / \$1,400 / \$400	391,191 / \$2,100 / \$600	521,589 / \$2,800 / \$800
5.5%	73,971 / \$420 / \$120	98,628 / \$560 / \$160	123,285 / \$700 / \$200	147,942 / \$840 / \$240	197,256 / \$1,120 / \$320	246,570 / \$1,400 / \$400	369,856 / \$2,100 / \$600	493,141 / \$2,800 / \$800
6.0%	70,052 / \$420 / \$120	93,403 / \$560 / \$160	116,754 / \$700 / \$200	140,105 / \$840 / \$240	186,807 / \$1,120 / \$320	233,508 / \$1,400 / \$400	350,262 / \$2,100 / \$600	467,017 / \$2,800 / \$800
6.5%	66,449 / \$420 / \$120	88,598 / \$560 / \$160	110,748 / \$700 / \$200	132,897 / \$840 / \$240	177,196 / \$1,120 / \$320	221,495 / \$1,400 / \$400	332,243 / \$2,100 / \$600	442,990 / \$2,800 / \$800
7.0%	63,129 / \$420 / \$120	84,172 / \$560 / \$160	105,215 / \$700 / \$200	126,258 / \$840 / \$240	168,344 / \$1,120 / \$320	210,431 / \$1,400 / \$400	315,646 / \$2,100 / \$600	420,861 / \$2,800 / \$800
7.5%	60,067 / \$420 / \$120	80,090 / \$560 / \$160	100,112 / \$700 / \$200	120,135 / \$840 / \$240	160,180 / \$1,120 / \$320	200,225 / \$1,400 / \$400	300,337 / \$2,100 / \$600	400,449 / \$2,800 / \$800
8.0%	57,239 / \$420 / \$120	76,319 / \$560 / \$160	95,398 / \$700 / \$200	114,478 / \$840 / \$240	152,638 / \$1,120 / \$320	190,797 / \$1,400 / \$400	286,195 / \$2,100 / \$600	381,594 / \$2,800 / \$800
8.5%	54,623 / \$420 / \$120	72,830 / \$560 / \$160	91,038 / \$700 / \$200	109,245 / \$840 / \$240	145,660 / \$1,120 / \$320	182,075 / \$1,400 / \$400	273,113 / \$2,100 / \$600	364,150 / \$2,800 / \$800
9.0%	52,198 / \$420 / \$120	69,598 / \$560 / \$160	86,997 / \$700 / \$200	104,397 / \$840 / \$240	139,196 / \$1,120 / \$320	173,995 / \$1,400 / \$400	260,992 / \$2,100 / \$600	347,989 / \$2,800 / \$800
9.5%	49,949 / \$420 / \$120	66,599 / \$560 / \$160	83,249 / \$700 / \$200	99,898 / \$840 / \$240	133,198 / \$1,120 / \$320	166,497 / \$1,400 / \$400	249,746 / \$2,100 / \$600	332,995 / \$2,800 / \$800
10.0%	47,859 / \$420 / \$120	63,812 / \$560 / \$160	79,766 / \$700 / \$200	95,719 / \$840 / \$240	127,625 / \$1,120 / \$320	159,531 / \$1,400 / \$400	239,297 / \$2,100 / \$600	319,062 / \$2,800 / \$800
10.5%	45,915 / \$420 / \$120	61,220 / \$560 / \$160	76,525 / \$700 / \$200	91,829 / \$840 / \$240	122,439 / \$1,120 / \$320	153,049 / \$1,400 / \$400	229,574 / \$2,100 / \$600	306,098 / \$2,800 / \$800
11.0%	44,103 / \$420 / \$120	58,804 / \$560 / \$160	73,504 / \$700 / \$200	88,205 / \$840 / \$240	117,607 / \$1,120 / \$320	147,009 / \$1,400 / \$400	220,513 / \$2,100 / \$600	294,018 / \$2,800 / \$800
11.5%	42,412 / \$420 / \$120	56,549 / \$560 / \$160	70,686 / \$700 / \$200	84,824 / \$840 / \$240	113,098 / \$1,120 / \$320	141,373 / \$1,400 / \$400	212,059 / \$2,100 / \$600	282,745 / \$2,800 / \$800
12.0%	40,832 / \$420 / \$120	54,442 / \$560 / \$160	68,053 / \$700 / \$200	81,663 / \$840 / \$240	108,885 / \$1,120 / \$320	136,106 / \$1,400 / \$400	204,158 / \$2,100 / \$600	272,211 / \$2,800 / \$800
12.5%	39,353 / \$420 / \$120	52,471 / \$560 / \$160	65,589 / \$700 / \$200	78,706 / \$840 / \$240	104,942 / \$1,120 / \$320	131,177 / \$1,400 / \$400	196,766 / \$2,100 / \$600	262,355 / \$2,800 / \$800
13.0%	37,968 / \$420 / \$120	50,624 / \$560 / \$160	63,280 / \$700 / \$200	75,936 / \$840 / \$240	101,248 / \$1,120 / \$320	126,559 / \$1,400 / \$400	189,839 / \$2,100 / \$600	253,119 / \$2,800 / \$800
13.5%	36,668 / \$420 / \$120	48,891 / \$560 / \$160	61,113 / \$700 / \$200	73,336 / \$840 / \$240	97,781 / \$1,120 / \$320	122,227 / \$1,400 / \$400	183,340 / \$2,100 / \$600	244,453 / \$2,800 / \$800
14.0%	35,447 / \$420 / \$120	47,262 / \$560 / \$160	59,078 / \$700 / \$200	70,894 / \$840 / \$240	94,525 / \$1,120 / \$320	118,156 / \$1,400 / \$400	177,234 / \$2,100 / \$600	236,312 / \$2,800 / \$800

1 = Maximum Mortgage Amount   2 = Maximum Monthly Mortgage Payment   3 = Maximum Monthly Debts

Table 4-3

It should be noted that the existence of these credit-scoring systems has created some inconsistency in findings. A big drawback in the system is caused by the fact that major determinants of credit capacity—income and assets—are not entered into the equation. This means that a higher income individual may show a lower credit score with perfect credit because his/her income level allows for a greater amount of open credit. Self-employed individuals may also be adversely affected because the system cannot distinguish between business expenses paid through personal accounts. An owner of a small business may run $10,000 or more monthly through his/her personal credit cards. In this case, a lender may allow removing these debts from the back ratio calculation with proof of payment from a business account. However, the cards cannot be removed from the credit score calculation.

Residual method

Gross monthly income
(-) Income and payroll taxes
(-) Monthly debts
(-) Family support
(-) Housing expense
= (+) or (-) Residual

Currently, FHA and VA do not use credit scores as a part of these underwriting guidelines. However, government loans are likely to be underwritten utilizing these automated underwriting systems and this in effect brings credit scores into play for government loans.

The residual method of qualification

While the ratio method of qualification calculates a percentage of income that can be applied to the housing and debt payments of an applicant,

VA Family Support Table of Residuals

Family Size	Northeast	Midwest/South	West
1	$390/$450	$382/$441	$425/$491
2	$654/$755	$641/$738	$713/$823
3	$788/$909	$772/$889	$859/$990
4	$888/$1,025	$868/$1,003	$967/$1,117
5	$921/$1,062	$902/$1,039	$1,004/$1,158

- First number is for loan amounts below $80,000.
- Add $75/$80 of each additional family member up to a family of 7.
- Northeast States: Connecticut, New Hampshire, Pennsylvania, Maine, New Jersey, Rhode Island, Massachusetts, New York, Vermont.
- West States: Alaska, Arizona, California, Colorado, Hawaii, Idaho, Montana, Nevada, New Mexico, Oregon, Utah, Washington, Wyoming.
- All other states are Midwest or Southern.
- Active duty servicemen or their families living close to a base and receiving benefits of such can reduce required residual by 5.0%.

Table 4-4

the residual method of qualification actually attempts to more directly calculate whether the applicant can afford the monthly mortgage payment. We can think of the residual method of qualification as the *family budget method*. That is, we take the income and subtract all expenses including the mortgage payment. If there is a positive *residual*, the applicant qualifies. If there is a negative *residual*, the applicant does not qualify.

Almost everyone can relate to the calculation of a family budget: income minus expenses. Yet, the calculation of the residual method is much more tedious than the ratio method because of the number of expenses that must be subtracted from the income:

- Federal income taxes
- State income taxes
- Social Security
- Rental negative
- Child support

Chapter 4

- Family Support
- Monthly debts
- Property taxes
- Utilities
- Housing maintenance
- Association fees
- Principal and interest

The cumbersome method of calculation may very well be a major reason why the majority of the industry has adopted the ratio method of qualification over the residual method. VA is the only major mortgage source continuing to rely on the residual method, though residual method continues to be an acceptable demonstration of affordability when a mortgage applicant needs to show compensating factors to exceed acceptable ratios on jumbo mortgages:

Monthly income:	$10,000
Monthly debts:	$2,000 (Alimony payment)
Monthly PITI:	$2,500
Debt ratio:	45%

In the above case, the debt ratio is 45%, much higher than the acceptable 36% conventional ratios. From a residual point of view, however, it can be seen that the applicant has plenty of disposable income, especially because the alimony payment is tax deductible:

Monthly Income:		$10,000	
Taxes:	(-)	$ 2,000	
Debts:	(-)	$ 2,000	
PITI:	(-)	$ 2,500	
Residual:		$ 3,500	For utilities, maintenance, family support

We will end this discussion of ratios and residuals with worksheets that combine the ratio and residual method and also present many notes help you work out qualification solutions. The pre-qualification worksheets walk you through an extra calculation to determine the lower interest rate needed for a larger mortgage amount. These are excellent pages for homebuyers, real estate agents, and loan originators to copy and use for multiple qualification and pre-qualification questions.

Qualifying for a Mortgage: Ratios and Residuals

Residual method example

Residual method example assumptions

Assumptions:
Husband and Wife
No Children
Property Taxes: $200   Monthly
Husband Income: $2,250   Taxable
Spouse Income: $1,250   Taxable
                 $840   Non-taxable[36]
Association Fees: $50   Monthly
Hazard Insurance: $25   Monthly
Interest Rate: 8.5%
Mortgage Amount: $165,000
Debts: $350   Car Loan
             150   Personal Loan
             $250   Monthly Credit Cards

Monthly tax chart Example

If Wages Are		Withholding Allowances		
At Least	But Less Than	0	1	2
960	1000	66	31	0
1960	2000	216	181	146

Residual Method Example

	Borrower	Co-Borrower
Monthly gross income	2,250	1,250
Federal Tax (-)	138	33
State Tax (-)		63
Social Security (-)	172	96
Retirement (-)		
Child Care (-)		
Monthly Debts (-)	750	
Rental Negative (-)		
Non-taxable Income (+)	840	
Subtotal	2,030	1058

Total		3,088
Taxes & Insurance (-)		225
Utilities (-)		215
Maintenance (-)		50
Association Fee (-)		50
Family Support (-)		823
Balance available for principal and interest (=)		1,725
$165,000 at 8.5% (-)		1,269
Positive Residual		+456

Notes:
- Actual tax tables are located in the Appendices. In this case we would use the married table with one exemption for each borrower.
- The State taxes are estimated at five percent of gross monthly income. This figure will change slightly from state to state. In addition, many states exempt income of the military from taxation.
- Social Security taxes are 7.65% of all taxable income in this case.
- Separate retirement may be paid by Federal, State and Local government employees. Military personnel do not contribute to their retirement plans.
- Rental negative would be in the case of another property owned by the applicants, and rented out to others. VA requires a veteran to have experience as a landlord in order to count rental income: as well as three months of mortgage payments as cash reserves after closing. On a multiple unit property purchase, the veteran is required to have six months cash reserves after closing.
- Monthly utilities is estimated at $1 per thousand plus $50 ($100,000 sales price would be $150 monthly).
- Maintenance: we usually estimate $50 for maintenance except for condominiums because the condominium assessment would cover a certain amount of maintenance. In the case of condominiums we would use $25.
- Family support is from a table issued by the VA (Table 4-4). The number used would depend upon the region of the country and the family size. In addition:
  – VA allows a 5% reduction in the required family support if the house is located near a military base and the veteran enjoys benefits from that base.
  – VA requires a 20% increase in family support if the debt ratio of the applicant(s) exceeds the required 41%. A positive residual with the 20% increase in family support is not mandatory, but is considered a significant compensating factor for anyone exceeding the 41% back ratio.
- Hazard insurance is from assumptions above. A general estimate is $2.50 for each $1,000 of sales price.

---

[36] Husband is active military and in addition to taxable base income he receives variable housing allowances, or VHA, Basic Allowance for Subsistence, or BAS, and Basic Allowance for Quarters, or BAQ, each of which is not taxable.

Chapter 4

Purchaser Qualification Sheet

_____ Date _____

Purchaser _____ Down payment & closing costs _____

Property _____ Liquid assets available _____

RATIO		RESIDUAL		
			(B)	(C)

A. **Monthly gross income** .... _____ (A) **Monthly gross income** .... _____ _____
B. **Housing expense** .... _____ Federal Tax (-) .... _____ _____
    Principal and Interest.................... _____ State Tax (-) .... _____ _____
    Taxes and Insurance .... _____ Social Security (-) .... _____ _____
    MI.. _____ Retirement (-) .... _____ _____
    Association Fee .... _____ Child Care (-) .... _____ _____
    PI for second Trust .... _____ Monthly Debts (-) .... _____ _____
    Total .... _____ (B) Rental Negative (-)...................... _____ _____
C. **Debt service** .... _____ Non-taxable Income (+) .... _____ _____
    Housing Expense **(B)** .... _____ **Subtotal** .... _____ _____
    Monthly Debt Payments .... _____ Total ....
    Rental Negatives .... _____ Taxes & Insurance (-) ....
    Total .... _____ (C) Utilities (-)....................................
Housing Ratio: Maintenance (-)............................
    (B) divided by **(A)** .... _____ % Association Fee (-).......................
Debt Ratio: Family Support (-) ....
    (C) divided by **(A)** .... _____ % **Balance available for principal**
                                                                          and interest ....

NOTES:
1. _Income_ must be averaged if variable (interest, commission, bonus, overtime, part-time). For self-employed use average of _Net_ income for 2 years. Do not include expense accounts.
2. _Debts:_ Monthly payments with more than 10 months remaining.
    Child support and/or alimony payments are monthly debts (child care only for VA).
    For credit cards use 5% of the outstanding balance or minimum of $10. For FHA, alimony can be taken as a reduction in income.
3. _Rental negative_: A vacancy facto 25% may be used to lower monthly rental income before a negative is calculated ($1,000 income with 25% factor is $750).
4. _PI_ for a second trust is in the first ratio only if secured on property being purchased.
5. _Association fee_ is included in first ratio in full. Condo fees that include utilities are sometimes reduced 30-40%. Condo fee in VA qualifying will reduce estimates for maintenance, insurance, and sometimes utilities.
6. _Social security_ for 2005 is 6.2% and 12.4% for self-employed on a maximum base of $90,000. Medicare Portion only (1.45%) is collected above that amount.
7. _Federal retirement_ is 8.5% with no maximum.
8. _State income tax_ is not paid by many active military.
9. _Utilities_ is $1 per 1,000 of sales price + $50.
10. _Maintenance:_ $50 estimate; $25 for condominiums.
11. _Insurance:_ Estimate $2.50 per 1,000 of sales price for annual premium.
12. Mortgage Insurance (MI) estimate .96% monthly for 95+% LTV, .78% monthly for 90% LTV.

Worksheet 4-1

Qualifying for a Mortgage: Ratios and Residuals

Conventional Pre-Qualification

FIRST RATIO

Monthly Gross Income _____

x .28

Less Property Taxes (-) _____

Less Hazard Insurance (-) _____

Less Mortgage Insurance (-) _____

Less HOA or Condo Fee (-) _____

Available for Principal & Interest (A) $_____

SECOND RATIO

Monthly Gross Income _____

x .36

Less Monthly Debts (-) _____

Less Property Taxes (-) _____

Less Hazard Insurance (-) _____

Less Mortgage Insurance (-) _____

Less HOA or Condo Fee (-) _____

Available for Principal & Interest (B) $_____

Divide the lower of (A) or (B) above by interest rate factor per $1,000 which is prevailing for program desired at time of pre-qualification

÷ _____ (factor)

= _____

Multiply answer by 1,000 to arrive at maximum loan amount

x ____1,000____

=$_____ maximum loan

To figure interest rate needed to qualify borrower when loan amount needed is known:

Carry lower of (A) or (B) above down to right $_____

Divide by loan amount, dropping the last three numbers (ex: $70,000 = 70)   ÷_____

Result is interest rate factor (Table on inside cover)   _____

Worksheet 4-2

Chapter 4

VA Pre-Qualification — Residual

	(B)	(CB
Monthly Gross Income	_____	_____
Less Federal Tax	(-) _____	(-) _____
Less State Tax	(-) _____	(-) _____
Less Social Security	(-) _____	(-) _____
Less Child Care	(-) _____	(-) _____
Less Monthly Debts	(-) _____	(-) _____
Less Rental Negative	(-) _____	(-) _____
Add Non-taxable Income	(+) _____	(+) _____
Sub-Total	_____	_____

Total		_____
Less Property Taxes	(-) _____	
Less Hazard Insurance	(-) _____	
Less Utilities	(-) _____	
Less Maintenance	(-) _____	
Less Association/Condo Fees	(-) _____	
Less Family Support	(-) _____	
Available for Principal & Interest	_____	

Divide the principal & interest by interest rate factor per $1,000 which is prevailing for program desired at time of pre-qualification

divide by _____ (factor)

= _____

Multiply answer by 1,000 to arrive at maximum loan amount

x _____

=$ _____ max loan

To figure interest rate needed to qualify borrower when loan amount needed is known:

Carry principal and interest down to right $ _____

Divide by loan amount, dropping the last three numbers (ex: $70,000 = 70)   ÷ _____

Result is interest rate factor (Table on inside cover)   _____

Worksheet 4-3

5

Comparing Mortgages

Thus far we have presented the characteristics of a multitude of mortgage types and sources. This information was imperative to arrive at the answer for the most significant question of this book:

"Which is the best mortgage alternative for me?"

Unfortunately, there may very well be no clear-cut answer to this question. Many mortgage applicants have very little choice when it comes to selecting a mortgage. This is because of limited cash assets and/or income necessary to qualify for the mortgage. Others have a choice but lack direction as to the proper way to compare mortgages. In the final analysis, even the most qualified and informed consumer still may not be able to make the best choice because there are always two undetermined variables at the time of mortgage selection:

- For how long will the mortgage be utilized?
- Where will interest rates move in the future?

If we could determine the answers to these questions, the selection of mortgage alternatives would be much simpler. Since it is unlikely that the prediction of the future will be within our reach, we will make any decision with a good measure of uncertainty. What we are forced to do is make assumptions about the future and then compare our alternatives under these assumptions. We then try to select from the scenario with which we are the most comfortable.

Comparing mortgage payments over the life of the mortgage

The cost of the mortgage over the life of the mortgage is obviously the consumer's main concern after home and/or mortgage acquisition has taken place. It is here that we must factor in the unknown variables of expected mortgage life and the future direction of interest rates. Let us take a simple example:

The choice is: $100,000 mortgage
    a.   8.00% 30 year fixed rate
    b.   5.00% one year adjustable
          2.00% annual cap
          6.00% life cap
          2.75% margin over one year *T* index

Chapter 5

In the first year, it is easy to see that the payments will be lower for the adjustable. If the mortgage has a five-year life, what will happen? Will the adjustable rate mortgage increase two percent every year?

If the adjustable increases by the maximum allowed under the adjustment caps, we are describing the *worst-case scenario*. The *worst-case scenario* for our one-year adjustable over a five-year period is shown in the example.

How do we compare this scenario to the fixed rate? The easiest way is to average the interest rate over the five-year period: 8.60%. Comparing payments over the period:

One year ARM:	8.60%	$46,560	total payments
30 year fixed:	8.00%	$44,025	total payments
Savings on fixed rate:		$ 2,535	

We should bring forward the following notations on this comparison:

1. The risk of the ARM averaging a higher rate than the fixed rate rises over time in the worst-case scenario. The average rate over four years for the ARM is actually identical to that of the fixed rate.
2. This analysis does not take into account of cost of money over time. The cost of money paid out in the future is worth less due to the existence of inflation.
3. The worst-case scenario actually presents adjustables in a negative light and this scenario is not the only valid method of comparison. For example, suppose we assumed that the mortgage was procured five years ago and we compare the average payments that would have occurred over the past five years as a model of prediction for the next five years? We call this the "historical case" scenario.

The example shows an average rate of 7.60% over five years, which is exactly 1% less than the average rate under the worst case scenario and less than the 8.00% fixed rate.

Another option for developing a scenario for predicting the behavior of an adjustable rate mortgage is to assume that the index value stays constant at the time of settlement for the life of the mortgage. This means that the adjustable rate mortgage will rise to the *Fully Indexed Accrual Rate*, or *FIAR*.

Which computation method is more accurate: the worst case, past track record, or FIAR scenario for ARMs? There is no way of knowing. Each has some element of merit:

Worst case scenario example

Year 1: 5.00%
Year 2: 7.00%
Year 3: 9.00% $776.01 average payments
Year 4: 11.00%
Year 5: 11.00% (11% is the life cap)
43.00%

43.00% ÷ 5 = 8.60% average

5-year "historical-case" comparison

Date of Mortgage: January 1, 1995
Interest rate year 1: 5.00% (start rate)
Interest rate year 2: 7.00% (index value January 1, 1996: 9.05 + 2.75 = 11.80%, which is higher than 2% annual cap)
Interest rate year 3: 9.00% (index value January 1, 1997: 7.92 + 2.75 = 10.67%, which is higher than 2% annual cap)
Interest rate year 4: 9.50% (index value January 1, 1998: 6.64 + 2.75 = 9.39%, or 9.5% rounded up to nearest .125%)
Interest rate year 5: 7.50% (index value January 1, 1999: 4.38 + 2.75 = 7.13%, which is lower than 2% annual cap)
Average rate 7.60%, less than 30-year fixed

FIAR example

5% One-year arm
2/6 Caps
2.75 Margin
Index value at the time of settlement: 7.00
Interest rate year 1: 5.00%
Interest rate year 2: 7.00% (7.00 + 2.75 = 9.75%, which is higher than 2% annual cap)
Interest rate year 3: 9.00% (7.00 + 2.75 = 9.75%, which is higher than 2% annual cap)
Interest rate year 4: 9.75% (7.00 + 2.75 = 9.75%, which means that ARM has reached its FIAR)
Interest rate year 5: 9.75% (this rate will hold for the term of the mortgage as we assume the index is stable)
Average rate for 5 years: 8.00%, the same as the fixed rate

Comparing Mortgages

- The worst-case scenario enables the consumer to determine the worst that can happen during the loan term. It is also to become more likely if the ARM was originated below market (with a *teaser rate*) or market rates are much lower than historical standards.
- The past track record enables the consumer to look back and determine how the ARM would have performed under market conditions that were in effect for the period directly before the settlement takes place. This would become more likely if the period used for comparison was not one that varied significantly from historical standards.
- The FIAR method assumes that today's market will be the standard for the future. This is to be more likely if today's market is typical of historical standards.

Worst Case Scenario Comparison for Different Mortgage Types

Mortgage amount: $100,000
 *30 year fixed rate of 8.00%
 *2-1 buydown of 30 year fixed rate of 8.25%
 *Three year adjustable at 6.50%
   2% cap every 3 years
   6% life cap
 *One year adjustable at 6.00%
   1% annual cap
   4% life cap

Year	30 Year Fixed	2-1 Buydown	Three Year	One Year
1	8.0%	6.25%	6.5%	6.0%
2	8.0%	7.25%	6.5%	7.0%
3	8.0%	8.25%	6.5%	8.0%
4	8.0%	8.25%	8.5%	9.0%
5	8.0%	8.25%	8.5%	10.0%
6	8.0%	8.25%	8.5%	10.0%
Average Rate:	8.0%	7.75%	7.5%	8.33%
Average Payment:	$733.76	$716.41	$699.21	$756.90
Total Payments:	$52,831	$51,581	$50,343	$54,497

The borrower actually should look at the performance of an ARM product under several conditions: the worst case, declining rates, stable rates and volatile rates. In this way the borrower will have an idea of all performances that are possible.

Because these calculations would be quite tedious for the average homebuyer, we have developed tables that should help in the determination of the performance level of different adjustable rate products under different scenarios.

Table 5-1 gives the average rates for each product type described under a worst-case scenario for a certain time period. For example, the one-year ARM with 2/6 caps will average 1% over the start rate for a two-year period. One can now use this table to compare any products with identical characteristics by just knowing the start rates.

Example: One year ARM
 Start rate of 5%
 Average rate for two
   years: 6% (5% + 1%)

Example: Three year ARM
 Start rate of 7%
 Average rate for five
   years: 7.8% (7% + 0.8%)

Chapter 5

Interest Rate Increases for Variable Mortgage
Average Interest rate increase as of given year
Assuming 0% start rate and worst case rate increase (5% increase for balloons)

Year	Fixed	2-1 Buydown	6 mo. ARM with 1/6 Caps	1 year ARM with 2/6 Caps	1 year ARM with 1/4 Caps	3 year ARM with 2/6 Caps	3/1 ARM with 2/6 Caps	5 year ARM with 2/6 Caps	5/1 ARM with 2/6 Caps	5/25 Balloon	7/23 Balloon
1	0.0%	0.0%	0.5%	0.0%	0.0%	0.0%	0.0%	0.0%	0.0%	0.0%	0.0%
2	0.0%	0.5%	1.5%	1.0%	0.5%	0.0%	0.0%	0.0%	0.0%	0.0%	0.0%
3	0.0%	1.0%	2.5%	2.0%	1.0%	0.0%	0.0%	0.0%	0.0%	0.0%	0.0%
4	0.0%	1.3%	3.4%	3.0%	1.5%	0.5%	0.5%	0.0%	0.0%	0.0%	0.0%
5	0.0%	1.4%	3.9%	3.6%	2.0%	0.8%	1.2%	0.0%	0.0%	0.0%	0.0%
6	0.0%	1.5%	4.3%	4.0%	2.3%	1.0%	2.0%	0.3%	0.3%	0.8%	0.0%
7	0.0%	1.6%	4.5%	4.3%	2.6%	1.4%	2.6%	0.6%	0.9%	1.4%	0.0%
8	0.0%	1.6%	4.7%	4.5%	2.8%	1.8%	3.0%	0.8%	1.5%	1.9%	0.6%
9	0.0%	1.7%	4.8%	4.7%	2.9%	2.0%	3.3%	0.9%	2.0%	2.2%	1.1%
10	0.0%	1.7%	5.0%	4.8%	3.0%	2.4%	3.6%	1.0%	2.4%	2.5%	1.5%
11	0.0%	1.7%	5.0%	4.9%	3.1%	2.7%	3.8%	1.3%	2.7%	2.7%	1.8%
12	0.0%	1.8%	5.1%	5.0%	3.2%	3.0%	4.0%	1.5%	3.0%	2.9%	2.1%
13	0.0%	1.8%	5.2%	5.1%	3.2%	3.2%	4.2%	1.7%	3.2%	3.1%	2.3%
14	0.0%	1.8%	5.3%	5.1%	3.3%	3.4%	4.3%	1.9%	3.4%	3.2%	2.5%
15	0.0%	1.8%	5.3%	5.2%	3.3%	3.6%	4.4%	2.0%	3.6%	3.3%	2.7%
16	0.0%	1.8%	5.3%	5.3%	3.4%	3.8%	4.5%	2.3%	3.8%	3.4%	2.8%
17	0.0%	1.8%	5.4%	5.3%	3.4%	3.9%	4.6%	2.5%	3.9%	3.5%	2.9%
18	0.0%	1.8%	5.4%	5.3%	3.4%	4.0%	4.7%	2.7%	4.0%	3.6%	3.1%
19	0.0%	1.8%	5.4%	5.4%	3.5%	4.1%	4.7%	2.8%	4.1%	3.7%	3.2%
20	0.0%	1.9%	5.5%	5.4%	3.5%	4.2%	4.8%	3.0%	4.2%	3.8%	3.3%
21	0.0%	1.9%	5.5%	5.4%	3.5%	4.3%	4.9%	3.1%	4.3%	3.8%	3.3%
22	0.0%	1.9%	5.5%	5.5%	3.5%	4.4%	4.9%	3.3%	4.4%	3.9%	3.4%
23	0.0%	1.9%	5.5%	5.5%	3.6%	4.4%	5.0%	3.4%	4.4%	3.9%	3.5%
24	0.0%	1.9%	5.6%	5.5%	3.6%	4.5%	5.0%	3.5%	4.5%	4.0%	3.5%
25	0.0%	1.9%	5.6%	5.5%	3.6%	4.6%	5.0%	3.6%	4.6%	4.0%	3.6%
26	0.0%	1.9%	5.6%	5.5%	3.6%	4.6%	5.1%	3.7%	4.6%	4.0%	3.7%
27	0.0%	1.9%	5.6%	5.6%	3.6%	4.7%	5.1%	3.8%	4.7%	4.1%	3.7%
28	0.0%	1.9%	5.6%	5.6%	3.6%	4.7%	5.1%	3.9%	4.7%	4.1%	3.8%
29	0.0%	1.9%	5.6%	5.6%	3.7%	4.8%	5.2%	3.9%	4.8%	4.1%	3.8%
30	0.0%	1.9%	5.7%	5.6%	3.7%	4.8%	5.2%	4.0%	4.8%	4.2%	3.8%

Table 5-1

Comparing mortgage payments for different mortgage terms

The consumer may actually desire higher mortgage payments if the result will be a shorter mortgage term. In this case, the consumer's goal will be to build up equity as quickly as possible, or reducing the interest owed over the life of the mortgage. Table 5-2 actually compares the total mortgage payments over the mortgage term and total interest paid for varied interest rates on a $100,000 mortgage.

The consumer can actually use these tables for any mortgage amount by a process of extrapolation:
- A mortgage amount of $150,000 would be 1.5 times any value in the tables
- A mortgage amount of $50,000 would be one-half of any value in the tables

Comparing Mortgages

Mortgage Term/Prepayment Comparison
Assuming $100,000 loan amount and 25% tax rate

Rate	Term (Years)	Monthly Payment	Additional Monthly Pmt vs. 30-Year	Total Interest Paid	Total of Payments	Lifetime Savings vs. 30-Year Term
5%	10	$1,060.66	$523.84	$27,278	$127,278	$65,978
	15	$790.79	$253.97	$42,343	$142,343	$50,913
	20	$659.96	$123.14	$58,389	$158,389	$34,867
	25	$584.59	$47.77	$75,377	$175,377	$17,879
	30	$536.82	$0.	$93,256	$193,256	$0
6%	10	$1,110.21	$510.66	$33,224	$133,224	$82,614
	15	$843.86	$244.31	$51,894	$151,894	$63,944
	20	$716.43	$116.88	$71,944	$171,944	$43,895
	25	$644.30	$44.75	$93,291	$193,291	$22,548
	30	$599.55	$0	$115,838	$215,838	$0
7%	10	$1,161.08	$495.78	$39,330	$139,330	$100,179
	15	$898.83	$233.53	$61,789	$161,789	$77,720
	20	$775.30	$110.00	$86,072	$186,072	$53,437
	25	$706.78	$41.48	$112,034	$212,034	$27,475
	30	$665.30	$0	$139,509	$239,509	$0
8%	10	$1,213.28	$479.51	$45,593	$145,593	$118,562
	15	$955.65	$221.89	$72,017	$172,017	$92,138
	20	$836.44	$102.68	$100,746	$200,746	$63,410
	25	$771.82	$38.05	$131,545	$231,545	$32,610
	30	$733.76	$0	$164,155	$264,155	$0
9%	10	$1,266.76	$462.14	$52,011	$152,011	$137,653
	15	$1,014.27	$209.64	$82,568	$182,568	$107,096
	20	$899.73	$95.10	$115,934	$215,934	$73,730
	25	$839.20	$34.57	$151,759	$251,759	$37,905
	30	$804.62	$0	$189,664	$289,664	$0
10%	10	$1,321.51	$443.94	$58,581	$158,581	$157,345
	15	$1,074.61	$197.03	$93,429	$193,429	$122,497
	20	$965.02	$87.45	$131,605	$231,605	$84,321
	25	$908.70	$31.13	$172,610	$272,610	$43,316
	30	$877.57	$0	$215,926	$315,926	$0

Table 5-2

We should note that if we merely compared the mortgage payments and interest paid over the term, we would not be able to realize the opportunity cost of not being able to invest certain money during the life of the mortgage. For example, if a 15-year mortgage requires an extra payment of $400 each month as compared to a 30-year instrument, the homeowner could invest this $400 each month in a bank account or mutual fund. The investment income will partially offset the interest savings on the 15-year mortgage. Another factor that is even harder to measure is the effect of deducting the taxes on the interest payments. Any interest savings will actually reduce the tax-deductible portion of the mortgage, thereby increasing the consumer's tax base. Of course, the investment interest gained will also be taxable.

Chapter 5

22-Year ARM Performance — Historical Method

Term (Years)	Index Value	ARM Rate	Cumulative Average	Five Year Average
1983	8.62	11.37	11.37	
1984	9.90	12.65	12.01	
1985	9.02	11.77	11.93	
1986	7.73	10.48	11.57	
1987	5.78	8.53	10.96	10.96
1988	6.99	9.74	10.76	
1989	9.05	11.80	10.91	
1990	7.92	10.67	10.88	
1991	6.64	9.39	10.71	
1992	4.15	6.90	10.33	9.70
1993	3.50	6.25	9.96	
1994	3.54	6.29	9.65	
1995	7.05	9.80	9.66	
1996	5.09	7.84	9.53	
1997	5.61	8.36	9.56	7.71
1998	5.24	7.99	9.36	
1999	4.51	7.26	8.24	
2000	6.21	8.87	9.22	
2001	4.81	7.56	9.13	
2002	2.16	4.91	8.92	7.32
2003	1.36	4.11	8.69	
2004	1.24	3.99	8.48	4.05 (2yr)

Notes:
- The Index is the 1 Year "T"
- The Index value used for comparison is January of each year.
- The Margin used is 2.75%
- For comparison purposes there are no caps. The ARM is fully indexed every January.
- The cumulative average is the average for the number of years since 1982 (e.g., 1985 would have a 4-year cumulative average).
- The 5-year average would have the average for the preceding five years only

Table 5-3

One should not make the assumption that the homeowner can easily convert a 30-year mortgage into a 20-year term. Most consumers put off prepayment until future years. Because of the "compounding" effect of interest, a dollar paid toward principal the first month of a mortgage is actually worth many times more than a dollar paid two years in the future.

Comparing points on mortgage programs

It is one thing to compare the performance of different mortgage instruments using the starting rates and potential rate increases in the future. What if the initial points charged are different? How does this affect the comparison?

1. When comparing different products with different point options, we can adjust easily for each point by adding one percent to the starting rate for each extra point charged.

    For example:
    >Fixed rate of 8.00% with 2 points
    >One year ARM of 5.00% with 3 points
    >(2% annual cap/6% life cap)

    When we provide the worst-case scenario comparison, we add one percent to the starting rate of the adjustable (for the first year only):

	Fixed Rate	Adjustable
Year 1:	8.00%	6.00% (instead of 5.00%)
Year 2:	8.00%	7.00%
Year 3:	8.00%	9.00%
Average rate:	8.00%	7.33%
Average rate without extra point:		7.00%

2. When comparing the same product with different point options, we are now trying to decide the answer to this question:

    > *"Should I choose a lower rate with more points or a higher rate with lower points?"*

    Assuming you have the income necessary to qualify for any interest rate available, and possess the cash assets necessary to pay any point options available, there remains only one factor important for the determination of the answer:

    > *How long will you have the mortgage?*

    Each extra point will be paid back over a period of time (from three to seven years typically) through a lower payment.

    Example:
$100,000 mortgage–30 year fixed rate	
Option 1:	8.25% with 0 points
Option 2:	7.75% with 2 points
Monthly payment at 8.25%:	$751.27
Monthly payment at 7.75%:	$716.41
Monthly savings at 7.75%:	$ 34.86
Extra cost of points at 8.25%:	$ 2,000
Months to recover cost of points:	$ 2,000
	$ 34.86 = 57.37, or *4.78 Years*

Our conclusion here is that the applicant will be better off paying the extra points if he/she stays with the mortgage for over five years. Generally, the longer one stays in the home, the more likely that extra points will pay off. We should note that this analysis is not entirely accurate because it compares points in today's dollars to future dollars with regard to monthly payments. We also don't compare the tax-deductibility of the points versus the extra monthly payment.

Chapter 5

Annual Percentage Rates
At varying terms and points
8% interest rate

Term (Years)	Points 0	1	2	3	4	5
6 mo.	8.000%	11.497%	15.049%	18.657%	22.322%	26.047%
1	8.000%	9.895%	11.818%	13.770%	15.751%	17.762%
2	8.000%	8.999%	10.012%	11.039%	12.082%	13.140%
3	8.000%	8.684%	9.378%	10.082%	10.796%	11.520%
4	8.000%	8.524%	9.055%	9.594%	10.141%	10.695%
5	8.000%	8.427%	8.859%	9.298%	9.744%	10.196%
6	8.000%	8.362%	8.728%	9.101%	9.478%	9.861%
7	8.000%	8.315%	8.635%	8.959%	9.288%	9.622%
8	8.000%	8.280%	8.564%	8.853%	9.145%	9.442%
9	8.000%	8.253%	8.510%	8.770%	9.034%	9.303%
10	8.000%	8.231%	8.466%	8.704%	8.946%	9.191%
15	8.000%	8.167%	8.336%	8.508%	8.683%	8.860%
20	8.000%	8.135%	8.273%	8.413%	8.555%	8.699%
25	8.000%	8.117%	8.237%	8.358%	8.481%	8.607%
30	8.000%	8.106%	8.214%	8.324%	8.435%	8.549%

Table 5-4

It should be noted that the volatility of rates may have much to do with the prediction of overall mortgage term. When rates are at an historic high, it is much more likely the homeowner will refinance out of the mortgage more quickly. When rates are historically low, it is more likely the mortgage will last longer. We are likely to advise clients to take actions that are contrary to these probabilities. For example, when rates are low, we tend to recommend no-cost refinances when they would be better served obtaining the lowest rate possible.

Once again we have developed tables to help you in the determination of the value of points. Through the *Truth-In-Lending Disclosure* (*TIL*), the Federal Government tries to standardize the cost of mortgages by combining extra fees with the interest rate. The figure that is compiled and disclosed is called the *Annual Percentage Rate*, or *APR*. Table 5-4 assumes that the only extra costs associated with the mortgage are points. We are utilizing a standard $100,000 mortgage and a base rate of 8.00%. The table varies the points paid and the life of the mortgage over which the points are utilized.

Comparing mortgage combinations

Often times the important comparison is not between two distinctly different programs. Instead we compare two mortgage combinations versus another for a particular consumer. Here are a few of the options that might require us to make such a comparison—

- Refinancing into a new mortgage versus adding a second onto an existing mortgage.
- Doing a combination of a first and second mortgage versus one mortgage (perhaps avoiding a jumbo rate and/or mortgage insurance).

To facilitate these comparisons, one would have to compute what is called a "blended" rate for a particular mortgage combination. For example, if there were a total mortgage amount of $100,000 and this total indebtedness consisted of—

$80,000 First at 7.0% interest
$20,000 Second at 8.0% interest, the calculation would be as follows—

    $80,000 x 7.0% = $5,600 annual interest
    $20,000 x 8.0% = $1,600 annual interest
    Total annual interest = $7,200, or a 7.2% interest rate (for a loan amount other than $100,000, divide the annual interest by the loan amount in thousands).

This calculation will enable us to make a comparison versus a new mortgage, perhaps at 6.75%. Are they better off refinancing the whole mortgage or better off just refinancing the second mortgage at 7.5%? Of course the points and other closing costs must be taken into account for this comparison.

The same calculation will help us determine whether they are better off obtaining a jumbo mortgage with a 7.50% interest rate or a conforming mortgage with a 7.25% interest rate and a second mortgage with an 8.0% interest rate. The larger the second is in this case, the higher the blended rate.

Comparing cash requirements for each mortgage

Sometimes the interest rate, payments, or points are not the overriding factors present within the mortgage selection process. Sometimes the one most important factor is:

"Which mortgage will enable me to get into the house with the least amount of cash invested?"

Cash Necessary for Home Purchase

Cash Requirement	FHA	VA	Conventional
Down Payment	1.25% to 2.85%	0	0 to 5.0%
Mortgage Insurance	0	0	0
Seller Contributions	6.0%	All normal costs	3.0% with minimum down
Prepaids	Seller can pay	Seller can pay	Varies
Total Cash	3.0%	0	3.0% to 5.0%
Gift	100%	100%	Borrower may be required to have 3.0% to 5.0% of own funds

Notes:
- Mortgage insurance not counted if it can be financed (escrow amount will be included under prepaids).
- Cash requirements based upon average closing costs of 3.0% and prepaids of 1.0%.
- Maximum seller contributions assumed for determining total cash requirements.
- 100% gift means that the borrower can use a gift for all necessary funds.
- Lender can pay prepaids with higher interest rate on FHA and some conventional mortgages.
- In the case of VA, the borrower pays a funding fee rather than mortgage insurance.
- Conventional 0 to 3.0% down payment programs may require maximum income or minimum credit score.

Table 5-5

As we have presented different mortgage sources, we have attempted to focus on all differences between these mortgage options. Table 5-5 attempts to summarize one characteristic: the cash necessary for home purchase.

Chapter 5

Comparing qualification requirements for each mortgage source

Qualification requirements comprise another factor that can be the determining variable in selecting a mortgage. The term and mortgage payment may not be relevant if the purchaser cannot purchase the home because their income is insufficient to qualify for a mortgage. Table 5-6 summarizes the income requirements for each mortgage source. These requirements are expressed in terms of mortgage ratios.

Qualification Requirements for Mortgage Sources

	FHA	**VA**	**Conventional**
Housing	29%	N/A	28%-33%
Debt Ratio	41%	41%	33%-38%
ARM Standard	Second year maximum rate	Second year maximum rate	Second year maximum rate or fully-indexed rate
Temporary buydown standard	Cannot qualify at reduced rate	Cannot qualify at reduced rate	Typically 2% below note rate

Notes:
- VA has second standard of a positive residual.
- ARM and temporary buydown standards are the rates at which the borrower will be qualified if these instruments are utilized to increase qualification (assumes maximum LTV). Hybrid adjustables qualify at the initial rate for all programs.
- VA will allow qualification at a reduced rate for a temporary buydown if the borrower provides proof of future increase in income of a definitive amount.
- The ratios for conventional mortgages will vary widely as to what is acceptable by automated systems.

Table 5-6

6

Refinancing a Mortgage

What is a refinance?

A refinance is the replacement of an existing mortgage with a new loan equal to, larger, or smaller in size than the original mortgage. In fact, if there was never a mortgage placed on the property (we say that it is owned *free and clear*), placing a mortgage on the property for the first time is considered a refinance as long as the owner remains the same. The placement of a second mortgage behind a first mortgage on a property after it is purchased is called a *refinance second*, or *home equity second*, as opposed to a *purchase-money second*.

There are two basic types of refinance mortgages:

- A *rate reduction refinance* replaces only the existing balance. The new mortgage balance can be increased to finance, or *roll in*, closing costs associated with procuring the new mortgage. It should be noted that not all rate reduction refinances carry a lower interest rate than the original mortgage. The important point is the primary purpose of the refinance, which will be to pay off the original mortgage and finance associated closing costs. Many loan programs allow a small amount of cash to be obtained without the transaction being considered a "cash-out." For example, Fannie Mae will allow up to 2% of the loan balance, or $2,000, whichever is less.

- A *cash-out refinance* replaces more than the existing balance and associated closing costs. The new mortgage balance is large enough to pay off the existing balance and associated closing costs *and* the homeowner will walk away with cash from the transaction. A second mortgage placed on the property for the purposes of *pulling cash or equity out* would be termed a *home equity* second. Second mortgages that open up *lines of credit* for future cash withdrawals are called *home equity lines of credit (HELOCs)*. It is not unusual for cash-out mortgages to carry a rate premium.

Rate reduction refinance

(With closing costs financed)

Existing mortgage balance:	$95,000
Closing costs on new mortgage:	$ 3,000
Refinance mortgage balance:	$98,000

Chapter 6

Cash out refinance

Existing mortgage balance:	$95,000
Closing costs on new mortgage:	$3,000
Refinance mortgage balance:	$110,000
Cash out to home owner:	$12,000

Rate and payment reduction refinance

Original mortgage balance:	$100,000
Original interest rate:	10.5%
Principal and interest payment:	$914.74
Present mortgage balance:	$98,500
Closing costs:	$1,800
Points:	$1,200
New mortgage balance:	$101,500
New interest rate:	8.5%
New principal and interest payment:	$780.45
Monthly savings:	$134.29
Total costs:	$ 3,000
Months to recover costs: ($3,000 ÷ $134.29)	22.34

Costs paid out-of-pocket

New mortgage balance	$98,500
New principal and interest payment:	$757.38
Monthly savings:	$157.36
Total costs:	$3,000
Months to recover costs: ($3,000 ÷ $157.36)	19.06

Why would someone want to refinance a home?

1. *Lower the interest rate and payment.* The most obvious reason someone would want to refinance a mortgage would be to lower the interest rate and payment on that mortgage.

   In the first example, *we rolled the costs into*, or *financed the costs of*, the refinance. This is the most common way to accomplish a refinance. Another way would be for the homeowner to pay the costs of the refinance from his/her own bank account. The costs would remain the same but the new mortgage balance would be the same as the original loan.

   One method is not more advantageous than the other. One cannot accurately measure the cost associated with increasing the present mortgage balance, or decreased equity in the home. Another cost that cannot be measured is the increased term of the loan:

   - Original balance and term: $100,000—30 years
   - Present balance and remaining term: $98,500-28.5 years
   - New balance and term: $101,500—30 years

   The new mortgage will actually cause the term to increase by one and one-half years. If the homeowner will own the home for this length of time without refinancing again, the extra cost at the end of the mortgage should be measured. Or, the terms should be made equivalent in the comparison as opposed to the examples on the left that do not make such an adjustment:

   - Present mortgage payment: $914.74
   - New mortgage payment: $789.60 at $101,500 balance
   - 8.5% interest rate
   - 28.5 years term
   - Recalculated monthly savings: $125.14
   - Recalculated recovery time: 23.97 months

At first glance, figuring the monthly savings and recovery time from reducing the interest rate is very simple: divide the costs of the refinance by the monthly savings to arrive at the recovery period. In reality, the actual monthly savings is not as easy to calculate as we figure in the factors of changing the loan term and financing the costs of the refinance. Since the length of time the homeowner will have the loan cannot be answered, the precise effect cannot be measured. Table 6-1 assumes that the costs are paid out of pocket and do not consider any change in mortgage term. It predicts monthly savings and gives the number of months until those savings equal the cost of the refinance. Although it assumes a 10% interest rate on the existing mortgage, the savings differentials will not vary much for interest rates from 5%-15%, and for loan terms of 20-40 years.

Months to Break Even After Refinance

Assuming 10% interest rate on existing mortgage and no change in 30 year term

Interest Rate Reduction	Payment Reduction Factor	Cost of Refinance							
		0.5%	1.0%	1.5%	2.0%	2.5%	3.0%	3.5%	4.0%
0.25%	0.184	27.1	54.3	81.4	108.6	135.7	162.9	190.0	217.2
0.50%	0.367	13.6	27.2	40.9	54.5	68.1	81.7	95.3	108.9
0.75%	0.549	9.1	18.2	27.3	36.4	45.5	54.6	63.8	72.9
1.00%	0.729	6.9	13.7	20.6	27.4	34.3	41.1	48.0	54.8
1.25%	0.909	5.5	11.0	16.5	22.0	27.5	33.0	38.5	44.0
1.50%	1.087	4.6	9.2	13.8	18.4	23.0	27.6	32.2	36.8
1.75%	1.263	4.0	7.9	11.9	15.8	19.8	23.8	27.7	31.7
2.00%	1.438	3.5	7.0	10.4	13.9	17.4	20.9	24.3	27.8
2.25%	1.612	3.1	6.2	9.3	12.4	15.5	18.6	21.7	24.8
2.50%	1.784	2.8	5.6	8.4	11.2	14.0	16.8	19.6	22.4
2.75%	1.954	2.6	5.1	7.7	10.2	12.8	15.4	17.9	20.5
3.00%	2.123	2.4	4.7	7.1	9.4	11.8	14.1	16.5	18.8
3.25%	2.290	2.2	4.4	6.6	8.7	10.9	13.1	15.3	17.5
3.50%	2.455	2.0	4.1	6.1	8.1	10.2	12.2	14.3	16.3
3.75%	2.619	1.9	3.8	5.7	7.6	9.5	11.5	13.4	15.3
4.00%	2.780	1.8	3.6	5.4	7.2	9.0	10.8	12.6	14.4

Note: to calculate monthly payment reduction, multiply the principal amount, in thousands, by the Payment Reduction Factor in the second column.

Table 6-1

In the example, the interest rate on a mortgage with $100,000 remaining principal was reduced from 10% to 7.5%. Using the table, the 2.5% reduction in the interest rate translates to a $178.40 reduction in monthly payment. If the refinance closing costs are $3,000, it will take 16.8 months for the monthly payment savings to total more than the closing costs.

One decision that will always have to be made when considering a rate reduction refinance is how many points to pay. Each point is equal to one percent of the new mortgage amount. Table 6-2 illustrates such a choice.

Refinance Example

Old interest rate	10.0%
New interest rate	- 7.5%
Rate reduction	2.5%
Principal amount	$100,000
Payment Reduction Factor ($/1,000)	x 1.784
Payment reduction	$178.40
Closing costs	3.0%
Months to break even	16.8

The conclusion? In the short term, higher points and a lower interest rate will cost more. In the long term, the higher the points and the lower the rate, the greater the savings. In other words, if you are going to have the loan for a long time, finance as many points as is possible.

Chapter 6

Points and Refinance Savings

Interest Rate	Points	Closing Costs Including Points	New Balance	New Payment	Savings	Months to Recover	Total Savings Over 30Years
6.25%	3	$4,800	$103,300	$636.58	$278.16	17.26	$100,138
6.5%	2	$3,800	$102,300	$647.12	$267.62	14.20	$96,343
6.75%	1	$2,800	$101,300	$657.52	$257.22	10.89	$92,599
7.0%	0	$1,800	$100,300	$667.77	$246.97	7.29	$88,909

Present Mortgage Balance: $ 98,500   Present Payment: $ 914.74   Closing Costs: Without Points: $ 1,800

Note: Total savings represents the monthly savings over a 30-year period, without taking into account the cost of the refinance. The refinance cost is not relevant over the term of the mortgage because after 30 years, the mortgage balance will be zero regardless of the alternative selected. It also does not take into account the increased term of the new mortgage as we are comparing these refinance alternatives to each other, not to the cost of keeping the original mortgage.

Table 6-2

2. *Reduce the term of the mortgage.* While a straight rate reduction refinance usually will increase the term of the mortgage, the homeowner may refinance for the purpose of reducing the term of his/her present mortgage to save interest payments over the life of the mortgage. A term reduction refinance will not make economic sense unless the new interest rate is lower than the interest rate on the existing mortgage. If the existing mortgage has a rate lower than market rates, the homeowner could simply increase the amount of existing monthly payments to reduce the term of the mortgage, as described by Table 6-3.

Effect of Monthly Payment on Typical $100,000 Loan at 7%, 30-Year Amortization

Extra Payment	Principal & Interest	Months to Payoff	Years to Payoff	Total of Payments	Interest Savings
$0	$665	360	30.00	$239,511	$0
$20	$685	328	27.33	$224,477	$15,034
$50	$715	291	24.25	$207,856	$31,655
$75	$740	267	22.25	$197,412	$42,099
$100	$765	247	20.58	$189,003	$50,508
$150	$815	217	18.08	$176,192	$63,319
$200	$865	193	16.08	$166,814	$72,697

Table 6-3

Note: Calculations do not take into account investing the payment savings over the term for the remainder of the term of the mortgage (from 15 to 30 years or from 20 to 30 years).

Let us take an example of the benefits of a term reduction refinance:

- Original mortgage balance: $100,000
- Original interest rate: 10.5%
- Present mortgage balance: $98,500
- Remaining mortgage term: 336 months
- Present mortgage payment: $914.74
- New interest rate: 7.0%
- New term: 15 years (180 months)
- Closing costs: $1,800
- Points: $1,200
- New mortgage balance: $101,500
- New mortgage payment: $914.11

- Remaining payments on
  present mortgage: $914.74 x 336 = $307,352.64
- Payments on new
  mortgage: $914.11 x 180 = $164,539.80
- Savings through term refinancing:

        $307,352.64
(-) $164,539.80
        $142,812.84   *The home owner saves over $140,000 in interest over the term of the mortgage!*

In this case, the homeowner is using the monthly savings from the lower interest rate towards a reduction in term. If the interest rate reduction is great enough, the applicant can reduce the term by 10 to 15 years without increasing the monthly payments on the mortgage.

3. *Change loan type.* It is very common for a homeowner to refinance in order to change the loan type from an adjustable rate mortgage or a balloon program to a fixed rate mortgage. Typically, the home owner originally opted for these mortgage instruments to:
    * Qualify at the lower starting rate; or
    * Lower the payments during the first few years of the mortgage.

A move may be made to refinance at a time when fixed rates have moved down to an acceptable level and/or the homeowner can qualify for a fixed rate. In the case of a balloon mortgage that has reached full term, the need may be more urgent. For example, in the sixth year of a seven year balloon mortgage, the homeowner may be 12 months or less from facing a balloon payment.

There are other examples of refinances that change the type of loan programs:
- The homeowner may refinance from an adjustable rate mortgage to another adjustable rate mortgage—taking advantage of the low initial rates in each case:

    - Original mortgage: 1998
    - One year adjustable: 2% annual cap
    - Initial rate: 5%
    - 1999 rate: 7%
    - 2000 rate: 9% (worst case scenario assumption)

Instead of risking another rate increase in 2001, the borrower refinances into another one year adjustable:

    - 2001 (initial rate): 5%
    - 2002 rate: 7%
    - 2003 rate: 9% (worst case scenario assumption)

Assuming the closing costs are reasonable, the costs of the refinance will be paid off in less than one year because of the drop in interest rates from 9.0% to 5.0%.
- The homeowner may move from a fixed rate mortgage to an adjustable or balloon instrument if the drop in interest rates is not enough to warrant refinancing into another

Chapter 6

fixed rate. The lower rate on the shorter term instruments may make a refinance worthwhile:
— Present mortgage fixed rate: 9.5%
— Present market fixed rates: 8.5% with 1 point
— Savings will not be attractive to refinance.
— Present 3/1 adjustable rate: 6.0% with 1 point (maximum adjustment cap of 2%)

- The move from 9.5% to 6.0% will yield a quick pay back (approximately 12 months). After the pay back of one year, the homeowner now enjoys two more years at 6.0% and one more year at a maximum of 8.0%. This makes sense for a homeowner who will have the mortgage from two to six years.
- Sometimes the move to an adjustable rate mortgage makes sense because of long-term safety as well. For example:
  — One year adjustable: caps 1% every adjustment and 5% over the life
  — Initial starting rate: 4.5%
  — Life cap: 9.5%
  — Present interest rate: 9.5%

  In this case, the life cap of the adjustable is identical to the present rate of the mortgage. The homeowner receives the benefit of the low starting rate and rate changes based upon a short-term treasury security instrument (one year "T"). There is no long-term risk of paying a higher rate than presently because of the low life cap.

- One variation of a refinance to change mortgage programs is a refinance with a primary purpose to consolidate a present first and second mortgage on the property. It is quite common for second mortgages to have terms that are not quite as attractive as first mortgages:
  — The rate may be higher;
  — The term may be shorter;
  — The mortgage may have rate adjustments with little or no cap protection.

4. *Take cash out to consolidate debts.* A debt consolidation refinance can benefit a home owner by converting existing debt payments to:
   - Lower payments because of the longer loan term; and
   - Tax deductible payments because only the mortgage interest is presently deductible.

The following is an example of how a debt consolidation refinance can help the monthly cash flow of a homeowner:
— Original mortgage balance: $100,000
— Present mortgage balance: $98,500
— Present interest rate: 9.5%
— Present monthly principal and interest: $840.85
— Present total monthly mortgage payment: $1,040
— Present value of the home: $185,000
— Present debt structure:

Loan	Monthly Payment	Balance
Credit cards	$250	$ 5,000
Auto loan	$500	$15,000
Personal loan	$250	$10,000
Personal loan	$300	$ 5,000
Totals:	$1,300	$35,000

Refinancing a Mortgage

— Present total monthly payments:

$1,040	Mortgage payment
$1,300	Monthly debts
$2,340	Total

— Debt consolidation refinance:

Present mortgage balance	$ 98,500
Closing costs	+ $ 1,800
Points	+ $ 2,200
Debt pay off	+ $ 35,000
Total new mortgage balance	$137,500
New interest rate	8.5%
New principal and interest payment	$1,057.26
New mortgage payment	$1,257
After taxes	$900
Present debt payments	$2,340
After taxes	$2,090
Monthly savings	$1,083
After taxes	$1,190

The following notations should be made upon analyzing this example:
- The home must have sufficient equity to allow this amount of cash-out. In this case the loan-to-value is 74.32% ($137,500 divided by $185,000).
- Not all mortgage interest is automatically tax deductible. It depends upon the use of the money and the cash basis of the home.
- Though the monthly payments are reduced almost $1,200 after taxes, it should be noted that a real drawback of this solution is the *spreading out of debt*. If the homeowner stayed with the original payments, the non-mortgage liabilities would be paid off in three to five years. Our solution causes the liabilities to be part of the mortgage that will be paid off in 30 years. If the homeowner stays in the home for 30 years, this disadvantage will be lessened. If the homeowner tries to sell the home two years later, a huge portion of the equity in the home will be gone. Of course, for homeowners who are having a rough time managing their finances, the benefits of lower monthly payments may outweigh the cost of home equity loss. In other words, if they are in pain, it must be fixed immediately. As an option, the homeowner may allocate a certain portion of the monthly savings to shorten the term of the mortgage. In this way, they will actually save additional money by ending the mortgage early.
- There is a second alternative. The homeowner can obtain a second mortgage on the present home instead of refinancing the whole mortgage debt. Generally, second

Opportunity costs of refinancing

Present mortgage balance:	$200,000
Present interest rate:	7.0%
Costs of refinance: (including points)	$ 4,000
New balance:	$214,000
New interest rate:	7.0%
Cash back to home owner:	$10.000

mortgages carry a higher interest rate than first mortgages (one to two percentage points higher) and/or the term of the second mortgages is shorter (15 years). If present market rates are higher than the rate on the existing mortgage, then the second mortgage alternative bears looking into. If the homeowner can lower the rate on the first mortgage at the same time as accomplishing the debt consolidation, then the first example may make more sense.

- Obtaining a second mortgage also may make more sense when the cash needed is very small compared to the overall size of the first mortgage. For example, if the first mortgage is $200,000 and the cash needed for debt consolidation is only $10,000, the borrowing costs would be too high for the procurement of the $10,000 cash unless the new mortgage rate is substantially below the present mortgage rate. In other words, there is a secondary benefit of rate reduction for the refinancing. In the example we say that the *opportunity costs* of borrowing are too high.

In the example, the homeowner only receives the benefit of $10,000 cash because the rate has not been lowered. The cost for borrowing this $10,000 is $4,000, a full 40% of the cash received!

5. *Obtain cash for other purposes.* Though debt consolidation remains a leading reason why home-owners remove equity from their home, obviously the homeowner may take cash out for many other reasons:
   - Purchase a vacation property or investment home;
   - College education;
   - Investment—including starting a retirement plan;
   - Major purchases such as a car.
   - Increase tax deductions by having a larger mortgage payment.

The loan-to-value limitations, tax considerations and additional considerations between taking a home-equity second versus a new first mortgage would mirror those discussed in the previous section's discussion of debt consolidation refinances.

Mortgage sources and refinancing

When considering a refinance, one of the first decisions a homeowner must make is what mortgage source to pursue for the refinance. The decision may be based upon:
- The qualifications of the homeowner;
- The source of the present mortgage;
- The loan-to-value of the proposed mortgage;
- The purpose of the refinance.

This section focuses on the industry guidelines for refinances so that the decision process will be ultimately clearer for someone considering refinance of a home for any reason.

1. *FHA refinances*
   - *Eligibility.* Anyone who presently holds an FHA mortgage can refinance through the FHA *Streamline* program[37]. If the present mortgage is not FHA, the homeowner can refinance only if the home is owner-occupied and the homeowner holds no other FHA mortgages.
   - *The streamline program.* The FHA streamline refinance program is for refinancing existing FHA mortgages. As long as the new payment is less than the old payment[38] and cash back

---

[37] If the present owner assumed the mortgage without credit qualification, then they must wait six months before accomplishing a non-credit qualifying streamline refinance.
[38] If refinancing to a shorter term, a $50 increase in payment is allowed.

to the borrower is no more than $250, the documentation required is limited to the following:
— Loan application;
— Previous 12-month mortgage payment history;
— An appraisal[39] of the property if the new mortgage amount finances the closing costs over and above the existing loan balance[40];
— No re-qualification of the applicant is required;
— The applicant can keep secondary financing in place without a new appraisal (must be subordinated).

If the property is no longer occupied by the applicant, FHA will allow a streamline refinance if the original loan balance is not increased. If the mortgage payment history shows delinquencies during the previous 12 months, the refinance may have to be approved under full documentation processing.

FHA streamline MIP

$90,000	Mortgage
$3,000	Closing costs to be financed
$1,350	New MIP (1.50% of base mortgage amount)
($1,190)	MIP refund from old mortgage
$93,000	Base mortgage amount
$93,160	Mortgage amount including new MIP ($1,350 - $1,190)

The FHA ARM program may not be used for a streamline refinance of an investor property, including FHA hybrid adjustables. If refinancing from a fixed rate on an owner occupied property to an FHA 1-year ARM, the new interest rate must be at least 2% lower than the rate on the existing mortgage. If refinancing from an FHA ARM to a fixed rate, the new rate can increase by 2% over the current rate.

The mortgage insurance charged for an FHA streamline refinance will be identical to that which is charged on a purchase transaction (See Chapter 2). However, if the applicant paid one-time MIP charges, the refund will be applied and subtracted from any new insurance premium.[41]

The applicant should be aware of the fact that the present lender may collect interest until the end of the month when an FHA mortgage is paid off (whether through a home sale or refinance). Therefore, if the new FHA mortgage causes the old mortgage to be paid off at the beginning of the month, the applicant will be charged duplicate interest.

- *Full documentation refinances.* As long as the home is occupied by an applicant who holds no other FHA mortgages, any existing mortgage may be refinanced under FHA mortgage programs with the following restrictions:
  — An appraisal, credit report, asset documentation, and income documentation must be obtained as required on an FHA purchase.

---

[39] Some lenders might require an appraisal even though FHA does not require such. If closing costs are financed, the 98.75/97.75 LTV rule applies.
[40] The borrower can finance closing costs through a higher interest rate, including accrued interest.
[41] The MIP structure that was in place before July 1, 1991 included 3.8% up front for 30-year FHA mortgages on all properties except condominiums. There was no monthly insurance requirement (except for condominiums).

Chapter 6

- The maximum mortgage amount cannot exceed FHA maximum mortgage limits published in the local area.
- The loan-to-value cannot exceed FHA loan-to-value limitations that exist for purchases. If paying off a second trust line of credit, the line must be seasoned at least one year.
- No temporary buydowns are allowed.
- FHA allows *cash-out* refinances up to 85% of the value of the property[42]. No qualification ratio exceptions are allowed for FHA cash-out refinances.
- If allowable under the maximum mortgage amount and loan-to-value calculations, all closing costs except prepaids may be included in the new mortgage amount. The applicant cannot pay miscellaneous lender charges such as a tax service fee or underwriting fees.
- Mortgage insurance charged will be identical to the schedule contained for purchase mortgages.

FHA payoff

New mortgage funding date	July 7th
Present mortgage is paid off	July 9th
Interest on new mortgage is collected for	July 7th through July 31st
Interest on present mortgage is collected for	July 1st through July 31st

VA full documentation refinance

Present mortgage amount:	$110,000
Appraised value of the property:	$120,000
Closing costs:	$2,000
Unused entitlement:	$25,000

Calculation 1:
$120,000 x 75% + $25,000 = $115,000
Calculation 2:
$120,000 x 90% = $108,000
The maximum mortgage amount is the lower of the two.

2. VA Refinances
   - *Eligibility.* All eligibility requirements for VA purchases apply: the program is limited to eligible active military, veterans, reservists and those in the national guard. Any veteran holding an existing VA mortgage can refinance through the VA Interest Rate Reduction Loan (IRRL) refinance program. A full documentation VA refinance requires unused entitlement as would be needed for a VA purchase.
   - *VA IRRL refinance.* A VA *IRRL* refinance is virtually identical to the FHA *streamline* refinance. The payment and the rate must be reduced and unless the term is being shortened, a one-year ARM is being refinanced or energy improvements are being financed. The documentation required:
     - Loan application.
     - Previous 12 month mortgage payment history.
     - Statement from the veteran acknowledging the effect of the new loan on their interest rate and payment, including how long it would take to recoup all closing costs.
     - An appraisal is not required, regardless whether the veteran still occupies the property. Closing costs can be financed regardless of the lack of an appraisal.

---

[42] The 85% is determined from the *acquisition cost*, or the appraised value plus any allowable closing costs that are paid by the applicant. If the house was purchased less than one year from the date of refinance, the 85% would be from the acquisition cost, or original sales price, whichever is lower.

The funding fee for rate reduction refinances is 0.5%. This funding fee can always be financed. If the mortgage payment history shows delinquencies within the last 12 months, the mortgage may have to be processed under full documentation guidelines. Otherwise, the veteran does not have to qualify for the new mortgage. If the current loan is more than 30 days past due, the loan must be submitted to VA for preapproval. No more than $500 in cash may be received from the transaction. The new term of the mortgage can be no more than ten years more than the existing term.

- *VA full documentation refinances.* If the present mortgage is not a VA mortgage, it still can be refinanced under VA full documentation guidelines as long as the veteran occupies the home and has unused entitlement. Full documentation refinances, including cash-out transactions, are limited to 90% of the appraised value of the property. VA also allows the financing of the costs energy-efficiency improvements of up to $6,000. In the example on the previous page, the veteran would not be able to refinance all the costs, as $108,000 does not even cover the existing mortgage amount.

It should be noted that the increase of entitlement starting in December of 2001 allowed use of the additional entitlement only for VA purchases over $144,000 sales price. Because refinances were specifically excluded, any unused entitlement utilized to effect a refinance transaction must come from a maximum of $36,000. Other VA rules:

— Prepaids can be financed.
— For FHA and VA refinances, the borrower cannot pay miscellaneous lender charges such as a tax service fee.

3. *Conventional refinances*
    - *Eligibility.* There are no restrictions on who is eligible for conventional refinances. Fannie Mae and Freddie Mac allow refinances on second homes and investor properties, though the products available will be restricted and loan-to-values allowed may be lower than for owner-occupied refinance transactions.
    - *Streamline refinances.* Both Fannie Mae and Freddie Mac have reduced documentation programs for the refinance of existing mortgages. The parameters may vary based on the results of automated underwriting systems, however, these are typical:
    — No cash-out (rate reduction only).
    — Original mortgage must have been purchased by Fannie Mae or Freddie Mac. If the original mortgage was purchased by Fannie Mae/Freddie Mac, the applicant can refinance with the present servicer of the mortgage under another Fannie Mae/Freddie Mac program.
    — For income documentation only a current pay stub is required. If self-employed, the most recent tax returns are required. If the original mortgage was originated under a no income documentation program, then full income documentation and qualification would be required.
    — All required assets must be verified.
    — No appraisal is required if current lender can certify that the value has not declined and the original appraisal supports the new mortgage amount.
    — The applicant does not have to be re-qualified if the loan is serviced by the originating mortgage company, original income verified has not declined, there are no mortgage delinquencies for the past 12 months, and the new payment is within 15% of the old mortgage payment.

Chapter 6

- Owner-occupied, 1-2 family properties only.
- *Full documentation conventional refinances.* Since there is a multitude of mortgage sources for conventional mortgages, the possibilities for refinances are actually quite numerous. Here are some general guidelines that will be found to be true for the majority of conventional refinance programs.
  - Owner-occupied no cash-out refinances may be typically limited to 95% of the value of the appraisal. Many non-conforming lenders will allow a loan-to-value of 100%.
  - Fannie Mae and Freddie Mac presently allow prepaids to be included in the new mortgage amount. Non-conforming lenders will vary in this regard.
  - Cash-out refinances are usually restricted to owner-occupied refinance transactions, with a maximum loan-to-value of 90%. Some non-conforming lenders will allow a loan-to-value of up to 100% or higher.
  - Refinances on second homes may not allow cash-out and may be limited to 95% of the value of the property. Non-conforming lenders may allow a loan-to-value of up to 95% and have more liberal guideline on cash-out alternatives. Under conforming guidelines, the applicant may not possess more than ten other properties that are mortgaged.
  - Refinances on investor properties may not allow cash-out and may be limited to 90% of the value of the property. Non-conforming lenders may allow loan-to-values of up to 100%. Under conforming guidelines, the applicant may not possess more than ten other properties that are mortgaged.
  - For rate reduction mortgages, if there is presently a second mortgage on the property and this second mortgage is to be included in the refinance, there may be a *seasoning* requirement of one to two years. A *seasoning* of the second mortgage means that the mortgage has been in place for a certain period of time. If the second mortgage is an *open line of credit*, conventional lenders will consider the mortgage to be in place since the last draw of equity of over $2,000. For the example in the margin, on January 1, 2000 the line of credit is *seasoned* for one and one-half years: July of 1998 until January of 2000. The draw of $1,000 in 1999 does not count. In February 2003, Fannie Mae changed its definition of cash-out to include the payoff of any second mortgage not used to finance the purchase of a property.
  - With the growth of the non-conforming market, many of these choices can be expanded with higher market rates. For example, this market might offer cash-out or investor mortgages to 100% loan-to-value. In addition, second mortgages are available to an LTV limit of 125% of the home's value.

  One can see how a seasoning requirement might be very important for investor refinance programs that do not allow cash to be taken out of the property. For example, if the homeowner has a mortgage of $50,000 and would like to remove $30,000 cash from his/her investor property, the homeowner might place a second trust on the property of $30,000 (perhaps borrowed from a relative for this *short-term* situation). The homeowner then applies to the lender for a *no cash-out* mortgage of $80,000 a few months later. Under the lender's guidelines, this may very well be a cash-out transaction.
4. *State and local bond issues.* State and local bond issues exist for the sole purpose of assisting people with low to moderate income with purchasing their first home. Refinances are not allowed under these mortgage programs.

Other considerations for refinances

Before embarking upon a refinance transaction, there are some other facts to note.

1. *Right of rescission.* The Federal Truth in Lending Law requires a lender to allow a three day *right of rescission* for an owner-occupied refinance transaction. A *right of rescission* can be considered a cooling off period during which the consumer may have a right to cancel the transaction and recover the costs incurred during the process. Though this law is designed to protect the consumer, one should be aware of the following drawbacks.

    - The three day right of rescission dictates that the lender does not fund the transaction until the rescission period expires. Therefore, if the mortgage closes on Monday, June 1st:

Monday, June 1st:	Closing date
Tuesday, June 2nd:	First rescission day
Wednesday, June 3rd:	Second rescission day
Thursday, June 4th:	Third rescission day
Friday, June 5th:	Funding date

        This means that the consumer will not receive the money from a cash-out refinance and/or the present mortgage will not be retired before the funding date. This is important to note when the present mortgage being paid off is an FHA or VA loan. One should remember the fact that the present lender is entitled to collect interest until the end of the month when an FHA or VA mortgage is paid off. If the rescission period causes the funding date to move into the next month, the applicant may end up paying duplicate interest for almost a whole month.

    - The mortgage will typically have to fund before the lock period expires. Normally, a mortgage applicant is given a lock-in, for a rate and points, that is good for a specified period of days:

        60 day lock   Lock-in date: July 1   Lock-in expiration date: August 29th

    In the above example, a mortgage purchase transaction must close on or before August 29th in order to preserve the locked-in rate. For a refinance transaction, the mortgage must fund by August 29th, so it must close five or seven days before August 29th. (Sundays and holidays are not counted as *rescission days*. In addition, the loan cannot fund on a weekend or bank holiday because financial institutions are not open for business). Basically, the lender has fewer days to process the mortgage application for a refinance transaction.

    The law provides that the right of rescission may be waived due to an emergency that creates a financial hardship. Unfortunately, the law does not specify what constitutes an emergency and lenders are extremely reticent to allow the right to be waived under this provision without such guidance. Because the lender would be in a position to allow the period to be waived, the lender would actually be rendering an opinion that an emergency exists. If the action were later challenged legally, there would be little or no basis to support that claim because of the lack of specific direction on this topic in the law. One exception to the rescission period is in the case where the law recognizes *no new financing* to be in place. If a refinance is affected through the original lender which is the present servicer and all closing costs are paid out-of-pocket, a rescission period is not required.

2. *Truth-in-Lending.* All loans require a *truth-in-lending (TIL)* disclosure. Mortgage lending is unique in that mortgages covered under RESPA, the *Real Estate Settlement Procedures Act*, require an initial *TIL* to be given to the applicant within three days of initial loan application, along with the *Good Faith Estimate of Closing Charges*. Refinances have been considered exempt from this three-day requirement at times, though a *TIL* must be given out sometime in the process and typically this was accomplished at closing. In 1992, RESPA was amended to require that a *Good Faith Estimate* be prepared for refinances within three days of loan application. There is still no requirement for an initial *TIL* disclosure on a refinance transaction, however it is customary to do so within the industry especially since it is not clear whether particular transactions are purchase or refinance transactions, for example, where there is change of title. In addition, the state may have a requirement for early disclosure.
3. *Getting to settlement.* When a typical homebuyer goes to settlement on a purchase transaction, the homebuyer has plenty of guidance from a real estate professional. The real estate agent typically guides the homebuyer by recommending a settlement agent, insurance company, procuring a pest inspection on the property, and taking care of a host of other settlement requirements. On a refinance transaction, there is no real estate agent involved. The applicant is literally on his/her own with respect to bringing the transaction to a settlement conclusion. The guidance of an experienced and diligent loan officer is essential.
4. *Closing costs.* One of the most prominent questions facing an applicant when going through a refinance transaction is:

How much is it going to cost?

Here are highlights of how some of the costs can be different for a refinancing a mortgage as opposed to a purchase:

- *Down payment.* Though refinance transactions do not typically require a down payment, the applicant must ensure the home appraises for a high enough value to allow the payoff of the present mortgage balance under the selected mortgage program. Additionally, if the applicant intends to finance closing costs, the value of the home must be even higher. Keep in mind that some refinance transactions, typically VA IRRLs, do not require an appraisal to establish the value. Some lenders may require an appraisal at their discretion.
- *Lender charges paid at loan application.* The appraisal and credit report charges for a refinance transaction will typically be no different than those incurred for a purchase. Some refinance programs require no appraisal and/or credit reports, the most prominent example once again being a VA IRRL. A lender may require a lock-in or application fee for a refinance mortgage application as opposed to a purchase. On a purchase transaction, the applicant must perform settlement within a certain time frame as usually specified in the contract. If rates go down after the mortgage rate is *locked-in*, what is to keep the applicant from making application and relocking with another lender on a refinance transaction? In this case, the applicant is just forfeiting the fee for appraisal and credit report. The lending institution has processed a mortgage without any income generated. The solution: collect *good faith money* up front from the applicant in the form of an application or lock fee.
- *Lender charges paid at settlement.* Origination fees and discount points charged by a lender on a refinance transaction are not normally any different than purchase mortgages. In the past, lenders charged higher discount points for refinances, especially for during periods of high refinancing activity; though this practice has become much less common recently. When rates

go down, many home owners try to refinance at once, causing log jams with lenders that may react by trying to slow activity down by raising rates and/or points.

Other lender fees are also going to be identical for purchase and refinance applications. The one exception will be miscellaneous lender fees on FHA and VA refinances. These fees are typically paid by the seller on FHA and VA purchase transactions. FHA and VA do not allow the lender to charge such fees at all on refinances, unless the fee is directly to a third party for such services as document preparation.

One time FHA mortgage insurance and the VA funding fee can be financed on all refinance transactions. VA charges a reduced funding fee of .50% on all IRRL refinances. FHA one time mortgage insurance will reflect a reduction by the amount of any refund of present FHA mortgage insurance if the present mortgage being refinanced is an FHA mortgage that was subject to one time mortgage insurance.

If the original mortgage had conventional mortgage insurance and the new loan is still above 80% LTV, the lender may achieve a discount on mortgage insurance by procuring such insurance from the original mortgage insurance company. This is termed a *reissue rate*.

- *Settlement agent charges.* Settlement agents will perform the same services on a purchase or refinance transaction, hence the charges will be similar. On a purchase transaction, the charges may be split between the buyer and the seller. On a refinance, the applicant must bear all settlement charges, including any fee for transmitting a pay off amount to the present lender.

  If the homeowner already has an owner's title insurance policy on the present home, the settlement agent can typically achieve a *reissue rate* on the new policy, which may mean a reduction of 25 to 50 percent on the cost of the insurance. If the home owner possesses a recent survey of the property (typically within five years) and no changes have been made within the boundary of the property since the date of that survey, the lender may accept a *survey affidavit* from the applicant, eliminating the cost of a new survey. A *survey affidavit* is merely a sworn statement attesting to the fact that there have been no changes. If not, some lenders may accept a *recertification* of the original survey by the original surveying company, which may lessen the cost.

- *Taxes.* Every jurisdiction will differ by their policy concerning taxation of refinance transactions. Some areas tax refinances as they would a purchase, but the majority have reduced fees or no taxes at all except for recordation fees. Even the recordation fees will typically be less because a new deed is not being recorded on the properties. Governments may charge less for owner-occupied as opposed to investor refinances. Others may charge more if the amount of the present mortgage is being increased.

- *Miscellaneous fees to complete the appraisal.* Most of these fees will not be applicable on a refinance. For example, a final inspection of a new home is a purchase transaction cost. On the other hand, if the appraisal dictates that repairs must be completed on the property, the refinance may incur final inspection charges. Some lenders do not require pest, well and septic inspection reports for refinance transactions. If the refinance is a full documentation FHA or VA mortgage, then the appraisal issued by the agency will dictate requirements for such.

- *Prepaids.* Prepaids are payable on a refinance transaction in the same manner as they are on a purchase. Some mortgage programs do not allow the financing of prepaid charges. The portion of prepaids placed into escrow with the new lender may very well be offset by an escrow refund from the present lender. If the applicant is refinancing with the present lender, that lender may give a credit for this escrow refund, alleviating the need for money changing hands. This is called an assignment of escrows. If the home has increased in value, the property taxes may have increased and therefore the homeowner may be behind on their escrow payments. In this situation, the escrow refund may not match the new escrow requirement. In addition, the new payment may not be as low as the consumer is expecting because their old payment was about to be increased because of this factor.

- *Prepaid Interest.* Though prepaid interest is paid at settlement on a refinance transaction, the homeowner should be made aware of the fact that accrued interest may still be due on the present mortgage since interest is paid *in-arrears*. This may seem as though the applicant is paying on both mortgages at the same time, but a new mortgage payment will not be due for some time after closing, which will cancel out this extra cost at closing. In effect, a mortgage payment must be made at closing, but the next payment is skipped. If prepaids can be financed under the program the applicant must decide whether to finance this interest payment. In the case of FHA mortgages, the present lender has the right to collect interest to the end of the month when the mortgage is paid off; therefore, the home owner may very well pay duplicate interest during the month of the refinance.

- *Subordination.* The homeowner may refinance a first mortgage and may desire to keep their second mortgage. In this case, the second mortgage would claim primary position at the point of payoff of the old first—without a subordination agreement. This agreement binds the second mortgage to stay in secondary position (or subordinate) while the new first is put into place. Investors may require approval of subordination agreements and the second mortgage company may take up to two weeks or more to prepare such an agreement as well as charging a fee for this service.

- *Cash-out Surcharge.* Many lenders charge a higher price for cash-out transactions—especially for higher loan-to-values. In 2003, the conforming agencies changed their definition of cash-out to encompass any second being paid off that was not acquired to purchase the property. Non-conforming lenders may vary in their definition, but many still use the older "seasoning" requirement. This requirement typically states that the second would have to have been in place for a certain period of time and that there were no recent draws on any home equity lines of credit.

- *Home For Sale.* Most lenders will not refinance a property if the intention is to sell the property. Therefore, if the home is presently or recently was listed for sale, this may present a problem. Some lenders may restrict refinances to properties not listed up to the past 12 months. In addition, for owner-occupied transactions most lenders require a written statement concerning intent to occupy after closing.

7

Applying and Packaging Your Loan for Approval

There is one secret to the loan application and approval process: preparation. Nothing will delay a mortgage approval process more than the lack of preparation. Even more significantly, nothing will reduce an applicant's chances for loan approval more greatly than the lack of preparation. A common complaint from loan applicants and Realtors is speed of the mortgage approval process and last minute problems that arise. Yet, it is the unprepared applicant who succeeds in causing many of these delays:

1. Don't push for a quick loan application. Go over the documentation requirements with the loan officer before the loan application and take the necessary time to procure this documentation so that the loan officer can review it at the loan application instead of afterwards.
2. Bring the loan officer everything necessary. Do not hold back on any documentation. Last minute surprises are often caused by information that surfaced later in the process, information that could have been gleaned from documentation provided at loan application.
3. Make loan application before offering a sales contract. It makes no sense that the homebuyer will spend weeks looking for a home with or without a Realtor, sign a sales contract, then ask a lender to process the mortgage in two weeks in order to effect a quick settlement. If the homebuyer made loan application when the home buying process started, there would be many more weeks to iron out problems. Approval may even be obtained before the home is selected, giving the purchaser more leverage with the seller.

Preparing the documentation

The next obvious question is:

"If I do need to prepare, then what do I need to bring to loan application?"

This section will provide a detailed analysis of most every situation that will warrant the provision of application documentation. Many lenders will provide *pre-application* packages that will help the applicant prepare by organizing the necessary information. Note that these requirements may vary widely by lender and program alternative—many streamline documentation programs now exist.

1. *The applicant's personal history*: The applicant should bring the following personal information to loan application:

Chapter 7

- Living address for the past two years.
- Employment address and phone number for the past two years.
- Social security number (social security card may be helpful).
- Drivers license or other photo identification.
- Address for any rental properties owned by the applicant.
- If the applicant is not a citizen, the *green card* and/or green card number.

2. *Information on the home being purchased or present home (for a refinance).*
   - Ratified sales contract for purchase.
   - Any ratified addenda for purchase.
   - Copy of listing data sheet if home was listed by a Realtor.
   - If no listing exists, information on yearly property taxes and monthly homeowners association dues.
   - Copy of the deed and existing note for a refinance (including for existing 2nd mortgage). The lender must have information regarding any prepayment penalties on your present mortgage(s).
   - If there are any *contingencies*, or conditions in the contract, the lender will want to see any future addenda removing these contingencies.
   - If the contract is amended in any way in the future, the lender must be provided with a copy of all addenda. New homes will often have increased sales prices with options added after the initial contract ratification.
   - If the home is a condominium, a pre-sale (condo cert) will need to be obtained from the Homeowner's Association. This document verifies the percentage of owner occupants in the project, in addition to other information.
   - If an investment property, a copy of the lease if currently rented.

3. *Information on the applicant's income.*
   - For those who are employed:
     - Pay stubs covering the most recent 30-day period.
     - W-2s for the past two years.
   - For those who are self-employed:
     - Year-to-date profit and loss from the business (if the tax returns end more than 90 days from the date of application).
     - Previous two years complete Federal individual tax returns (signed).
     - Previous two years complete Federal corporate or partnership tax returns (signed) if there is a corporation or partnership.
   - Two years individual tax returns are also needed for those who earn more than 25% of their income from commission, bonus, or overtime. Any interest or dividend income used to qualify must also be shown on individual tax returns.
   - For those who are using a variable income such as overtime, part-time, commission or bonus—any information breaking down the types of income for the past two years. This may be the last pay stub for each year, or a letter from the employer.
   - For rental properties, a current one-year lease and two years Federal tax returns may be required.
   - For note receivable income, a copy of the ratified note and two years tax returns.

Applying and Packaging Your Loan for Approval

- For alimony, child support and/or separate maintenance income, a copy of the separation agreement and divorce decree or other evidence of support payments and proof of receipt of regular payments for the previous 12 months.
- For social security, retirement, or disability, a copy of the award letter, the letter issued with the past payment change, and proof of receipt of payments (usually using a 1099, which is the equivalent of a W-2 for miscellaneous income).
- If there is a raise due in the near future and the increased income is necessary for qualification, the employer must provide a letter specifying the amount and effective date. The lender may ask to see a pay stub at the new salary level, either before or after settlement takes place.

4. *Information on the applicant's assets.*
   - For all liquid assets (savings, checking, mutual funds, money market, stocks, etc.) held with a financial institution, the prior three months statements. The most recent statement will do if these are issued quarterly instead of monthly. FHA and VA require only two monthly statements.
   - For a retirement plan, 401K, or IRAs, the latest statement. Statements covering the previous quarter are necessary if these assets are to be liquidated in order to purchase the home.
   - For the sale of an asset that is going to produce the necessary cash to fund the transaction, a copy of the agreement and proof of receipt of funds. In the case of the sale of the present home, the ratified sales contract will be needed at loan application or when received. The settlement statement (HUD-1) on the previous home may be brought to settlement on the new home if both settlements are occurring on the same day, or *back-to-back*.
   - If the cash needed is coming from a loan, proof of loan approval must be provided, as well as the terms of the loan. Later in the process, proof of receipt of funds must be provided.
   - If the cash needed is coming from a gift, the lender will provide an acceptable gift letter that must be filled out by whomever is giving the funds. Most lenders will accept a copy of the donor's bank statement as evidence of ability to give the gift. The lender also will typically want to see proof of receipt of funds later in the process.
   - If the applicant's employer is paying closing costs before settlement, a copy of the benefits package or relocation letter must be provided. The lender may want to see receipt of funds later in the process if these funds are necessary to complete the transaction.
   - If the applicant's employer or a relocation company is providing an equity advance on the applicant's present home and the home's sale is guaranteed, provide the terms of the equity advance, proof of guarantee with minimum sales price, and proof of receipt of funds.
   - If the seller is paying closing costs, the terms of such must be specified in the sales contract.
   - Always provide a copy of the deposit or escrow check that was used as a deposit on the home purchased. If not a bank or cashier's check, the lender will typically want a copy of the canceled check (copy front and back) after it clears the bank account. This ensures the funds in the applicant's bank account are in addition to the amount placed upon deposit under the terms of the sales contract.

5. *Information on the applicant's liabilities.*
   - The balance, monthly payment, account number, and lender address should be provided for all outstanding liabilities. A copy of the latest statement and/or a page from the payment coupon book will suffice. If you review a copy of your credit report—you could provide these only for loans that are incorrect on the report.

- If the applicant owes child support, alimony or separate maintenance, a copy of the complete ratified separation agreement and divorce decree or similar evidence.
- For those presently paying rent, the name and address of the landlord.
- If the present mortgage is held by a private individual rather than a financial institution or the present landlord is a private individual rather than a management company, it may be helpful to provide copies of canceled checks of payments (front and back copied) for the prior 12 months.
- If a home is owned free of liens (is *free and clear*), the applicant must provide proof that there is no mortgage on the property. This may include the original settlement sheet, a deed of satisfaction, or tax returns showing no interest deduction. In addition, proof of the amount of real estate tax, insurance, and homeowners association payments must be provided.
- If a car is less than four years old and there is no car loan or lease outstanding, the applicant may be asked to provide a copy of the car title showing no lien.
- If any liabilities are being paid off in order to qualify for this mortgage (unless being paid at settlement from the funds of a cash out refinance or sale of present home), the lender will want to see proof of payoff and verify the funds utilized.
- If this transaction is a relocation in which the applicant's employer is guaranteeing the sale of the present home, proof that the employer will make the present mortgage payments during any time period in which the applicant owns two homes.

6. *Explanations to provide at loan application.* The applicant must provide written explanations for any of the following situations:
   - A gap in employment of more than one month during the previous two years.
   - A decrease in income from year-to-year.
   - A complex job history (for example, a switch from employed to self-employed and back to employed again).
   - Any bank accounts opened in the previous 90 days, including proof of source of funds.
   - Any significant increase in funds in existing accounts during the prior 90 days, including proof of source of funds. (FHA accepts cash saved at home with documentation of ability to save.)
   - Explanation of use of any cash being taken from the property if a cash out refinance transaction.
   - Explanation for late payments of which the applicant is aware. If significant credit blemishes such as bankruptcies, judgments, etc. have occurred, the applicant should provide documentation to back up the explanation.

Application

So you have brought two tons of information to the lender. Now what happens? Good loan officers review the information while taking the loan application. They will be looking for such things as:

1. Pay stubs.
   - Does the year-to-date income amount shown match the monthly salary? For example, if the applicant reports earning $50,000 annually, does the pay stub on June

What does the loan officer do with the documents

30th show $25,000 of income earned for the year? If not, what is the explanation? One reasonable explanation would be a recent raise to $50,000 salary.
- Are there any regular withdrawals from the pay stub that could be construed as debt payments? An applicant may have taken a loan from the employer's credit union last year.
- Does the entire personal information match on the pay stub, for example the name and social security number? Is the pay stub dated within the past 30 days of loan application?
- If there is overtime, bonus, or commission income, is it broken out on the pay stub? Many times the applicant will report his/her income as salary but a second look at the pay stub will reveal overtime that will affect the final income calculation.

2. W-2s.
   - Are there W-2s for the prior two years? Is the social security number and name correct for each year? What about the employer's name? Quite often the employer's name or ownership of the company will change. The employee could have transferred to a different subsidiary from the same company.
   - Does the income match the salary level reported? Minor increases each year would be expected, but what if the income shown decreased from year-to-year? Can we get a breakout of overtime or bonus directly from the employer?

3. Tax Returns.
   - Once again we would match the personal information: names, social security numbers and dates. Are the returns signed and are all schedules included? If there is a separate corporation and/or partnership, are these returns included as well? Watch out for returns that are not current because of extensions filed. In addition, some corporations are on a fiscal year that will not match up directly to the calendar years contained in the individual returns. This may affect the final income calculation or at least the data necessary in order to calculate the final income.
   - Does the income on the returns match what is disclosed? For example, if the applicant is a sole proprietorship (Schedule C), does the bottom line of the Schedule C averaged for two years match the monthly income disclosed?
   - If the applicant is self-employed, is there a profit and loss statement on the business covering the period from the end of the tax returns to the time of the loan application (or within the most recent quarter)?

4. Bank statements.
   - Is each bank statement complete (all pages) and do you have bank statements current for the past 90 days (there must be three consecutive months)? Is the personal information correct? Watch for another name on the bank statements that could mean that the account is joint with another person not involved in the transaction. Does the applicant have permission to use the money, or a portion of the money?
   - The last balance on the most current bank statement is the amount that would be utilized for calculation of the asset figure. Is this enough to support the transaction, or are they counting on a deposit recently made (or to be made)? If so, where did the funds come from?
   - Are there regular withdrawals of the same amount each month that might indicate debts not disclosed? Large withdrawals and deposits (outside of which the regular pay would support) must be explained. Returned checks also must be explained as an item of derogatory credit.

Chapter 7

5. Sales contract.
   - Is the contract fully ratified (signed) and are all addenda included? Are all purchasers making loan application? Is the information contained in the sales contract accurate?
   - If the seller is paying closing costs, are contributions within the program's guidelines? A common mistake is to specify that the seller will pay prepaids when the program does not allow this. Is the contract clear on who will pay what points and loan fees?
   - Is there personal property conveying that cannot be financed? Perhaps the purchaser is also buying the furniture in the home.
   - Does the listing attached to the sales contract indicate that the home is a condominium? If so, is the project approved for the loan program? Does the listing indicate large acreage that might make the land-to-value ratio too high to support a residential home mortgage?

It is important for the loan officer to obtain the answers to any questions concerning loan approval up-front in the process. For example, if the applicant has been self-employed for only 18 months, is this acceptable and how is the income to be calculated? With the right information present at loan application and a proper review of the information by the mortgage representative, the loan officer will be in a position to pose the question within a few days of loan application.

Processing

Loan set-up

You have given the mortgage company a bundle of information that has been reviewed by a loan officer for any questions that may hold up your loan approval. What happens now?

The loan application is then turned over to the *processing* department of the mortgage lender. The processing department is responsible for getting the loan ready for submission to the underwriting department for final approval. This procedure is called *processing the mortgage*. Today, it is more likely that portions of the processing and underwriting process may be automated—with appraisals, credit reports, and other documentation ordered directly via a laptop by the loan officer. In this case, we will describe the process as if completed by a separate individual.

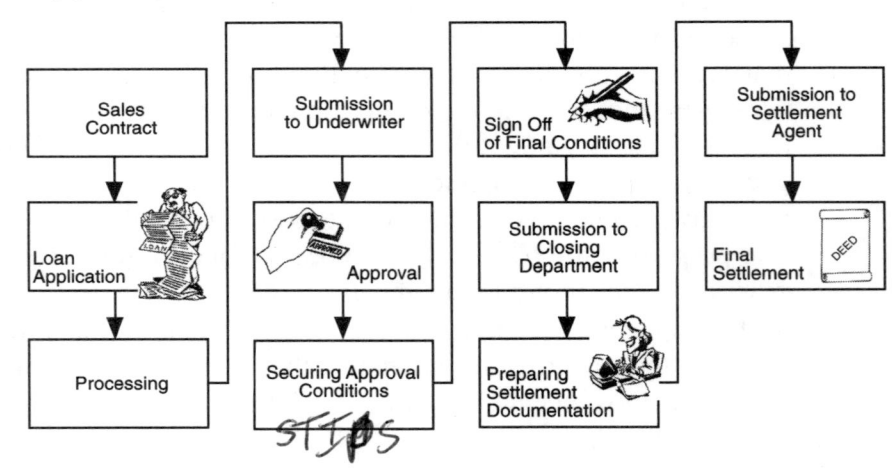

The first thing a processor does *is set-up the loan*. The set-up process consists of the following:
1. *Registering the application*. Every mortgage lender has a way of keeping track of all mortgage applications that are brought in by loan officers.
2. *Sending the disclosures*. The processor must send the Truth-in-Lending Disclosure within three business days of loan application for all purchase transactions, though most loan officers provide this at loan application. Typically most other required disclosures are signed at loan application:

- *The Program Disclosure*, that describes the mortgage program if it is not a fixed rate;
- The *Transfer of Servicing Disclosure*, which describes the mortgage lender's policies and track record concerning selling the servicing rights of the mortgages the lender originates;
- The *Good Faith Estimate of Settlement Costs*, which discloses the estimated closing costs;
- The *Settlement Cost Booklet*, a HUD guide that describes each settlement charge and the process;
- *Consumer Handbook on Adjustable Rate Mortgages* and program disclosures, required for ARM applications;
- The *Certification and Authorization*, which authorizes conventional lenders to investigate your credit history and reverify any information provided by the applicant (including on no-income verification mortgages); and,
- The *Lock-in Agreement*, which will give the mortgage rate terms and conditions.
- The *Marketing "Opt-out" Disclosure* which discloses the lender's practice of using information collected (including sharing it with partners) from loan documents, credit reports, etc. The applicant is given the ability to "opt out" of such practice.
- The *Patriot Act Disclosure,* which proves that the lender as identified the applicant.
- The *Credit Score Disclosure,* which proves that the lender has disclosed the applicant's credit score and the effect of this score in the decision-making process.

If the loan application is missing any of these disclosures, the processor sends these with the Truth-in-Lending. There are also several disclosures that are unique to FHA and VA applications.

Required disclosures for FHA mortgages:
- *Addendum to the Uniform Residential Loan Application*. This addendum includes a variety of certifications by the lender and the applicant. It also incorporates the *Privacy Act Notice* and *Assumption Disclosure*.
- *Important Notice to Homebuyer*. Informs the applicant that FHA does not warrant the condition or the value of the property, warns of the penalties for commission of loan fraud, and states that FHA does not set the rate and discount points and that these are negotiable with the lender. It also explains the mortgage insurance costs and the refund process.
- The *Lead Paint Disclosure* warns about the dangers of lead based paint in homes constructed before 1978.
- The *Assumption Disclosure* describes FHA policies concerning future assumptions of FHA mortgages. FHA assumption policies have changed several times in the past, but all presently originated FHA mortgages need credit approval for assumption and cannot be assumed by investors. Informs the applicant that he/she must receive a release of liability from FHA in order not to be responsible for payments after an assumption takes place.
- *For Your Protection: Get a Home Inspection*. Inform buyers that an FHA appraisal is not a home inspection and advise them that an inspection is recommended.
- *Informed Consumer Choice Disclosure Notice*. Compares the cost of an FHA Mortgage to Conventional alternatives, including the costs of Mortgage Insurance.
- *Notice to Homebuyer (Homebuyer Summary)*. Provided by the FHA appraiser indicating whether the home meets minimum FHA minimum property standards.
- *Real Estate Certification*. Certifies that the terms of the sales contract are true and correct and all terms are disclosed. It is signed by the seller and purchaser. Typically incorporated into most sales contracts.

Chapter 7

- *Settlement Disclosure.* In addition to the HUD-1 addendum, the FHA requires a notice to the settlement agent that funds are not to be dispersed unless the funds required of the purchaser are coming from the purchaser and not any other party. There is also a notice to the borrower concerning his/her right to prepay and the fact that he/she may be expected to pay interest through the end of the month if the prepayment is not received by the lender by the first day of the month.

Required disclosures for VA mortgages:

- The *Interest Rate and Discount Disclosure Statement* states that the rate and points are not set by VA and are negotiable with the lender.
- The *Verification of VA Benefit Related Indebtedness (VA Indebtedness Letter)* enables the lender to verify from VA that the applicant/veteran does not have any unpaid or unscheduled indebtedness to the agency. Also gives VA an opportunity to indicate that the applicant/veteran is exempt from the funding fee due to receipt of VA disability
- The *Federal Collection Policy Notice* informs the applicant/veteran of actions the government can take if scheduled payments are not made.
- *Assumption of VA Guaranteed Mortgages* discloses VA's policy with regard to assumption of mortgages made after March 1, 1988. This includes credit approval, payment of 1/2 point VA funding fee, a lender processing charge, and assumption of liability by the person assuming the mortgage.
- For homes built before 1978—*Notice of Possible Lead Based Paint* and/or *Lead Based Paint Hazards (VA Form 26-6705e)* which includes a 10 day opportunity to conduct an evaluation.
- The *VA Debt Questionnaire* asks the veteran about past foreclosure or judgment problems. Also asks the veteran about present delinquencies or defaults on Federal obligations.
- *Counseling Checklist for Military Homeowners.* Active duty borrowers must sign to certify that they have received homeownership and loan obligation counseling.

3. *Ordering the credit report and appraisal.* If not accomplished by the loan officer, the processor orders the credit report and appraisal from vendors selected by the mortgage company. The appraiser selected may be an employee of the lender (a *staff appraiser*), an independent company selected by the lender, or selected by VA from their panel of approved appraisers. When ordering the appraisal, it is important to indicate:

   - *The type of transaction.* For example, if the application is for an investor transaction an *operating income statement* and *comparable rental schedule* will have to be ordered with the appraisal.
   - *The type of property.* For newer condominiums, special forms may have to be ordered that describe the complex and ownership. For 2-4 unit properties, *operating income statements* will have to be ordered.
   - *The approval status of condominium.* If a certain condo is not approved by the FHA or the VA, the appraisal request will be rejected.

4. *Ordering verification forms.* The vast majority of mortgage programs will now accept the documentation brought to the lender by the applicant as the final income and asset documentation needed for loan approval. Use of W-2s, pay

What happens after the processor "sets-up" the loan application?

118

subs, and bank statements is called *alternative documentation*. A full documentation loan would consist of *verification forms* sent to the employers and banks:
- A *Verification of Employment*, is sent to current and former employers for the past 2 years;
- A *Verification of Deposit*, is sent to all banks where liquid assets are held;
- A *Verification of Mortgage or Rent* is sent to the present landlord or mortgage holder.

Almost all lenders now accept alternative documentation in lieu of sending out these verification forms. The processor will be required to verify the employment of the applicant via the telephone with the employer for a measure of independent verification of the information contained in alternative documentation.

Processor Review

The processor then waits for the credit report, appraisal, and verifications to arrive. Also to be arriving from the applicant will be a list of information missing at loan application. For example, perhaps a profit and loss was not prepared for a self-employed applicant. What does the processor review these documents for?

1. *Credit report review.* A credit report is reviewed for the following:
   - Verification that all personal information such as the social security number is correct. The wrong social security number could cause some or all of the data to be incorrect.
   - Verify that all disclosed debts are present and the payment and balances are accurate. If payments are higher than what was disclosed at loan application, the applicant may be re-qualified.
   - Verify that any undisclosed debts are not present. If there are any significant undisclosed debts, the applicant must write a letter as to why they were not disclosed and must be re-qualified with the extra payments.
   - Look for any late payments, judgments, tax liens, bankruptcies, or collections. Any significant late payments will require a letter from the applicant. Significant credit blemishes such as a tax lien may also require back up documentation to accompany the explanation. Any outstanding bad debts must be satisfied—such as unsatisfied judgments.
   - If the credit score does not meet minimum program guidelines, there may have to be actions taken to raise the score, including correcting mistakes, paying off debts, etc.
2. *Appraisal review.* An appraisal is reviewed for the following:
   - Verification that property information is correct—address, legal description, etc.
   - Verification that the property has appraised for at least the sales price or minimum value necessary to effect the refinance transaction.
   - Verification that the appraiser did not specify any conditions, for example repairs to be completed before settlement.
   - Verification that there is no negative information contained in the appraisal. Negative information might include poor condition of the property, declining property values, above the value range for the area, exceedingly high land-to-value, etc.
   - Make sure the comparables selected are adequate: recent, closed and that the adjustments made for size, condition, location options and rooms are reasonable.
   - Make sure that additional forms required, such as an *operating income statement* and *comparable rental schedule* for investor transactions, are included.
3. *Verification review.* If full documentation, the verifications of employment, deposit, mortgage and rent are reviewed for:

Chapter 7

- Are the forms signed and dated by the proper authority? No *cross-outs* or *whiteout* are allowed that are not initialed.
- Does the information on the verification match the information on the loan application, including:
  - employment dates and salary information;
  - bank account value;
  - monthly payments and balance.
- Is there any information that will have to be explained such as:
  - Increases in the balance of bank accounts.
  - Undisclosed debts such as open credit lines on these accounts.
  - Recently opened debts or bank accounts.
  - Late payments.
  - Poor probability of continued employment.
  - Gaps in employment dates.
  - Decrease in salary.

What does an underwriter do with a loan application submission

After the information is all received and reviewed

After all information has been received and reviewed by the processor or loan officer and any discrepancies have been explained, the loan application is then *worked-up* to be submitted to the underwriter for final approval. *Work-up* consists of producing the final loan application (which typically is signed at settlement), preparing a *transmittal form*, and putting all documents in final submission order.

Underwriting

If one has ever communicated with a mortgage company after a mortgage application was submitted to the underwriting department or the investor, one would think that there is some closed room where no one dared to enter until a magical process was completed. The truth is, there is no magic or mystery to the underwriting process. If the loan is packaged the way we described in this Chapter and any questions concerning discrepancies such as the acceptability of high ratios were asked up front, then the underwriting process should be quite rote. If the loan package is packaged poorly with no explanations and missing documentation, then we will hear the dreaded words:

"There are some last minute conditions the underwriter wants to see before making a decision. I don't think that we will close as scheduled this Thursday"

What last minute conditions? Here are a few of the typical conditions:

- Explain the source of funds for the down payment, focusing on the large deposit in the borrower's account last month.
- Back up documentation is needed to support borrower's explanation of a car accident and hospital bills that caused the late payments.
- The separation agreement shows a joint property owned by the applicant and his ex-spouse. Show proof of disposition of the property, proof that the spouse is making payments since that time, or verify and add the mortgage to the debt ratio.
- The appraisal's value is higher than the predominant value range for the neighborhood. Have the appraiser explain why the home is not an over improvement.

- The tax returns show a limited partnership with losses of $5,000 each year. Provide K-1's to show that the applicant does not own over 25% of the partnership and does not contribute significant capital each year.

This is all documentation that should have been provided to the underwriter before underwriting. If the underwriter has a complete package, then the process is simply a check to make sure that the loan does not exceed limits for the program:

- Is the loan-to-value correct for the property type and transaction?
- Is there any excess seller contributions?
- Are the ratios within acceptable guidelines, or are there compensating factors present to allow higher ratios (supported by a cover letter from the originator)?

If the underwriter sees a complete package that is well documented and explained, the loan will be returned with an approval and the conditions assigned will be standard settlement conditions such as:

- Pest inspection report;
- Survey;
- Final truth-in-lending disclosure;
- Title commitment, or binder, from settlement agent;
- Homeowners insurance policy;
- Rate lock-in, if floating;
- Seller contributions to match those in contract;
- Three day right of rescission for refinances.

Either the processing or closing department will procure these final conditions in order for settlement to occur. Most mortgage lenders require that the final settlement conditions be received at least 48 to 72 hours before settlement is to occur. The key to the whole process is the provision of documents up front. A mortgage application can take a few minutes to achieve approval, or three months. The greatest variable is the way documentation is provided, examined and explained.

Automated Underwriting

Automated underwriting has significantly altered the way the loan application process takes place. With complete information, a loan officer can enter the data on a laptop, order a credit report and have the loan decision within minutes. This is especially helpful if the applicant has not purchased a home as of yet and wants a "pre-approval" before making an offer on a house. If the credit score is low, it is likely the loan may come back as requiring a closer review by an underwriter—and the process will more than likely resemble the description of the previous pages. These systems allow the underwriters to spend their time with the files that need the closest review. For those with good credit histories, income and assets— much of documentation required by the lender can be eliminated or at least lessened. For example, why request a copy of a deposit check when there are more than enough liquid assets to close the loan?

Items Needed For Loan Application

1. Fully ratified sales contract and addenda or copy of Deed and Note(s) for refinances.
2. Most recent original pay stubs, covering a 30-day period.
3. Original W-2s for past two years.
4. For self employed and commissioned only. Two most recent years complete, ratified federal individual and corporate tax returns. Year-to-date profit and loss dated within 90 days.
5. One year lease and tax returns for all investment properties.
6. Proof of any additional income needed to qualify.
7. Gift letter and proof of donor's ability to give.
8. Original bank statements (all pages) covering most recent three-month period.
9. Child care statement (VA loans), divorce decree, separation agreement.
10. List of all debts owed, account numbers, balances and monthly payments. Copy of payment books or statements for these loans if not on credit report.
11. Name, address and phone number of current landlord (if renting). Copy of listing, lease and/or sales contract for present home (if own).
12. Copy of car title if auto is owned free and clear and less than four years old.
13. Social security card and picture ID.
14. DD-214 and Certificate of Eligibility (VA Loans).
15. Check for application fee.

Table 7-1

8

Mortgages, Home Ownership and Taxes

We began this book by indicating one of the main economic motivations behind the ownership of real estate is the tax advantages. We end the book by summarizing the implications of real estate holdings upon one's obligation to pay taxes. This Chapter should by no means serve as a replacement for qualified advice from a tax professional. Tax laws and interpretations thereof change on a periodic basis and the information we present is accurate to our knowledge only as of the date of printing. On the other hand, we cannot imagine someone learning about real estate without wanting an overview of the topic's implication regarding taxation.

Purchasing a Home

When one purchases a home, will any or all of the costs paid at settlement affect tax obligations? This has long been a gray area of tax law, especially with regard to the deductibility of points paid by the purchaser. IRS has indicated that:

- Points computed as a percentage of the loan are tax deductible by the borrower in full for the tax year in which the points were paid. This is true for owner-occupied (primary residences) purchase transactions only. For refinances, the points must be deducted over the life of the mortgage except the portion of the proceeds utilized for home improvements.[43]
- The purchaser does not have to write a separate check at settlement for the points for them to be deductible.
- Any points paid by the seller can be deducted by the purchaser but will reduce the cost basis of the home. This will affect the calculation of a gain when the home is sold.
- The amount of points must conform to established business practice of charging points for loans in the area in which the property is located.
- The points cannot be paid by the lender (lender closing cost credit).

Of the additional costs paid at home purchase, the following are deductible:
- *Prepaid Interest.* Any interest paid to the lender at settlement would be deductible. This will be expanded upon later in this Chapter.

---

[43] The U.S. Court of Appeals for the Eighth Circuit has allowed the full deduction in the year paid for points on a long-term home mortgage loan refinancing a short-term balloon loan used to acquire a home.

Chapter 8

- *Real Estate Property Taxes.* Any real estate property taxes paid by the borrower during the purchase of the home will be deductible, but only after money is actually paid to the taxing authority:

    Example: Settlement Date: November 30, 2002

    Tax Escrow: Six Months @ $150 ($900)

    Tax Payment Due: July 1, 2003 (12 months)

The above tax escrow would not be paid out by the lender until 2003, and therefore is not deductible in 2002.

The following costs paid at home purchase are not deductible:
- *Insurance.* Hazard, homeowners, mortgage, flood, and title insurance are not deductible;
- *Taxes.* Recordation taxes, recording fees, and transfer taxes are not deductible;
- *Services.* Fees for services such as attorney fees, miscellaneous mortgage lender/broker fees, survey preparation, pest inspection report, appraisal and underwriting fees are not deductible.

Does this suggest that a borrower paying the lender a $300 underwriting fee should actually ask the lender to charge a proportional higher amount of points rather than the underwriting fee? Sounds like this would be a winning tax reduction strategy—as long as it can be argued that it is within established business practices.

Just because a particular cost is not deductible at settlement does not mean it will not factor into the tax equation at a later date. It is important to keep copious records of the purchase transaction and we will explain why in the section covering the home sale.

Deduction of Regular Mortgage Payments

A typical mortgage payment consists of the following components:
- Principal;
- Interest;
- Real Estate Taxes;
- Homeowners Insurance;
- Mortgage Insurance;
- Homeowners Association Fees.

Deductible Portion	*Non-Deductible Portion*
Mortgage Interest	Insurance
Real Estate Taxes	Homeowners or Condominium Association Fees
	(except portion that goes to pay real estate taxes)

Mortgage Interest Deductions. As Congress has lowered the tax rates, many tax deductions have been eliminated. Mortgage interest has stood the test of time as a deduction but it has not remained unscathed:

Interest on mortgages made before October 13, 1987 is fully deductible as an itemized deduction. For mortgages made after that date, there are two classifications of mortgages:
- *Acquisition Debt*: A mortgage secured by a primary residence or second home that is incurred when you buy, build or substantially improve your home. This is deductible to a limit of

$1,000,000 ($500,000 if married and filing separate returns). The acquisition of the home must be made within 90 days before or after incurring the mortgage.
- *Home-Equity Debt.* A mortgage secured by a primary residence or second home that is incurred after home purchase. The maximum amount of deductible home-equity debt is $100,000, however the acquisition debt and the home-equity debt cannot exceed the fair market value of the residence at the time of incurring the home-equity debt. This is important because there have been offered home equity loans on the market that have exceeded the fair market value of the home (125% loans).

In the case of a second mortgage, the calculation of home-equity debt is easy -- the full amount of the second mortgage is home-equity debt and is deductible up to $100,000. In the case of a refinance:

$300,000 Sales Price

$250,000 Original Mortgage

$245,000 Principal Balance at Time of Refinance

$500,000 Value at Refinance

$300,000 Mortgage at Refinance

The new first mortgage would have $245,000 of acquisition debt and $55,000 of home-equity debt, both of which would be deductible.
- *Home Construction Loans* are fully deductible as acquisition debt from the time construction begins to a period of up to 24 months or 90 days after the construction is completed, whichever comes first.
- *Home Improvement Loans* secured by the property can be added to the original acquisition debt (up to $1,000,000) because they add to the value of the home. This does not include loans made for the purpose of funding maintenance repairs.
- *Second Home Residences* qualify if used for personal (non-rental) purposes for the greater of 14 days or 10% of the rental days per year.
- *Cooperatives* qualify for the home mortgage interest deduction even though the shareholders do not own their apartments. The IRS considers indebtedness secured by stock in the cooperative deductible as long as it is occupied as the primary or secondary residence.

Mortgage interest as an itemized deduction is subject to an overall floor on itemized deductions that is applied to higher income taxpayers. This floor is indexed annually to the inflation rate.

Real Estate Property Tax Deductions. Real estate property taxes are deductible on the date paid by the homeowner or the lender on behalf of the applicant in the case of a lender-held escrow account. This is important to note because the date the homeowner pays into the escrow account for property taxes is not relevant. The date the lender pays the governmental authority is relevant.

In the case of a condominium association, the portion of the condominium association fee that is allocated for real estate property taxes on the common areas is also deductible. In the same manner, tenant-stockholders of cooperative apartments may deduct a proportion of the taxes paid by the cooperative.

Chapter 8

Example: $100 Monthly Condominium Association Fee

$100,000 Annual Condominium Association Budget

$5,000 Annual Condominium Association Property Taxes

(equals 5% of budget for property taxes)

$100 x 5% x 12 = $60 of annual fees are tax deductible

Tax Deductions and Refinances

We have already touched on the deduction of mortgage interest after a refinance takes place. What about the costs of a refinance — are they deductible? Basically, the costs outside of interest and taxes paid are not deductible. Points paid in conjunction with a refinancing can be deducted, but must be deducted over the life of the mortgage unless the purpose of the refinance was to pay off a short-term or bridge loan on the property. If you sell your home before the points are fully written off, the residual value may be written off when calculating the final gain on the sale.

There has been much controversy with regard to the IRS position with regard to the deductibility of points paid on refinance transactions. Some have taken the position that refinances for the purpose of home improvements can be treated as purchases with regard to this issue. Others have taken the position that points that are financed by rolling in the costs into the new mortgage are never deductible. In other words, the borrower must pay refinance loan points "*out of pocket.*"

Rental Property Deductions

The cash flow loss on a rental property is fully deductible on an individual's tax returns as long as the individual is actively involved in the management of that property, the losses do not exceed $25,000 each year, and the adjusted gross income of the individual does not exceed $100,000. The allowable deduction is phased out between $100,000 and $150,000 annual adjusted gross income.

Example of Schedule E Rental Loss:

$12,000	Annual Rental Income
$ 5,000	Mortgage Interest
$ 2,000	Real Estate Taxes
$ 500	Advertising
$ 1,000	Insurance
$ 1,800	Homeowners Association Fees
$ 1,500	Maintenance
$ 2,500	Repairs—Painting and Electrical
$ 300	Travel
$ 3,000	Depreciation
$17,600	Total Expenses
($ 5,600)	Rental Loss

Depreciation for real estate placed into service after December 31, 1986 is 27.5 years for residential rental property. The method of depreciation is the "*straight-line method*," which means an equal amount of depreciation is taken each year. "*ACRS*" depreciation methods previously allowed accelerated depreciation of a property over a smaller number of years, which increased the yearly deductions for a rental property. It should be noted that any depreciation will have to be *recaptured* upon sale of the property—and the gain is taxable. That is, the calculation of gain would increase by the amount of any real property depreciation previously taken on the property.

Taxation upon Sale of Residential Real Estate

The sale of real estate can result in a capital gain just as the sale of any assets such as stocks and bonds. Unlike other assets, the sale of your primary residence receives significant preferential tax treatment:

The *Taxpayer Relief Act of 1997* eliminated the rule that required homeowners to *rollover* home sale gains until they were able to take a one-time exclusion over the age of 55. In its place, the profits of the sale of a principal residence are excluded from income up to a maximum of $500,000 for joint filers, including married couples, and $250,000 for individuals. This rule applies to home sales after May 7, 1997 and you must have owned the home at least two years and used it as your primary residence at least two out of the past five years. Even those who have already taken the one-time exclusion before this date can participate as long as they meet the principal residence test. The only exception to the "two-years-out-of-five" standard is if a sale was necessitated by a change in place of employment, health or unforeseen circumstance. In this case, the IRS will allow a percentage of the exclusion based upon how long the property was owned and used. In 2004, The IRS issued final regulations more specifically defining the term *unforeseen circumstance* as well the practice of prorating the period of use as primary residence. Depreciation taken on principal residences for home offices would be taxed regardless of the exclusion. If the residence contains a separate apartment such as a duplex—this would accounted-for separately because it produced income.

Gains above the $250,000 or $500,000 exclusionary amounts are taxed at a long-term capital gains rate of 15% (maximum tax bracket). There is a 5.0% capital gains rate for those in either a 10% or 15% tax bracket. Sales of homes utilized for investment purposes would also be subject to long-term capital gain rates. There is no provision that allows one to take a capital loss if the sale of a personal residence results in a loss. A loss can be taken on income-producing properties, however.

How is the gain of a home calculated? The following is the formula and a sample calculation:

Selling Price:	$100,000
Less:	
Selling Expenses:	$ 8,000
Cost of Home:	$40,000
Cost of Purchase:	$ 5,000
Cost of Improvements:	$20,000
Total Deductions:	$73,000
Total Gain:	$27,000

Let's take a brief definition of each of these deductions:

- *Selling Expenses* are the costs a seller incurs upon sale, for example the sales commission to a real estate agent, transfer taxes and closing costs paid on behalf of the purchaser.
- *The Cost of the Home* is the purchase price that should be supported by a HUD-1 and the original sales contract.
- *The Costs of Purchase* includes the closing costs that were not deductible as itemized deductions in previous years. These may include transfer taxes, attorney fees, appraisal fees, survey, etc. They do not include regular expenses such as homeowners association fees and homeowners insurance.
- *The Costs of Improvements* are the capital improvements made to the home after purchase and before the sale. The types of improvements are those that would increase the value of the home, but are not for repair of items already located in the home. For example, replacement of a water heater would be a repair. The installation of a deck in a home that did not previously have a deck would be considered an improvement. Replacement of an old deck with a newer, bigger deck would be considered both a repair and an improvement. The IRS publishes a list that delineates acceptable improvements on the outside and inside the home. A few examples of inclusions:

Shrubs	Driveway
Dishwasher	Additional Acreage
Bathtub	Sprinkler System
Air Conditioning	Finish Basement
Intercom	Built-in Furniture

- *Fix-Up Expenses* as defined as the costs incurred to prepare the house for home sale are no longer a subtraction against the selling price. These were defined as expenses that were incurred within the period 90 days before and 30 days after the sales contract is ratified (for owner-occupied properties).

A few notes on two types of real estate transactions that will differ from the IRS taxation treatment described above:

- *Sale of Rental Property*. The sale of rental property is not eligible for the same income tax breaks as the sale of a primary residence. There is no possibility of rolling over the gain and no exclusion. In addition, any depreciation of the rental property must be *recaptured* upon the sale of the home. *Recapturing* refers to subtracting all real property depreciation from the original purchase price when figuring the gain on the sale. In other words, the gain will be increased by the amount of depreciation taken. The tax rate on the portion of the gain resulting from recapture of depreciation is 25%.
- There is one way to avoid tax on the sale of a rental property. A *tax-free, like kind* or *Starker* exchange involves the exchange of a property used for income producing purposes for another rental property of equal value at the same time. In this way, the gain is not realized for tax purposes until the second property is sold. In September of 2000, the IRS issued new rules allowing the purchase of the new property before the present property is sold (*Reverse Starker Exchange*) as long as it was held in a "qualified exchange accommodation arrangement," or QEAA.

- *State Bond Issues.* The sale of property purchased under a state or local bond issue program may be subject to a *recapture tax*. Purchasers may be subject to this tax if the home is disposed of in less than ten years from purchase and the income of the purchaser at the time of sale exceeds the maximum gross income limits for the program in effect at the time of purchase. The maximum gross income is adjusted upward to include tax-exempt interest and downward to include the gain on the sale.

Each program publishes a formula that calculates the maximum amount of tax. For example, original loan amount multiplied by 6.25%, reduced by a percentage that is determined by the holding period. The homeowner would pay 100% of this tax if the adjusted gross income is exceeded by $5,000 or more. If the adjusted gross income were exceeded by $1,000, then 20% of the tax would be paid.

Example:

Original Mortgage Amount:	$100,000
Times 6.25%:	$ 6,250
Held for 6 years (60% of tax):	$ 3,750
Exceeds the income limits by $3,000 (60% of above):	$ 2,250

Special IRA Provision

The Taxpayer Relief Act of 1997 contained a special provision with regard to the purchase of a first home. Withdrawals can be made penalty-free up to $10,000 for the purpose of purchasing a home. A *first-time homebuyer* is defined to include someone who has not owned a home within the past two years. Though the homebuyer would be exempt from the 10% penalty, they would not be exempt from paying regular income taxes on the money withdrawn—unless the money came from a *Roth IRA* and was taxed in the year the contributions were made.

Appendix A   *Federal Withholding Tax Tables*

SINGLE Persons—MONTHLY Payroll Period
(For Wages Paid in 2005)

If the wages are—		And the number of withholding allowances claimed is—										
At least	But less than	0	1	2	3	4	5	6	7	8	9	10
		The amount of income tax to be withheld is—										
$0	$230	$0	$0	$0	$0	$0	$0	$0	$0	$0	$0	$0
230	240	1	0	0	0	0	0	0	0	0	0	0
240	250	2	0	0	0	0	0	0	0	0	0	0
250	260	3	0	0	0	0	0	0	0	0	0	0
260	270	4	0	0	0	0	0	0	0	0	0	0
270	280	5	0	0	0	0	0	0	0	0	0	0
280	290	6	0	0	0	0	0	0	0	0	0	0
290	300	7	0	0	0	0	0	0	0	0	0	0
300	320	9	0	0	0	0	0	0	0	0	0	0
320	340	11	0	0	0	0	0	0	0	0	0	0
340	360	13	0	0	0	0	0	0	0	0	0	0
360	380	15	0	0	0	0	0	0	0	0	0	0
380	400	17	0	0	0	0	0	0	0	0	0	0
400	420	19	0	0	0	0	0	0	0	0	0	0
420	440	21	0	0	0	0	0	0	0	0	0	0
440	460	23	0	0	0	0	0	0	0	0	0	0
460	480	25	0	0	0	0	0	0	0	0	0	0
480	500	27	0	0	0	0	0	0	0	0	0	0
500	520	29	2	0	0	0	0	0	0	0	0	0
520	540	31	4	0	0	0	0	0	0	0	0	0
540	560	33	6	0	0	0	0	0	0	0	0	0
560	580	35	8	0	0	0	0	0	0	0	0	0
580	600	37	10	0	0	0	0	0	0	0	0	0
600	640	40	13	0	0	0	0	0	0	0	0	0
640	680	44	17	0	0	0	0	0	0	0	0	0
680	720	48	21	0	0	0	0	0	0	0	0	0
720	760	52	25	0	0	0	0	0	0	0	0	0
760	800	56	29	3	0	0	0	0	0	0	0	0
800	840	60	33	7	0	0	0	0	0	0	0	0
840	880	66	37	11	0	0	0	0	0	0	0	0
880	920	72	41	15	0	0	0	0	0	0	0	0
920	960	78	45	19	0	0	0	0	0	0	0	0
960	1,000	84	49	23	0	0	0	0	0	0	0	0
1,000	1,040	90	53	27	0	0	0	0	0	0	0	0
1,040	1,080	96	57	31	4	0	0	0	0	0	0	0
1,080	1,120	102	62	35	8	0	0	0	0	0	0	0
1,120	1,160	108	68	39	12	0	0	0	0	0	0	0
1,160	1,200	114	74	43	16	0	0	0	0	0	0	0
1,200	1,240	120	80	47	20	0	0	0	0	0	0	0
1,240	1,280	126	86	51	24	0	0	0	0	0	0	0
1,280	1,320	132	92	55	28	1	0	0	0	0	0	0
1,320	1,360	138	98	59	32	5	0	0	0	0	0	0
1,360	1,400	144	104	64	36	9	0	0	0	0	0	0
1,400	1,440	150	110	70	40	13	0	0	0	0	0	0
1,440	1,480	156	116	76	44	17	0	0	0	0	0	0
1,480	1,520	162	122	82	48	21	0	0	0	0	0	0
1,520	1,560	168	128	88	52	25	0	0	0	0	0	0
1,560	1,600	174	134	94	56	29	3	0	0	0	0	0
1,600	1,640	180	140	100	60	33	7	0	0	0	0	0
1,640	1,680	186	146	106	66	37	11	0	0	0	0	0
1,680	1,720	192	152	112	72	41	15	0	0	0	0	0
1,720	1,760	198	158	118	78	45	19	0	0	0	0	0
1,760	1,800	204	164	124	84	49	23	0	0	0	0	0
1,800	1,840	210	170	130	90	53	27	0	0	0	0	0
1,840	1,880	216	176	136	96	57	31	4	0	0	0	0
1,880	1,920	222	182	142	102	62	35	8	0	0	0	0
1,920	1,960	228	188	148	108	68	39	12	0	0	0	0
1,960	2,000	234	194	154	114	74	43	16	0	0	0	0
2,000	2,040	240	200	160	120	80	47	20	0	0	0	0
2,040	2,080	246	206	166	126	86	51	24	0	0	0	0
2,080	2,120	252	212	172	132	92	55	28	1	0	0	0
2,120	2,160	258	218	178	138	98	59	32	5	0	0	0
2,160	2,200	264	224	184	144	104	64	36	9	0	0	0
2,200	2,240	270	230	190	150	110	70	40	13	0	0	0
2,240	2,280	276	236	196	156	116	76	44	17	0	0	0
2,280	2,320	282	242	202	162	122	82	48	21	0	0	0
2,320	2,360	288	248	208	168	128	88	52	25	0	0	0
2,360	2,400	294	254	214	174	134	94	56	29	3	0	0
2,400	2,440	300	260	220	180	140	100	60	33	7	0	0
2,440	2,480	306	266	226	186	146	106	66	37	11	0	0

Appendix A   Federal Withholding Tax Tables

SINGLE Persons—MONTHLY Payroll Period
(For Wages Paid in 2005)

If the wages are—		And the number of withholding allowances claimed is—										
At least	But less than	0	1	2	3	4	5	6	7	8	9	10
		The amount of income tax to be withheld is—										
$2,480	$2,520	$312	$272	$232	$192	$152	$112	$72	$41	$15	$0	$0
2,520	2,560	318	278	238	198	158	118	78	45	19	0	0
2,560	2,600	324	284	244	204	164	124	84	49	23	0	0
2,600	2,640	330	290	250	210	170	130	90	53	27	0	0
2,640	2,680	340	296	256	216	176	136	96	57	31	4	0
2,680	2,720	350	302	262	222	182	142	102	62	35	8	0
2,720	2,760	360	308	268	228	188	148	108	68	39	12	0
2,760	2,800	370	314	274	234	194	154	114	74	43	16	0
2,800	2,840	380	320	280	240	200	160	120	80	47	20	0
2,840	2,880	390	326	286	246	206	166	126	86	51	24	0
2,880	2,920	400	333	292	252	212	172	132	92	55	28	1
2,920	2,960	410	343	298	258	218	178	138	98	59	32	5
2,960	3,000	420	353	304	264	224	184	144	104	64	36	9
3,000	3,040	430	363	310	270	230	190	150	110	70	40	13
3,040	3,080	440	373	316	276	236	196	156	116	76	44	17
3,080	3,120	450	383	322	282	242	202	162	122	82	48	21
3,120	3,160	460	393	328	288	248	208	168	128	88	52	25
3,160	3,200	470	403	336	294	254	214	174	134	94	56	29
3,200	3,240	480	413	346	300	260	220	180	140	100	60	33
3,240	3,280	490	423	356	306	266	226	186	146	106	66	37
3,280	3,320	500	433	366	312	272	232	192	152	112	72	41
3,320	3,360	510	443	376	318	278	238	198	158	118	78	45
3,360	3,400	520	453	386	324	284	244	204	164	124	84	49
3,400	3,440	530	463	396	330	290	250	210	170	130	90	53
3,440	3,480	540	473	406	340	296	256	216	176	136	96	57
3,480	3,520	550	483	416	350	302	262	222	182	142	102	62
3,520	3,560	560	493	426	360	308	268	228	188	148	108	68
3,560	3,600	570	503	436	370	314	274	234	194	154	114	74
3,600	3,640	580	513	446	380	320	280	240	200	160	120	80
3,640	3,680	590	523	456	390	326	286	246	206	166	126	86
3,680	3,720	600	533	466	400	333	292	252	212	172	132	92
3,720	3,760	610	543	476	410	343	298	258	218	178	138	98
3,760	3,800	620	553	486	420	353	304	264	224	184	144	104
3,800	3,840	630	563	496	430	363	310	270	230	190	150	110
3,840	3,880	640	573	506	440	373	316	276	236	196	156	116
3,880	3,920	650	583	516	450	383	322	282	242	202	162	122
3,920	3,960	660	593	526	460	393	328	288	248	208	168	128
3,960	4,000	670	603	536	470	403	336	294	254	214	174	134
4,000	4,040	680	613	546	480	413	346	300	260	220	180	140
4,040	4,080	690	623	556	490	423	356	306	266	226	186	146
4,080	4,120	700	633	566	500	433	366	312	272	232	192	152
4,120	4,160	710	643	576	510	443	376	318	278	238	198	158
4,160	4,200	720	653	586	520	453	386	324	284	244	204	164
4,200	4,240	730	663	596	530	463	396	330	290	250	210	170
4,240	4,280	740	673	606	540	473	406	340	296	256	216	176
4,280	4,320	750	683	616	550	483	416	350	302	262	222	182
4,320	4,360	760	693	626	560	493	426	360	308	268	228	188
4,360	4,400	770	703	636	570	503	436	370	314	274	234	194
4,400	4,440	780	713	646	580	513	446	380	320	280	240	200
4,440	4,480	790	723	656	590	523	456	390	326	286	246	206
4,480	4,520	800	733	666	600	533	466	400	333	292	252	212
4,520	4,560	810	743	676	610	543	476	410	343	298	258	218
4,560	4,600	820	753	686	620	553	486	420	353	304	264	224
4,600	4,640	830	763	696	630	563	496	430	363	310	270	230
4,640	4,680	840	773	706	640	573	506	440	373	316	276	236
4,680	4,720	850	783	716	650	583	516	450	383	322	282	242
4,720	4,760	860	793	726	660	593	526	460	393	328	288	248
4,760	4,800	870	803	736	670	603	536	470	403	336	294	254
4,800	4,840	880	813	746	680	613	546	480	413	346	300	260
4,840	4,880	890	823	756	690	623	556	490	423	356	306	266
4,880	4,920	900	833	766	700	633	566	500	433	366	312	272
4,920	4,960	910	843	776	710	643	576	510	443	376	318	278
4,960	5,000	920	853	786	720	653	586	520	453	386	324	284
5,000	5,040	930	863	796	730	663	596	530	463	396	330	290
5,040	5,080	940	873	806	740	673	606	540	473	406	340	296

$5,080 and over   Use Table 4(a) for a **SINGLE** person on page 36. Also see the instructions on page 34.

From $2,625 to $5,813 use $330.80 plus 25% of the excess over $2,625; from $5,813 to $12,663 use $1,127.80 plus 28% of the excess over $5,813; from $12,663 to $27,354 use $3,045.80 plus 33% of the excess over $12,663; over $27,354 use $7,893.83 plus 35% of the excess over $27,354

Appendix A — Federal Withholding Tax Tables

MARRIED Persons—MONTHLY Payroll Period
(For Wages Paid in 2005)

If the wages are—		And the number of withholding allowances claimed is—										
At least	But less than	0	1	2	3	4	5	6	7	8	9	10
			The amount of income tax to be withheld is—										
$0	$540	$0	$0	$0	$0	$0	$0	$0	$0	$0	$0	$0
540	560	0	0	0	0	0	0	0	0	0	0	0
560	580	0	0	0	0	0	0	0	0	0	0	0
580	600	0	0	0	0	0	0	0	0	0	0	0
600	640	0	0	0	0	0	0	0	0	0	0	0
640	680	0	0	0	0	0	0	0	0	0	0	0
680	720	3	0	0	0	0	0	0	0	0	0	0
720	760	7	0	0	0	0	0	0	0	0	0	0
760	800	11	0	0	0	0	0	0	0	0	0	0
800	840	15	0	0	0	0	0	0	0	0	0	0
840	880	19	0	0	0	0	0	0	0	0	0	0
880	920	23	0	0	0	0	0	0	0	0	0	0
920	960	27	1	0	0	0	0	0	0	0	0	0
960	1,000	31	5	0	0	0	0	0	0	0	0	0
1,000	1,040	35	9	0	0	0	0	0	0	0	0	0
1,040	1,080	39	13	0	0	0	0	0	0	0	0	0
1,080	1,120	43	17	0	0	0	0	0	0	0	0	0
1,120	1,160	47	21	0	0	0	0	0	0	0	0	0
1,160	1,200	51	25	0	0	0	0	0	0	0	0	0
1,200	1,240	55	29	2	0	0	0	0	0	0	0	0
1,240	1,280	59	33	6	0	0	0	0	0	0	0	0
1,280	1,320	63	37	10	0	0	0	0	0	0	0	0
1,320	1,360	67	41	14	0	0	0	0	0	0	0	0
1,360	1,400	71	45	18	0	0	0	0	0	0	0	0
1,400	1,440	75	49	22	0	0	0	0	0	0	0	0
1,440	1,480	79	53	26	0	0	0	0	0	0	0	0
1,480	1,520	83	57	30	3	0	0	0	0	0	0	0
1,520	1,560	87	61	34	7	0	0	0	0	0	0	0
1,560	1,600	91	65	38	11	0	0	0	0	0	0	0
1,600	1,640	95	69	42	15	0	0	0	0	0	0	0
1,640	1,680	99	73	46	19	0	0	0	0	0	0	0
1,680	1,720	103	77	50	23	0	0	0	0	0	0	0
1,720	1,760	107	81	54	27	1	0	0	0	0	0	0
1,760	1,800	111	85	58	31	5	0	0	0	0	0	0
1,800	1,840	115	89	62	35	9	0	0	0	0	0	0
1,840	1,880	119	93	66	39	13	0	0	0	0	0	0
1,880	1,920	124	97	70	43	17	0	0	0	0	0	0
1,920	1,960	130	101	74	47	21	0	0	0	0	0	0
1,960	2,000	136	105	78	51	25	0	0	0	0	0	0
2,000	2,040	142	109	82	55	29	2	0	0	0	0	0
2,040	2,080	148	113	86	59	33	6	0	0	0	0	0
2,080	2,120	154	117	90	63	37	10	0	0	0	0	0
2,120	2,160	160	121	94	67	41	14	0	0	0	0	0
2,160	2,200	166	126	98	71	45	18	0	0	0	0	0
2,200	2,240	172	132	102	75	49	22	0	0	0	0	0
2,240	2,280	178	138	106	79	53	26	0	0	0	0	0
2,280	2,320	184	144	110	83	57	30	3	0	0	0	0
2,320	2,360	190	150	114	87	61	34	7	0	0	0	0
2,360	2,400	196	156	118	91	65	38	11	0	0	0	0
2,400	2,440	202	162	122	95	69	42	15	0	0	0	0
2,440	2,480	208	168	128	99	73	46	19	0	0	0	0
2,480	2,520	214	174	134	103	77	50	23	0	0	0	0
2,520	2,560	220	180	140	107	81	54	27	1	0	0	0
2,560	2,600	226	186	146	111	85	58	31	5	0	0	0
2,600	2,640	232	192	152	115	89	62	35	9	0	0	0
2,640	2,680	238	198	158	119	93	66	39	13	0	0	0
2,680	2,720	244	204	164	124	97	70	43	17	0	0	0
2,720	2,760	250	210	170	130	101	74	47	21	0	0	0
2,760	2,800	256	216	176	136	105	78	51	25	0	0	0
2,800	2,840	262	222	182	142	109	82	55	29	2	0	0
2,840	2,880	268	228	188	148	113	86	59	33	6	0	0
2,880	2,920	274	234	194	154	117	90	63	37	10	0	0
2,920	2,960	280	240	200	160	121	94	67	41	14	0	0
2,960	3,000	286	246	206	166	126	98	71	45	18	0	0
3,000	3,040	292	252	212	172	132	102	75	49	22	0	0
3,040	3,080	298	258	218	178	138	106	79	53	26	0	0
3,080	3,120	304	264	224	184	144	110	83	57	30	3	0
3,120	3,160	310	270	230	190	150	114	87	61	34	7	0
3,160	3,200	316	276	236	196	156	118	91	65	38	11	0
3,200	3,240	322	282	242	202	162	122	95	69	42	15	0

Federal Withholding Tax Tables

MARRIED Persons—MONTHLY Payroll Period
(For Wages Paid in 2005)

If the wages are— At least	But less than	0	1	2	3	4	5	6	7	8	9	10
		\multicolumn{11}{c}{The amount of income tax to be withheld is—}
$3,240	$3,280	$328	$288	$248	$208	$168	$128	$99	$73	$46	$19	$0
3,280	3,320	334	294	254	214	174	134	103	77	50	23	0
3,320	3,360	340	300	260	220	180	140	107	81	54	27	1
3,360	3,400	346	306	266	226	186	146	111	85	58	31	5
3,400	3,440	352	312	272	232	192	152	115	89	62	35	9
3,440	3,480	358	318	278	238	198	158	119	93	66	39	13
3,480	3,520	364	324	284	244	204	164	124	97	70	43	17
3,520	3,560	370	330	290	250	210	170	130	101	74	47	21
3,560	3,600	376	336	296	256	216	176	136	105	78	51	25
3,600	3,640	382	342	302	262	222	182	142	109	82	55	29
3,640	3,680	388	348	308	268	228	188	148	113	86	59	33
3,680	3,720	394	354	314	274	234	194	154	117	90	63	37
3,720	3,760	400	360	320	280	240	200	160	121	94	67	41
3,760	3,800	406	366	326	286	246	206	166	126	98	71	45
3,800	3,840	412	372	332	292	252	212	172	132	102	75	49
3,840	3,880	418	378	338	298	258	218	178	138	106	79	53
3,880	3,920	424	384	344	304	264	224	184	144	110	83	57
3,920	3,960	430	390	350	310	270	230	190	150	114	87	61
3,960	4,000	436	396	356	316	276	236	196	156	118	91	65
4,000	4,040	442	402	362	322	282	242	202	162	122	95	69
4,040	4,080	448	408	368	328	288	248	208	168	128	99	73
4,080	4,120	454	414	374	334	294	254	214	174	134	103	77
4,120	4,160	460	420	380	340	300	260	220	180	140	107	81
4,160	4,200	466	426	386	346	306	266	226	186	146	111	85
4,200	4,240	472	432	392	352	312	272	232	192	152	115	89
4,240	4,280	478	438	398	358	318	278	238	198	158	119	93
4,280	4,320	484	444	404	364	324	284	244	204	164	124	97
4,320	4,360	490	450	410	370	330	290	250	210	170	130	101
4,360	4,400	496	456	416	376	336	296	256	216	176	136	105
4,400	4,440	502	462	422	382	342	302	262	222	182	142	109
4,440	4,480	508	468	428	388	348	308	268	228	188	148	113
4,480	4,520	514	474	434	394	354	314	274	234	194	154	117
4,520	4,560	520	480	440	400	360	320	280	240	200	160	121
4,560	4,600	526	486	446	406	366	326	286	246	206	166	126
4,600	4,640	532	492	452	412	372	332	292	252	212	172	132
4,640	4,680	538	498	458	418	378	338	298	258	218	178	138
4,680	4,720	544	504	464	424	384	344	304	264	224	184	144
4,720	4,760	550	510	470	430	390	350	310	270	230	190	150
4,760	4,800	556	516	476	436	396	356	316	276	236	196	156
4,800	4,840	562	522	482	442	402	362	322	282	242	202	162
4,840	4,880	568	528	488	448	408	368	328	288	248	208	168
4,880	4,920	574	534	494	454	414	374	334	294	254	214	174
4,920	4,960	580	540	500	460	420	380	340	300	260	220	180
4,960	5,000	586	546	506	466	426	386	346	306	266	226	186
5,000	5,040	592	552	512	472	432	392	352	312	272	232	192
5,040	5,080	598	558	518	478	438	398	358	318	278	238	198
5,080	5,120	604	564	524	484	444	404	364	324	284	244	204
5,120	5,160	610	570	530	490	450	410	370	330	290	250	210
5,160	5,200	616	576	536	496	456	416	376	336	296	256	216
5,200	5,240	622	582	542	502	462	422	382	342	302	262	222
5,240	5,280	628	588	548	508	468	428	388	348	308	268	228
5,280	5,320	634	594	554	514	474	434	394	354	314	274	234
5,320	5,360	640	600	560	520	480	440	400	360	320	280	240
5,360	5,400	646	606	566	526	486	446	406	366	326	286	246
5,400	5,440	652	612	572	532	492	452	412	372	332	292	252
5,440	5,480	658	618	578	538	498	458	418	378	338	298	258
5,480	5,520	664	624	584	544	504	464	424	384	344	304	264
5,520	5,560	673	630	590	550	510	470	430	390	350	310	270
5,560	5,600	683	636	596	556	516	476	436	396	356	316	276
5,600	5,640	693	642	602	562	522	482	442	402	362	322	282
5,640	5,680	703	648	608	568	528	488	448	408	368	328	288
5,680	5,720	713	654	614	574	534	494	454	414	374	334	294
5,720	5,760	723	660	620	580	540	500	460	420	380	340	300
5,760	5,800	733	666	626	586	546	506	466	426	386	346	306
5,800	5,840	743	676	632	592	552	512	472	432	392	352	312
5,840	5,880	753	686	638	598	558	518	478	438	398	358	318

$5,880 and over   Use Table 4(b) for a **MARRIED** person on page 36. Also see the instructions on page 34.

From $5,517 to $10,063 use $666.70 plus 25% of the excess over $5,517; from $10,063 to $15,800 use $1,803.20 plus 28% of the excess over $10,063; from $15,800 to $27,771 use $3,409.56 plus 33% of the excess over $15,800; over $27,771 use $7,359.99 plus 35% of the excess over $27,771

ESTIMATE OF SETTLEMENT COSTS OF A MORTGAGE TRANSACTION

A. ITEMS PAID FOR AT LOAN APPLICATION:

1. **APPRAISAL**... _____

          Conventional $250 - $450
          FHA/VA   Add $75-$150

   NOTE: Add $75-125 for 2-4 unit or investor property. Homes over $500,000 may be more.

2. **CREDIT REPORT**.. _____

                                     $15 - $75

   NOTE: Extra report non-married coborrowers. If lender uses an "in-file" charge may be less.

3. **APPLICATION/LOCK FEE**.. _____

                                  .25-1.00%
                                  of Loan Amt

   NOTE: If charged, may be applied to closing costs at settlement. If so, do not add in total.

SUBTOTAL .... _____

B. PREPAID ITEMS

1. **ONE YEARS HOMEOWNERS INSURANCE**................................... _____
   (First Year Premium) $2.00 to $3.00 per
                                          $1,000 Loan Amt

   NOTE: Paid Directly by Applicant (may be credit if refinance)

2. **PRIVATE MORTGAGE INSURANCE**... _____
   (First Year Premium)   .25% to 1.20%
                                         of Loan Amt

   NOTE: Applicable over 80% LTV conventional mortgages. Varies by loan type, LTV, and Company. Not applicable for monthly mortgage insurance.

3. **ESCROWS**
   NOTE: On refinances, escrow account will be refunded by present lender

   3A. REAL ESTATE TAXES... _____
                                        2 to 14 Months
   NOTE: Will be higher in states collecting only one time each year

   3B. HOMEOWNERS INSURANCE... _____
                                          2 Months
   NOTE: From annual estimate above

   3C. MORTGAGE INSURANCE... _____
   (Monthly Premium)   2 Months
   NOTE: .20% to 1.30% monthly conventional over 80% LTV depending upon loan type, LTV and company. May eliminate the need for first year premium (above). 50% for FHA loans (15-year mortgages are .25%)--up-front premium is financed.

4. **PREPAID INTEREST**... _____
                                       Estimate 15 Days
   NOTE: Actual amount will vary in accordance with settlement date.

SUBTOTAL .... _____

C. LENDER CHARGES

N/A
1. **LOAN ORIGINATION FEE**.. _____
   Up to 1% of Loan Amt
   NOTE: Figured on base loan amount for FHA, including funding fee for VA

2. **DISCOUNT POINTS**.. _____
   Varies
   NOTE: Each discount point is 1.0% of the loan amount including funding fee or FHA MIP

3. **DOCUMENT PREPARATION/REVIEW OR CLOSING FEE** .... _____
   $150-$350

4. **LENDER INSPECTION/COURIER FEES** .... _____
   $50-$125

5. **TAX SERVICE FEE**... _____
   $50-100
   NOTE: 3-5 above cannot be paid by applicant on FHA/VA loans except if paying for 3rd party service. Cannot be charged on FHA/VA refinances except for 3rd party services.

6. **VA FUNDING FEE** .... _____
   If Not Financed
   NOTE: 2.15% for no downpayment purchases and refinances. 1.50% for 5% down purchases and 1.25% for 10% down purchases and .50% for all VA rate reduction refinances. Can be financed. Higher for second time users and reservists.

7. **FHA MORTGAGE INSURANCE** .... _____
   If Not Financed
   NOTE: 1.50% for all loans except condominiums and 203K. Can be financed

SUBTOTAL .... _____

D. ATTORNEY CHARGES

1. **ATTORNEY FEES**:.. _____
   $300-$700
   NOTE: May be separate charge to seller. Includes preparation of documents, title exam, courier charges, payoff fees.

2. **SURVEY** .... _____
   $150-$400
   NOTE: Recertification of present survey or survey affidavit acceptable on most refinances

3. **TITLE INSURANCE:**
   3A. Owners Policy: Based upon sales price (optional) .... _____
   $350-$700/$1,000
   NOTE: Owner policy includes lender policy below

   3B. LENDER POLICY: Based upon loan amount (mandatory) .... _____
   $250-$600/$1,000
   NOTE: May be additional charges for endorsements for condos, Leasehold, etc. ($25-$100)

SUBTOTAL.. _____

Appendix B   *Estimate of Settlement Costs of A Mortgage Transaction*

E. TAXES

    1. RECORDING FEES .... _____
                                                    $20-$70
        NOTE: Will vary based upon property type (condos higher) Reduce by 30-40% if a refinance

    2. RECORDATION/INTANGIBLE/TRANSFER TAXES .... _____
        NOTE: Will vary from zero in many states (ex California, Ohio) to over 2% of the sales price (Maryland). Most states reduce or do not charge taxes on a refinance

    SUBTOTAL .... _____

F. MISC. FEES TO COMPLETE APPRAISAL OF HOME

    1. FINAL INSPECTION .... _____
                                                    $50-$100
        NOTE: For new homes or other appraisal requirements such as repairs

    2. PEST INSPECTION .... _____
                                                    $40-$60
        NOTE: May not be required for high rise condos over the fourth floor or refinances

    3. WELL/SEPTIC INSPECTION .... _____
                                                    $75-$250
        NOTE: VA will require hook-up to public water supply if available

    4. HOME INSPECTION FEE .... _____
                                                    $150-$300
        NOTE: May be financed on FHA loans up to $200

    5. FLOOD CERTIFICATION .... _____
                                                    $12-$20

    SUBTOTAL .... _____

TOTAL CASH REQUIRED

    A.   **Items Paid for At Loan Application** .... _____
    B.   **Prepaid Items** .... _____
    C.   **Lender Charges** .... _____
    D.   **Attorney Fees** .... _____
    E.   **Taxes** .... _____
    F.   **Misc. Fees to Complete Appraisal of Home** .... _____

    Downpayment .... _____

                                                                     TOTAL CASH   _____

National Real Estate Transaction Taxes and Title Insurance Costs

Note: These charges will vary from local jurisdiction to local jurisdiction within each State and are subject to change. They will also vary in accordance with the sales price and the type of transaction (for example, refinances may not be taxed). The designation of which party pays is also customary and may vary. Recordation fees (usually less than $100 per transaction) are not included. The title insurance charges shown are approximate for a $100,000 sales price. The cost per thousand will typically be higher at a lower sales price and lower at a higher sales price.

Northeast

Connecticut*
.61% of sales price by seller
$400 for owner's title

Delaware
2-3% of sales price split
$325 for owner's title

Maine*
.44% of sales price split
$250 for owner's title

Massachusetts*
.228% of sales price by seller
$275 for owner's title

New Hampshire*
1.05% of sales price split
$275 for owner's title

New Jersey
.35% up to $150,000
.50% over $150,000
of sales price by seller
$553 for owner's title

New York*
.4% of sales price by seller
+1.0% NY City
(.25% on mortgage)
$650 for owner's title

Pennsylvania
2.0% of sales price split
+some higher local taxes
$783 for owner's title

Rhode Island*
.28% of sales price by seller
$390 for owner's title

Vermont*
.5%-1.0% of sales price by purchaser
$225 for owner's title

Southeast

Alabama
.1% of sales price
.15% of mortgage amount split
$572 for owner's title

Arkansas
.22% of sales price by seller
$325 for owner's title

District of Columbia
2.2% of sales price split
$350 for owner's title

Florida
.6-1.5% of sales price by seller
.55% of mortgage amount by buyer
$685 for owner's title

Georgia
.1% of sales price by seller
.3% of mortgage amount by buyer
Owner's title varies by locality

Kentucky
.1% of sales price split
$325 for owner's title

Louisiana
Local taxes only
$429 for owner's title

Maryland*
1.5-2.1% of sales price split
.44-.70% of sales price split
$350 for owner's title

Mississippi
None
Owner's title varies by locality

North Carolina
.2% of equity by seller
$200 for owner's title

South Carolina
.33% of sales price by seller
$275 for owner's title

Tennessee
@.115% of mortgage
@.37% of sales price
varies by locality
$325-$396 for owner's title

Texas
None
$1,023 for owner's title

Virginia
.2% of sales price
.2% of mortgage
by buyer
.1% of sales price by seller
$390 for owner's title

West Virginia
.44% of sales price by seller
$390 for owner's title

C-1

Midwest

Idaho
.2-.3% of sales price split
$590 for owner's title

Illinois varies
.15-.65% of sales price:
$432 for owner's title

Indiana
None
$500 for owner's title

Iowa*
.16% of sales price by seller
Title insurance cost varies

Kansas
.25% of mortgage by buyer
$325 for owner's title

Michigan
.11% of sales price by seller
$520 for owner's title

Minnesota*
.23% of mortgage by buyer
.33% of sales price by buyer
$350 for owner's title

Missouri
None
$325 for owner's title

Nebraska
.15% of sales price by seller
$382 for owner's title

North Dakota
None
$325 for owner's title

Ohio
.1-.4% of sales price by seller
$500 for owner's title

South Dakota
.1% of sales price by seller
$450 for owner's title

Wisconsin*
.3% of sales price by seller
$575 for owner's title

West

Alaska
None
$582 for owner's title

Arizona
None
$572 for owner's title

California*
.11-.61% of sales price by seller
$622 for owner's title

Colorado
.01% of sales price by seller
$678 for owner's title

Hawaii
4.01% of sales price split
$380 for owner's title

Montana
None
$553 for owner's title

Nevada
.13% of equity by seller
$520 for owner's title

New Mexico
None
$773 for owner's title

Oklahoma
.15% of sales price by seller
$380 for owner's title

Oregon*
None
$455 for owner's title

Utah*
None
$605 for owner's title

Washington
1.75% of sales price by seller
$520 for owner's title

Note: *indicates that State may require payment of interest on escrows for some mortgages. Sources include First American Title Company and Mortgage Bankers Association.

Glossary

Above Par. When a mortgage is sold for more than its face value because it has an above market interest rate. For example, a $100,000 mortgage may be sold for 101.00, or $101,000.

A Credit Mortgages. Mortgages which generally meet the credit underwriting guidelines of Fannie Mae, Freddie Mac, FHA, VA or major jumbo purchasers. Those who have credit ratings or other qualification deficiencies would be rated as *B, C* or *D* credit.

Acquisition Cost. The sales price of a property plus FHA allowable closing costs. Before down payment simplification, FHA allowed certain closing costs to be financed by adding them to the sales price before calculating the required down payment. This is now reflected in tables for low closing cost and high closing cost states with different down payment requirements for each.

Adjustable Rate Mortgage. A mortgage in which the interest rate changes at certain intervals during the term of the mortgage.

Adjusted Sales Price. IRS term for the sales price of a home minus the costs of the sale. Used to calculate capital gains.

Adjustment Period. The length of time that dictates interest rate adjustments on an adjustable rate mortgage. A *six month ARM* would have an adjustment every six months.

Adjustment Period Cap. The amount that the interest rate is allowed to increase or decrease at the time of adjustment of an adjustable rate mortgage. A one-year adjustable would have an *annual cap*, since the adjustment period is every year.

Alternative Documentation. Use of bank statements, W-2's, and pay stubs to document an applicant's income and assets instead of verification forms mailed by the lender.

Amortization Schedule. A table that shows the principal changes of a mortgage balance on a monthly or annual basis.

Annual Percentage Rate (APR). Calculation that standardizes rates, points and other costs of a financing instrument such as a mortgage loan. This figure is disclosed as part of the *truth-in-lending statement* that is required by the *Federal Truth-in-Lending Act*. The statement is required on all consumer loans but is required to be disclosed within three working days of application for residential owner-occupied mortgage loans pursuant to the *Real Estate Settlement Procedures Act (RESPA)*.

Application Fee. Fee charged by a lender at the time of loan application. This fee may include the cost of an appraisal, credit report, lock-in fee or other closing costs which are incurred during the process or the fee may be in addition to other charges.

Appraisal. An estimate of value—in this case for real property. For residential properties the appraiser would utilize the *Uniform Residential Appraisal Report, or URAR*.

Appreciation. The increase in value of property over time.

Assumption. The act of taking over the previous borrower's obligation of a mortgage note. Assumptions may be advantageous if the terms of the mortgage are advantageous and these terms are not changed by the lender when the mortgage is assumed.

Automated Underwriting Systems. Technological systems that take into account credit scores and other characteristics of borrowers (such as job histories) to develop a rating upon which an underwriting decision can be based. These systems include *Desktop Underwriter* (Fannie Mae) and *Loan Prospector* (Freddie Mac).

Glossary

Back-to-Back Settlement. Transactions involving selling one home and purchasing another on the same day, usually within hours of one another. The seller typically moves from one settlement table to the next in order to accomplish the purchase transaction.

Balloon. A mortgage that does not fully amortize over the term of the mortgage. The principal remaining at the end of the term is called a balloon payment.

Base Mortgage Amount. The mortgage amount before mortgage insurance or VA funding fee is added.

Bi-weekly Mortgage. A mortgage that requires one-half of one monthly payment every two weeks. The resulting extra monthly payment each year lowers the mortgage term to approximately 22-25 years.

Bridge Loan. Short-term mortgage, usually interest only, utilized to help a purchaser settle on a home before his/her present home is sold.

Buydown. To lower the interest rate on a mortgage. A *permanent buydown* would lower the rate for the entire term of the mortgage. A *temporary buydown* would lower the rate for a certain portion of the mortgage term, usually the first few years.

Capital Gains Income. Income derived through the sale of assets such as real estate.

Capped Rate. A rate commitment by a lender which locks-in a maximum rate but allows the borrower to relock if market rates decrease. Also referred to as cap and float.

Cash Out Refinance. A refinance in which the borrower takes cash, or equity out of the property.

Certificate of Deposit Index (CODI). The average of the most recently published monthly yields on 3-month certificates of deposits for the 12 most recent calendar months as published by the Federal Reserve Board.

Certificate of Eligibility (COE). Issued by VA to certify the amount of entitlement available to a veteran.

Certificate of Insurance. Document which adds the mortgage holder on a particular unit to the master insurance policy for a condominium development.

Certificate of Reasonable Value (CRV). Appraisal of a property for a VA mortgage. Appraisal of a subdivision would be a *Master Certificate of Reasonable Value*, or *MCRV*.

Certificate of Veteran Status. FHA form filled out by the Department of Veteran Affairs in order to establish a borrower's eligibility for an *FHA Vet Mortgage*.

Closing Costs. The costs incurred in order to purchase real estate. May include points, taxes, fees and more.

Co-borrower. Two or more borrowers obtaining the same mortgage. If a co-borrower is not living in the house he/she would be known as a *non-owner occupant co-borrower*.

Combined Loan-to-Value. The principal balance of all mortgages on the property (including second and third trusts) divided by the value of the property.

Commercial Mortgage. A loan that secures commercial real estate.

Commercial Real Estate. Office buildings, shopping centers, apartment buildings and other property which is utilized for the production of income rather than as residences. If residential real estate has more than four units it is considered commercial real estate.

Commitment. An agreement for future action. A *rate commitment* would be an agreement to lend at a certain rate. A *loan commitment* would be an agreement to lend and represents another term for *loan approval*.

Comparables. Properties utilized in an appraisal to determine the value of the property being appraised.

Compensating Factor. A positive characteristic of a mortgage application that may offset a negative factor.

Compressed Buydown. A temporary buydown that has rate changes every six months as opposed to annually.

Glossary

Conditional Right to Refinance. A provision of a balloon mortgage which, at the time of the scheduled balloon payment, allows the borrower to covert to a fixed rate for the remainder of the loan term.

Conditional Commitment. Term for an FHA appraisal. An FHA appraisal for a subdivision would be called a *Master Conditional Commitment*, or MCC.

Condominium. A project in which each unit owner has title to a unit and has an undivided interest to the common areas.

Condominium Association Fee. A fee paid by the homeowner to the association that governs a condominium complex for his/her part of the maintenance and management of the project.

Conforming Mortgage. A mortgage that can be purchased by Fannie Mae or Freddie Mac.

Construction Mortgage. A loan secured by real estate which is for the purpose of funding the construction of improvements, or building(s), upon the property.

Construction-to-Permanent Mortgage. A loan secured by real estate that is for the purpose of replacing a construction mortgage soon after the improvements are completed.

Consumer Price Index. An index of the Federal Government's measure of price increases at the retail level.

Contingencies. Conditions without which a transaction would be voided.

Contribution. Cash or other concession by the seller of a property in order to induce a purchaser to buy that property.

Conventional Mortgage. A mortgage not guaranteed by VA or insured by FHA, Rural Housing or State Bond Agencies.

Conversion Feature. A feature of a mortgage that allows the conversion to another interest rate, mortgage term, or type of mortgage instrument.

Cooperative (COOP). A form of ownership in which the right to occupy the unit is obtained by the purchase of shares in a corporation which owns the building.

Cost of Funds Index. An index that is made up of the cost to depository institutions of acquiring funds.

Coverage. The portion of the mortgage that mortgage insurance insures against default.

Credit Package. The portion of a loan application and documentation that is comprised of the information regarding the applicant's credit, income and asset history. The additional aspect of a loan application concerns the property being financed (appraisal).

Credit Report. A report run by an independent credit agency that verifies certain information concerning an applicant's credit history.

Credit Score. Automated systems that compile the credit characteristics of an individual into a single numeric rating. The rating would take into consideration the amount of open credit, credit payment history, number of credit inquiries, as well as other indications.

Deed of Trust. A legal document that enables the lender, or *mortgagee*, to hold legal claim or title to a property while the note is outstanding. *The Deed of Trust* transfers title to a *trustee* designated by the lender.

Default. The non-payment of a mortgage or other loan in accordance with the terms as specified in the note.

Delegated Underwriting. The delegation of underwriting authority from an investor or agency to the lender.

Department of Housing and Urban Development. A cabinet level Federal Agency which houses the Federal Housing Administration (FHA) and Government National Mortgage Association (Ginnie Mae).

Department of Veterans Affairs (VA). Cabinet level Federal Agency whose chief purpose is to aid veterans through a variety of programs.

Glossary

Depreciation. The decrease in value of an asset over a fixed period of time.

Desktop Underwriter (DU). Fannie Mae's automated underwriting system (Desktop Originator is used by mortgage brokers).

Discount Point. A charge by a lender levied to *buy down* the interest rate (equals 1% of the loan amount).

Distributive Shares. Increments of FHA insurance from a pool of mortgages insured during the same time period. In the past unused shares were distributed by FHA to the holders of the mortgages within that pool.

Down Payment. Money given by the purchaser of a property to the seller to acquire the mortgage and hence the property. The difference between the sales price and mortgage amount is the down payment.

Draws. Money taken out of an escrow account to finance the rehabilitation or construction of a house.

Easement. A right to utilize another property other than one's own. For example, a utility company may be granted an easement for utility lines.

Encroachment. The existence of a protrusion or infringement of a structure such as a fence on a property.

Equity. The net value of an asset. In the case of real estate, it would be the difference between the present value of the property and the mortgage amount on that property.

Escrow. Money held by a third party on behalf of the first party to be utilized for requirements of a second party. A *servicer* is a third party that holds an escrow on behalf of a borrower to pay taxes and insurance payments to the applicable entities when they become due.

Extended Locks. Mortgage rate commitments that are for longer than the typical 60-day lock-in term.

Farmers Home Administration (FmHA). Federal agency that guarantees mortgages in rural areas. Renamed as the Rural Housing Authority or the Rural Housing Program.

Federal Bond Subsidy Act. Federal legislation empowering state and local governments to issue tax free bonds to fund mortgages for lower and middle-income borrowers.

Federal Home Loan Mortgage Corporation (Freddie Mac) and *Federal National Mortgage Association (Fannie Mae).* Government Sponsored Enterprises (GSEs) that are publicly traded corporations supervised by the Federal Government. The purpose of the entities are to help facilitate the access of mortgage money by creating a secondary market for conventional mortgages. Conventional mortgages purchased by Freddie Mac and Fannie Mae are called *conforming* mortgages.

Federal Housing Administration (FHA). Government agency located within the Department of Housing and Urban Development. Administers the FHA mortgage program.

Fee Simple. Unrestricted ownership of real property.

FHA Direct Endorsement. FHA program in which lenders approve FHA mortgages directly as opposed to submitting the applications to the agency for approval.

FHA Lender Connection. Internet-based system that allows lenders to work with FHA online.

Final Inspection. Home inspection made by a lender, VA, FHA or the appraiser after a new home or repairs have been completed.

First Mortgage. The primary or original loan secured upon real estate.

Fixed Rate Mortgage. A mortgage in which the interest rate (and usually the payment) does not change over the term of the mortgage.

Fixed Payment Mortgage. A mortgage in which the payment does not change over the term of the mortgage. This is usually due to the interest rate being fixed.

Float. Application in which the lender has not committed to lend at a particular interest rate (not *locked-in*).

Floor. The lowest interest rate of an adjustable rate mortgage.

Free and Clear. A property with no mortgage liability placed upon it.

FSBO. An acronym that stands for *for sale by owner*, as opposed to a home that is listed for sale through a real estate company.

Full Documentation. Mortgage verification process that relies upon verification forms sent by the lender rather than alternative documentation (such as pay stubs) provided by the applicant.

Fully Amortized. A mortgage that has a zero balance at the end of the mortgage term.

Fully Indexed Accrual Rate. The index plus the margin for an adjustable rate mortgage (FIAR).

Grace Period. A length of time (usually 15 days) after a mortgage payment is due in which the lender will not charge a late penalty or report the payment as late.

Graduated Payment Mortgage (GPM). A mortgage which has regularly scheduled payment increases during some portion of the mortgage term.

Green Card. Immigration status which permits the holder to work in the United States, obtain a social security number and become an apprentice to attain citizenship (the permit is no longer green in color).

Gross Monthly Income. A person's income before deductions for taxes, medical insurance, etc. After deductions, the income is referred to as *take home pay* or *net income*.

Ground Rent. The land upon which a home is located is under a long-term lease (*leasehold ownership* as opposed to *fee simple*).

Growing Equity Mortgage (GEM). A type of graduated payment mortgage that has a shorter mortgage term due to future payment increases.

Government Mortgages. Mortgages insured or guaranteed by the government (FHA, VA, Rural Housing, or State Bond Agencies).

Government National Mortgage Association (Ginnie Mae). Government agency located within the Department of Housing and Urban Development. Created in 1968, its purpose is to facilitate the access of mortgages through creation of a secondary market for government mortgages (FHA and VA).

Grossing-Up Income. Increasing the value of income that is not taxed when qualifying for a mortgage application.

Guaranty. Amount of money VA will reimburse a lender upon default of a VA mortgage. Also referred to as the amount of *entitlement* or *eligibility*.

Home Equity Line of Credit (HELOC). An open line of credit against the equity in a home (typically a second mortgage).

Homeowners Association Fees (HOA Fees). A fee typically paid monthly by a homeowner to a homeowners association in order for the association to take care of areas owned in common by all homeowners within a *planned unit development*.

Homeowners Insurance. Insurance carried by the homeowner to protect the dwelling against fire and other hazards. Also known as "fire insurance."

Index. An indicator that is typically measured by an average of a variable over a certain period of time. Adjustable rate mortgage indices are measures of the movement of interest rates.

In-File Credit Report. Report directly from the credit repositories without any investigative data such as interviews with employers. Many loan programs will now base decisions using "in-files" merged from two or three repositories.

Glossary

Intangible Tax. The tax of something that is not tangible. The taxation of a real estate transaction would be considered an example of an intangible tax and sometimes is referred to as such.

Interest Only Mortgages. Mortgage programs that require no repayment of principal. Typical of bridge loans, which will balloon at the end of their term.

Interest Rate Cap. A limit on interest rate increases and/or decreases during each interest rate adjustment *(adjustment period cap)* or over the term *(life cap)* of the mortgage.

Investor Purchase. The purchase of a home for the purpose of generating income by renting the property.

IRS 4506/Request for Copy of Tax Form. IRS Form required that allows the lender to pull tax returns on the borrower directly from the IRS, usually accomplished as a quality control check on a certain number of cases after closing. More recently has been replaced by the IRS 8801.

Jumbo Mortgage. A mortgage that is larger than the purchase limits of Fannie Mae and Freddie Mac.

K-1. Federal tax form that reports the income of an individual from a Partnership or Subchapter S Corporation. Other important information on this form includes the percentage of ownership by the individual as well as capital contributed to the entity.

Land-to-Value. The value of the land divided by the total value of the property, including both the land and the home.

Lender Appraisal Processing Program (LAPP). VA program that allows lenders to directly issue appraisals, or *CRVs*.

Lender-Paid Mortgage Insurance. Mortgage insurance program that allows the lender to collect a higher interest rate from the borrower and forward the excess payment to the mortgage insurance company to pay for the mortgage insurance.

Lender Subsidized Buydown. A buydown that has a higher note rate than market. The higher rate funds the initial costs, or *subsidy*, of the temporary buydown.

Leverage. Ability to control a large asset with a smaller asset.

LIBOR Index. London Interbank Offered Rates, which is the average rate of interest that major world banks are willing to pay each other for U.S. dollar deposits for various terms on the London market.

Lien. A claim against a property. A mortgage is one form of a lien.

Life Cap. The amount the interest rate is allowed to increase during the term of the mortgage.

Limited Documentation. A mortgage that does not verify income, assets or another aspect of the credit package.

Loan Prospector (LP). Freddie Mac's automated underwriting system.

Loan-to-Value (LTV). The principal amount of a mortgage on a property divided by the value of that property.

Lock-in Fee. A fee that may be charged by lenders at the time of lock-in.

Lock-in. The process by which a lender commits to lend at a particular rate as long as the mortgage transaction closes within a specified time period. The document that specifies the terms of the *lock-in* is called a *rate commitment* or *lock-in agreement.*

Lot Mortgage or Lot Loan. A loan secured by real estate that contains no improvements or buildings (land).

Low/Mod Programs. Acronym for mortgage programs aimed to serve the low-to-moderate income populace.

Margin. The amount added to the index on an adjustable rate mortgage to determine the interest rate at each adjustment.

Master Conditional Commitment (MCC). An FHA appraisal accomplished for a subdivision.

Mortgage. A loan secured against real estate as opposed to personal property. States which are not *Trust States* utilize a *mortgage* as the legal instrument to secure the lien against the real estate which means that the owner holds title rather than a trustee.

Mortgagee. The lender of money that is secured by real estate

Mortgagor. The borrower of money that is secured by real estate.

Mortgagee Clause. Verbiage in the homeowners and title insurance policies which identifies the mortgage holder and it's successors and/or assigns.

Mortgage Insurance. Insurance that protects the lender against *default*. Insurance can be issued by private sources (private mortgage insurance) or the Federal Housing Administration (MIP).

Mortgage Insurance Premium (MIP). Mortgage insurance charged by FHA to insure a mortgage.

Moving Treasury Average (MTA). The 12-month average of the monthly yields of U.S. Treasury securities adjusted to a constant maturity of one year.

Negatively Amortized Mortgage (Negative Amortization). A mortgage whose balance may increase with all (scheduled negative) or certain (potential negative) payments.

Net Proceeds. Amount of cash that accrues to the seller after expenses are deducted from a home sale.

Non-conforming Mortgage. A mortgage that cannot be sold to Fannie Mae or Freddie Mac.

No-Income Verification Mortgage (Limited Documentation). A mortgage that does not verify the income stated by the applicant.

No Point Mortgage. A mortgage that carries a higher interest rate in exchange for no discount points or origination fee.

No Ratio Mortgage. A mortgage that requires no income qualification (as opposed to no-income documentation). In this case—the income level does not matter.

Note. A legal instrument that specifies the terms of any debt. When someone borrows money secured against real estate, a note will be signed.

Open Equity Line. A second trust mortgage that is an *open line of credit*. That is, the balance can be increased by future draws up to a set amount. Also known as a Home Equity Line of Credit (HELOC).

Operating Income Statement. Form that determines the probable cash flow on a property which is to be used for rental purposes.

Origination Fee. A charge by a lender for the costs of *originating* a mortgage. Usually equal to one point, or 1% of the mortgage amount.

Owner-Occupied Purchase. The purchase of a property for the purpose of the primary residence of the owner.

Partial Entitlement. The entitlement remaining after the veteran has used part of his/her full entitlement in obtaining a VA mortgage. The partial entitlement may result from a legislated increase in entitlement that occurs after the veteran has purchased a home.

Payment Cap. The limitation on increases or decreases in the payment amount of an adjustable rate mortgage or fixed rate hybrid. Will be associated with potential negative amortization.

Personal Property. All other property besides real estate (for example, furnishings).

PITI. Total mortgage payment assuming an escrow fund is set up by the lender for real estate taxes (T) and insurance (I). The PI is the principal and interest, or loan payment.

Planned Unit Development. A project in which there is land and/or facilities owned in common by owners within the development. Typical common areas might be recreational facilities, wooded areas or parking lots.

Glossary

Plans and Specs. The plans and specifications upon which the construction of a home is based. An appraiser will typically appraise a new property conditionally upon completion of plans and specs. A final inspection is then performed after the house is completed.

POC. A charge that is paid outside of closing. This would include closing costs such as the appraisal and credit report which an applicant pays up-front to the lender.

Point. A charge by a lender. One point is equal to 1% of the mortgage amount.

Post Closing Reserves. The liquid assets of an applicant required by a lender after closing on the mortgage.

Potential Negative Amortization. An adjustable rate mortgage that may have principal balance increases at some time during the mortgage term, depending upon the future direction of the index upon which rate adjustments are based and whether a payment cap is invoked.

Positively Amortized Mortgage. A mortgage that has a balance decrease with each payment.

Prepaids. Closing costs that are actually paid at closing for charges that will occur in the future. One example would be prepaid interest that will accrue after the closing date until the starting date of the note.

Prepayment. To apply a payment to the principal of the mortgage balance before the payment is actually due under the terms of the mortgage. Will cause a mortgage to be retired early.

Prepayment Penalty. A charge specified in the note that is levied if a mortgage is paid off before the end of the mortgage term.

Pre-qualification. The process of determining one's qualifications for a mortgage and home purchase before the actual home is identified.

Principal Reduction. The reduction in loan balance that occurs with each payment of a positively amortized mortgage.

Processing. The procedure in which a lender takes a loan application and brings it to the point to *underwriting* for loan approval.

Profit and Loss Statement (P&L). A financial statement provided by the applicant that reports the income and expenses for a business during a certain time period. The statement would typically be required of self-employed applicants if the tax returns are not current within 90 days.

Purchase Money Mortgage. A mortgage obtained to finance the purchase of real estate.

Qualification. The process that determines whether an applicant can be approved for a mortgage loan.

Rate Reduction Refinance. The refinance of an existing mortgage balance solely to lower the interest rate.

Ratio Method. Method of qualifying which divides the monthly mortgage payment by the gross monthly income of the borrower (*housing* or *first ratio*) and then divides the monthly mortgage payment and monthly debt payments by the gross monthly income (*debt* or *second ratio*).

Real Estate Settlement Procedures Act (RESPA). Federal law that regulates the settlement practices within the real estate industry. This law requires the provision of *Good Faith Estimates of Closing Costs*, prohibits kickbacks for referrals of related services, and standardizes the closing with a required form (*HUD-1*).

Real Estate Taxes. Local government taxes levied on the ownership of real estate. Also known as real estate property taxes.

Real Property. The ownership of real estate.

Recapture Tax. A federal tax required on the gain of sale of certain properties financed under the *Federal Bond Subsidy Act* which are sold within 10 years of purchase. This tax is in effect for homes purchased after December 31, 1990.

Recordation Fees. Fees charged by a local government to record the documents of a real estate transaction.

Reduced Closing Cost Mortgage. A mortgage that carries a higher interest rate in exchange for no points and/or a credit towards other closing costs from the lender.

Refinance Mortgage. Money borrowed by the present owner of real estate to replace an existing loan secured by the same real estate or to place a mortgage on *free and clear* property.

Rehabilitate. The process of reconstructing or improving property that is in the state of disrepair. A mortgage for such purpose would be referred to as a *rehab mortgage*.

Rental Equivalency. A mortgage payment (PITI) after the tax deductions are taken into consideration.

Rental Negative. The monthly cash flow loss on an investment property.

Residential Mortgage. A loan that is secured by *residential real estate.*

Residential Real Estate. Housing built and owned for the purpose of a person(s) making the property his/her home or a property to be rented to tenants. For purposes of classification, residential real estate contains one to four units. Larger rental properties are considered commercial real estate (such as apartment complexes).

Residual Method. Method of qualifying that subtracts all expenses from a borrower's income to determine whether there remains a positive *residual*.

Reverse Annuity Mortgage. A mortgage which uses present equity in the property to fund monthly payments from the lender to the borrower—in lieu of the borrower receiving the proceeds of the loan in a lump sum.

Revolving Credit. Open lines of credit that are subject to variable payments in accordance with the balance. Credit cards are examples of revolving credit.

Right of Rescission. Period of three full days after closing in which the consumer is allowed to negate an owner occupied refinance transaction. Loan funding does not occur until this period expires.

Right to Financial Privacy Act. Places restrictions upon governmental authorities having access to copies of the financial records of any mortgage applicant.

Rolled-in. To include the closing costs of a refinance transaction in the balance of the new mortgage — i.e., to finance the closing costs of the refinance so that they are not paid in cash by the borrower, or *out-of-pocket*.

Sales Concession. Cash a seller pays on behalf of a purchaser in order to entice the purchaser to buy the home. Another term for *seller contribution*. For example, the seller may pay a certain number of dollars towards a purchaser's closing costs.

Scheduled Negative Amortization. A mortgage that has planned increases in the balance of the mortgage during some portion of the mortgage term. Typically associated with *Graduated Payment Mortgages*.

Second Home Purchase. A property purchased for occupancy by the owner but is not the primary residence. Usually recreational or vacation properties.

Second Mortgage. A loan that is secured by real estate that is already secured by another loan that is the *first mortgage*.

Second Trust. Another term for a *second mortgage*. More common term in *Trust* states.

Secondary Market. A market that exists for the purchase and sale of mortgages and *servicing rights* as commodities.

Self-Employment. A person who owns at least 25% of the entity (such as a corporation or partnership) that generates income for that person. There may be no separate legal entity, such as the case of a sole proprietor.

Glossary

Servicing. The process by which a lender collects monthly mortgage payments and forwards applicable portions of the payments to the investor, local government and insurance agencies. *Servicing rights* are the right to service these mortgages. These rights are commodities that can be sold via the secondary markets.

Settlement Agent. A person or entity that coordinates or conducts a closing or settlement.

Settlement. Another term for *closing* of a real estate transaction.

Shared Appreciation Mortgage. A mortgage that offers the lender the ability to realize future gains based upon future appreciation of the property, in exchange for a below market interest rate.

Sole Proprietorship. A form of self-employment in which the individual that is self-employed has formed no separate legal entity such as a corporation.

Staff Appraiser. An appraiser who works as an employee for a mortgage company as opposed to the company hiring an independent firm to appraise properties.

Streamline. A rate reduction refinance requiring less documentation than a *full package* mortgage application.

Subsidize. A term referring to some type of aid. Federally subsidize mortgages typically have an interest rate lower than market because of government assistance. Temporary buydowns are considered *subsidized mortgages,* because there is money placed in an escrow fund to supplement the regular payment for a certain period of time.

Survey. The measurement of the boundaries of a parcel of land, including any improvements, easements or encroachments within the boundaries of the property. A *staked survey* is a higher costs but marks the boundaries via wooden or metal stakes.

Take Home Pay. One's paycheck after taxes and other deductions have been subtracted.

Take-Back. When the seller uses the equity in the property to provide a private mortgage for the purposes of financing the purchase for the buyer. Also known as *owner take-back.*

Tax Deduction. An expense that the government allows you to subtract from your income before the tax liability is computed. The Federal Government allows you to subtract certain *itemized deductions* such as mortgage interest in lieu of utilizing the standard deduction.

Tax Service Contract. A service performed by a tax service company which identifies the payment due date of local taxes for the servicer of the mortgage.

Teaser Rate. A starting rate which is below the *fully indexed accrual rate (FIAR)* on an adjustable rate mortgage.

Temporary Buydown. A lower interest rate on a mortgage for a fixed period at the beginning of the term.

Term. The full period or life over which a mortgage is scheduled to exist.

Title. Ownership record of the property. A settlement agent will conduct a title search to make sure the seller has clear title to the property before conducting settlement. If there is no clear title, it is said that the title has *clouds* or *defects. Title Insurance* is typically required to cover the lender against such defects.

Transfer Taxes. Taxes levied by a state or local government upon the transfer of real property. Also may be known as *tax stamps.*

Transmittal Form. Form that summarizes the data contained within a loan application so that it can be considered by underwriting.

Treasury Constant Maturities Indices. A series of indices issued by the Federal Government that measure the yield of treasury securities maturing for a term measured by the index. For example, the one-year *TCM* would measure all outstanding securities with one-year left to maturity.

Truth-In-Lending Act. Federal law that requires a truth-in-lending statement to be disclosed for consumer loans. This statement would include disclosure of the *annual percentage rate*, or *APR*, as well as other facets of the mortgage program. The law also requires the *right of rescission* period that follows the closings of owner-occupied refinances.

Two-Step®. An adjustable rate mortgage marketed by Fannie Mae which, instead of a five or seven year balloon payment, has a feature for conversion to a fixed rate to fully amortize the mortgage or to a one-year adjustable.

Uniform Residential Loan Application Form (Fannie Mae/Freddie Mac 1003/FHA 2900/VA 1802). The form that is accepted by all major mortgage sources for application of residential mortgages.

Uniform Residential Appraisal Report (URAR). The appraisal form that is utilized by appraisers of residential properties to estimate the value of properties to be financed with FHA, VA and conventional mortgages.

Uniform Settlement Statement (HUD-1). Settlement summary form required by *RESPA* to be used by closing agents settling a real estate transaction.

Underwrite. The process by which a lender analyzes risk in order to determine whether a loan application should be approved and under what conditions that loan should be funded. Automated underwriting does so through automated systems utilizing, among other things, credit scores.

VA Automatic. A Department of Veterans Affairs program that allows the lender to approve VA mortgage applications directly instead of sending the applications to the Department for approval.

VA IRRL Refinance. Another term for a VA interest rate reduction refinance which is a VA-to-VA refinance accomplished solely to lower the interest rate.

VA Funding Fee. Fee charged on VA mortgages to cover the administrative costs of the program.

Variable Income. Income that will vary from year to year. Examples of income that will vary include: self-employment, commission, bonus, overtime, part-time employment, and investment income.

Verification of Deposit. Form that verifies an applicant's liquid assets held with a particular financial institution. Not needed if alternative documentation (bank statements) is provided.

Verification of Employment. Form that verifies an applicant's job history, including employment date, salary, year-to-date income, income for the past year, and probability of continued employment. This form is sent directly from the lender to the applicant's employer. Not needed if alternative documentation (W-2's and paystubs) is provided.

Verification of Mortgage. Form that verifies an applicant's mortgage history with a financial institution, including the date of the mortgage, present balance, present payment, and history of late payments. The *Verification of Loan* and *Verification of Rental History* would garner similar information for personal loans and the applicant's landlord (if renting). Not needed if credit report discloses this information.

W-2. IRS form that reports income paid and taxes withheld by an employer for a particular employee during a calendar year.

W-4. IRS form which determines the amount of Federal taxes the employer will withhold from a person's paycheck each pay period.

Worked-Up. Process by which a fully verified loan application is prepared by the processor for underwriting.

Worst Case Scenario. A scenario in which the rate of an adjustable rate mortgage increases as fast as the caps will allow, i.e. the worst that can happen.

LoanOfficerSchool.Com Catalog

Our introductory Loan Officer Course teaches industry-specific concepts and proven techniques to new loan professionals. With an A to Z approach to loan origination, this class covers a vast array of information, including how to review a credit report, how to qualify a customer, how to develop a client list, the variety of loan programs available, how to get loans, and much more! **$595**

Our **Advanced Loan Officer Training Course** is absolutely the Most Intense, Comprehensive Training Available in the Mortgage Industry! **$800** ($675 Early Registration)

Day One: Become an expert in real estate finance by learning facets of the industry only understood by less than 5.0% of brokers in the industry.
Day Two: Use your expertise to deliver top-notch customer service within the mortgage process.
Day Three: Learn to leverage your expertise and establish the most powerful referral network ever!

The ultimate marketing tool for any mortgage brokerage or loan officer has just arrived. **The Complete Mortgage Marketing Kit** is a must for anyone within the mortgage industry who is tired of not having a professional presentation for his or her products and services. If you are serious about your success, you must have the advanced marketing tools necessary to market effectively.
This Kit has EVERYTHING you will need with almost 500 pages of valuable and professional marketing tools! **$495**

The Complete Home Study Course! Join us as you enjoy the complete Beginners Loan Officer Course taped on 7 VHS tapes! You will enjoy a front row seat and see and hear every word our Senior Trainer delivers to the live class.
To complete the package, you will receive one of the most comprehensive collections of training materials ever compiled into a step-by-step training course. Over 300 pages of course materials and handouts that will generate business and closed loans if you follow our simple formulas. **$495**

Our interactive CD-ROM's listed below utilize video, multi-media presentations and short quizzes that require the trainee to interact to learn the responsibilities for either the loan officer or processor. **$295**
Basic Loan Officer Training
Advanced Loan Officer Training
You're Approved - Interactive Case Study
Basic Loan Officer Training - Nonconforming
Basic Loan Officer Training - FHA
Basic Processor Training
Advanced Processor Training

The Complete FHA & VA Originators Guide
Adding FHA and VA expertise to your product line opens up a whole new world for your success. From low-to-moderate income borrowers to streamline refinances, these are truly powerful tools. Learn and use this knowledge not only to become more successful. Use these tools to help bring the dream of homeownership to immigrants and those citizens who will really appreciate the blessing we have in America. **$149**

To order any of the products shown, call 866-623-1250 — Or order on-line at www.LoanOfficerSchool.com

QUALIFYING PRINCIPLES & CALCULATIONS

TABLE OF CONTENTS

Introduction		Page 1
Unit 1:	**Principal and Interest Payments**	Page 2
Unit 2:	**Income Computations**	Page 3
	Hourly	
	Biweekly Salary	
	Annual Salaries	
	Self Employed, Commissioned, and Trade Workers	
Unit 3:	**Ratios**	Page 5
	Debt Ratios	
	Loan-to-Value	
Unit 4:	**Points and Premiums**	Page 7
	Discount Points	
	Basis Points	
	Yield Spread Premium	
	Mortgage Insurance Premiums	
Unit 5:	**Per-diem Interest**	Page 7
Unit 6:	**Breakeven Point**	Page 8
Unit 7:	**Prepayment Penalties**	Page 8
Unit 8:	**ARM Adjustments**	Page 9
	Worst Case Calculations	
	Sample Rate Calculations	

QUALIFYING PRINCIPLES & CALCULATIONS: PRETEST

Please read each question carefully and select the one **best** response.

1. What is the principal and interest (PI) payment on a loan of $165,000 at 6.75% interest for 30 years?
   a. $995.54
   b. $1,070.19
   c. $1,140.00
   d. $1,254.60

2. John Davis works as a machinist for a local manufacturer. He is paid $22.50/hour and works a 40-hour workweek with no overtime. His wife, Judy, is an office manager for a medical office and is paid $1,850 biweekly. What is their approximate combined monthly income?
   a. $7,300
   b. $7,600
   c. $7,900
   d. $8,200

3. The Johnson family is considering the purchase of a home for $280,000. They have sufficient cash on hand to cover a 20% down payment and closing costs. They will receive a 30-year fixed rate mortgage at 6.5% interest, with property taxes of $3,700 per year and homeowners insurance of $980 per year. They also have a car payment of $458 per month, $6,400 in credit card debt, and a personal loan with payments of $225 per month for two years. What is the minimum monthly income needed to qualify for this loan using a back ratio of 38%?
   a. $4,467
   b. $7,105
   c. $7,442
   d. $6,805

4. A borrower has a verifiable income of $3,400/mo, with no other debts. Using standard FHA ratios of 29% and 41%, approximately how large a mortgage could the borrower qualify for if the 30-year fixed interest rate is 6.50%?
   a. $139,858.00
   b. $155,995.00
   c. $166,754.00
   d. $220,545.00

5. A borrower is considering refinancing their first mortgage of $235,000. Their current rate is 7.375% for 30 years, and their PI payment is $1,623.09. The new interest rate would be 6.625%, with $5,400 in fees and closing costs. About how long will it take for the borrower to recover the cost of refinancing?
   a. 46 months
   b. 50 months
   c. 56 months
   d. 60 months

6. A loan of $325,000 for 20 years at 6.625% will be closing in the middle of the month. The borrower wants to know how much prepaid interest will be collected. Using a 360-day year, calculate the per diem interest that will need to be collected for each day they close before the end of the month.
   a. $58.98
   b. $59.80
   c. $64.37
   d. $81.57

How did you do? Turn the page to review your answers.

QUALIFYING CALCULATIONS

QUALIFYING PRINCIPLES & CALCULATIONS: PRETEST ANSWERS

Compare your selection to the correct response.

1. What is the principal and interest (PI) payment on a loan of $165,000 at 6.75% interest for 30 years?
   b. $1,070.19
   Common mistakes when calculating the PI payment include failing to clear the calculator before starting a new calculation, entering the data incorrectly, and using a calculator with a low battery.
   See p. 5

2. John Davis works as a machinist for a local manufacturer. He is paid $22.50/hour and works a 40-hour workweek with no overtime. His wife, Judy, is an office manager for a medical office and is paid $1,850 biweekly. What is their approximate combined monthly income?
   c. $7,900
   John's monthly income is $3,900. Judy's is $4,008. Therefore, their combined monthly income is approximately $7,900.
   See p. 6

3. The Johnson family is considering the purchase of a home for $280,000. They have sufficient cash on hand to cover a 20% down payment and closing costs. They will receive a 30-year fixed rate mortgage at 6.5% interest, with property taxes of $3,700 per year and homeowners insurance of $980 per year. They also have a car payment of $458 per month, $6,400 in credit card debt, and a personal loan with payments of $225 per month for two years. What is the minimum monthly income needed to qualify for this loan using a back ratio of 38%?
   b. $7,105
   A detailed explanation of the calculations in this problem begins on page 8.

4. A borrower has a verifiable income of $3,400/mo, with no other debts. Using standard FHA ratios of 29% and 41%, approximately how large a mortgage could the borrower qualify for if the 30-year fixed interest rate is 6.50%?
   b. $ 155,995.00
   To solve this problem, you must be able to use ratios and solve for loan amount.
   See pages 5 and 8

5. A borrower is considering refinancing their first mortgage of $235,000. Their current rate is 7.375% for 30 years, and their PI payment is $1,623.09. The new interest rate would be 6.625%, with $5,400 in fees and closing costs. About how long will it take for the borrower to recover the cost of refinancing?
   a. 46 months
   This three-step equation answers a common question from borrowers. To answer it, you must calculate the new PI payment, subtract the new payment from the existing payment, and divide the cost by the result.
   See p. 11

6. A loan of $325,000 for 20 years at 6.625% will be closing in the middle of the month. The borrower wants to know how much prepaid interest will be collected. Using a 360-day year, calculate the per diem interest that will need to be collected for each day they close before the end of the month.
   b. $59.80
   This equation is easier than it seems. Just divide the rate by 360 and multiply the loan amount by the result. The term of the loan is irrelevant.
   See p. 10

Refer to the pages listed after each question for more information.

QUALIFYING PRINCIPLES AND CALCULATIONS

Can I afford to buy this house?
How large of a loan can I qualify for?
What would the payments be?
Does it make sense to refinance now?

These are the most common questions a loan originator is asked. The knowledge and skills needed to answer them define the basic proficiencies needed to be a good mortgage loan originator. To meet this requirement, an originator needs a basic understanding of the math used in mortgage lending. Fortunately, it isn't difficult math.

The following calculations are covered in this chapter:

- Monthly principal and interest payments
- Income calculations
- Debt-to-income and loan-to-value ratios
- Points and premiums
- Per-diem interest
- Break-even point
- Prepayment penalties
- ARM adjustments

QUALIFYING PRINCIPLES AND CALCULATIONS: Q & A

My computer does all of these calculations, so why should I learn how to use a calculator?

There are two good answers to that question. First, you won't have your computer with you when you take the licensing exam. You will have to use a calculator. Second, and more importantly, once you learn how to use a calculator you will find it much easier to use than your computer for those times when you are running through different loan scenarios with a potential client.

What type of calculator should I use?

Any financial calculator will do, as long as you are comfortable using it before you go to take your licensing exam. We recommend the *Mortgage PaymentCalc*™ by Calculated Industries®. It can be purchased from TrainingPro for $35. It is very easy to use.

I sometimes get a different answer on my calculator than the one my computer gives me. Why is that?

Both the calculator and the computer use the same HUD approved amortization formulas. If you are getting different answers, check the following:

- Are both programs using the same assumptions? Clear all data and start over with both.
- Make sure that the calculator is set on month-end (if applicable) and that the future value {FV} field is empty.
- Does the calculator need a new battery? Low batteries can lead to wrong answers—even though the calculator seems normal.
- If you are using Excel on your computer, it may contain rounding errors.

QUALIFYING CALCULATIONS

In this chapter, the math associated with each step of the qualifying process is explained. The focus is on measuring capacity by calculating the monthly income, determining front and back debt ratios, and calculating the loan-to-value ratio. A section on determining the time needed to break even on discount points or the costs of a refinance is also included.

Prerequisite! Students must have access to a financial calculator to successfully complete this chapter. Any financial calculator will work, but students should be familiar with how to compute a principal and interest payment on a calculator before starting this course. We recommend the *Mortgage PaymentCalc*™ by Calculated Industries® and have based the instructions in this course on that calculator.

CALCULATING THE PRINCIPAL AND INTEREST PAYMENT

All financial calculators need the same three pieces of information to determine what the principal and interest payment (PI) on a normally amortized mortgage will be. However, the calculator key names and exact procedures may vary. The three pieces of information needed include:

- The loan amount, which is entered using the [Loan Amt] key
- The term of the loan in years, which is entered using the [Term] key
- The annual interest rate, which is entered using the [Int] key

All financial calculators have some provision for converting the term from years to months and the interest rate from annual to monthly. The *Mortgage PaymentCalc*™ does so automatically. Other calculators typically require the use of the second function [2nd F] key, which might be green or blue. Some calculators also need the present value to be entered as a negative amount, by using the [+/-] key. Consult your calculator's manual for more information.

Once these three pieces of data have been entered, the calculator will compute the PI payment. This is initiated by pressing the [PMT] key. Originators wanting to see how a change in interest rate, term, or loan amount would affect a borrower's payment need simply re-enter that data to compute the new payment.

For example, suppose a borrower wants to know what the payment would be on a $175,000 mortgage at a 6.75% interest rate for 40 years. The steps are as follows:

QUALIFYING CALCULATIONS

1. Enter 175,000, and then hit [Loan Amt]
2. Enter 6.75, then hit [Int]
3. Enter 40, then hit [Term]
4. Then hit [PMT]

The result should be $1,055.87. This is the principal and interest payment. The monthly homeowner's insurance premium and property tax impounds need to be added to calculate the PITI payment. "PITI" stands for **P**rincipal, **I**nterest, **T**axes, and **I**nsurance.

Most financial calculators will allow the user to compute any one item in the payment equation, as long as the other three have been entered. For example, if a borrower wanted to know how much they could borrow for a given monthly payment, the originator could enter the payment, rate, and term, and then compute the loan amount by hitting [Loan Amt]. Here is an example.

The Anderson family is not comfortable with a principal and interest payment higher than $1,800. If the prevailing interest rate is 7.00% and the term is 30 years, the calculation would go like this:

1. Enter 7.00, then hit [Int]
2. Enter 30, then hit [Term]
3. Enter 1800, then hit [Pmt]
4. Then hit [Loan Amt]

The result is $270,553.62. That is the maximum loan that they could receive given an interest rate of 7.00%, a term of 30 years, and a payment of $1,800 per month. Knowing that, you might also want to know what the loan amount would be for a 40-year term. To calculate that, just enter 40, hit [Term], and hit [Loan Amt] again. The result is $289,653.91.

The same steps can be used to look at the impact of different interest rates. It might be possible that the Anderson's could afford to buy down the rate to 6.75%. To determine what impact that change would have, just enter 6.75, hit [Int], and hit [Loan Amt] again. The result is $298,330.92.

You can examine a nearly infinite number of rate, term, and payment combinations using this method. In addition, you can do this much more easily on your calculator than on the computer. A seasoned originator can turn these skills into a powerful sales tool. Practice these steps until they become second nature to you.

INCOME CALCULATIONS

The first calculations an originator typically makes during the loan interview regard income. Most borrowers are paid on either an hourly basis or a salary. The salary might be given on an annual, monthly, or bi-weekly basis. Borrowers who are self-employed or commissioned sales people require special considerations. This discussion will follow standard conforming guidelines in the consideration of income.

A pay stub will provide most of the needed information. However, the originator will need to ask questions about the frequency of any overtime pay, how the employer handles vacation time, and when the potential buyer last received a raise. Once these questions are answered, the rest is just basic math!

Hourly

To compute the income of an hourly worker, you need to know the base hourly rate of pay, the number of hours worked in a typical week, the number of overtime hours received on average, and the number of weeks worked each year.

The formula is as follows:

1. {base rate} X {hours} = {weekly base income}

2. {OT rate} X {OT hours} = {OT weekly income}

3. {weekly base} + {OT income} = {**weekly income**}

4. {**weekly income**} X {weeks worked} = {**annual income**}

5. {**annual income**} ÷ 12 = {**monthly income**}

Overtime income can only be used to qualify for a loan if the borrower can show a history of receiving overtime and the employer verifies that overtime is likely to continue.

Annual vacation days are included at the base rate.

QUALIFYING CALCULATIONS

Bi-weekly Salary

To compute a bi-weekly salary, all you need to know is the borrower's salary and how the borrower's vacation time is treated. If the borrower receives a paid vacation (as most do), the calculation is simple. Remember that there are 26 bi-weekly pay periods in a year.

The formula is as follows:

1. {bi-weekly salary} X 26 = {**annual income**}

2. {**annual income**} ÷ 12 = {**monthly income**}

If the borrower does not receive a paid vacation, determine the typical amount of days that he or she takes off each year and subtract that income from the annual income before calculating the monthly income.

Annual Salaries

A borrower's income will occasionally be reported as an annual salary. This is common for educators and business executives. If this is the case, the formula is as follows:

{annual income} ÷ 12 = {**monthly income**}

Self-Employed, Commissioned, and Trade Workers

Self-employed, commissioned, and trade workers are treated in much the same way. Their income is usually averaged over a two-year period. For the self-employed, the loan originator uses the income shown on the individual's tax return. For commissioned and trade workers, the originator uses the income shown on their W-2 form. In both cases, the calculation begins with adding the income from the previous two years and dividing it by 24.

The formula is as follows:

1. {year one income} + {year two income} = {**income base**}

2. {**income base**} ÷ 24 = {**monthly income**}

This more restrictive standard is used because the income of these workers is less stable than the income of hourly or salaried workers. Therefore, a lender must be more cautious when evaluating the capacity of these borrowers' ability to repay a loan.

When evaluating a person's tax returns, remember to add back into the annual income those expenses that will not recur and any depreciation taken on capital expenditures. For example, a person might have relocated his or her office, which would be expensed and lower the net income. However, this expense is unlikely to recur, so the loan originator can add those costs back into the net income when determining the borrower's annual income.

Other Income

Annual bonuses, summer income, or other recurring additional income may be averaged over a two-year period and included in a borrower's annual income prior to calculating the monthly income. Child support and separate maintenance may be used if it is court ordered and if the borrower can show a stable history of receiving the payments.

CALCULATING RATIOS

Ratios are used to describe the relationship between two related events or characteristics. In mortgage lending we use ratios to describe the relationship between a borrower's debts and his or her income, and the relationship between a loan's balance and the property's value.

Ratios that are used in mortgage lending are not expressed using standard ratio notation. For example, lenders do not say that a person making $3 for every $1 in debt payments has a 3:1 ratio. Rather, ratios are expressed as percentages of the whole, or proportions. Therefore, a person spending $1 on debt for every $3 in income would have a 33% debt ratio.

Proportions are always calculated by dividing the part by the whole. For example, if there were 40 golf balls in a bucket, and you had hit eight of them, the proportion you had hit would be determined by dividing 8 by 40, like this:

$$\begin{aligned} \{part\} &= 8 \\ \div \{whole\} &= 40 \\ \{proportion\} &= 0.20 \end{aligned}$$

To express the proportion as a percentage, just move the decimal point two places to the right and add a percentage sign. In this case, it is 20%.

QUALIFYING CALCULATIONS

Debt Ratios

There are two debt ratios commonly used in qualifying a person for a mortgage loan. The housing expense to income, or "front," ratio is calculated by adding the monthly PI payment to all other fixed monthly housing expenses, such as property tax impounds, insurance impounds, mortgage insurance (MI), and homeowner's association dues. The total is then divided by the gross monthly income to determine the debt ratio.

The formulas are as follows:

1. {PI}+{impounds}+{MI}+{dues} = {**housing expense**}

2. {**housing expense**) ÷ {monthly income} = {**front ratio**}

The second debt ratio is the total debt-to-income ratio, sometimes called the "DTI" or "back" ratio. To compute the back ratio, you add all other monthly debt payments to the housing expense, and then divide by the monthly income.

1. {housing expense} + {monthly debt} = {**total debt**}

2. {**total debt**} ÷ {monthly income} = {**back ratio**}

For most investors, only those debts that will take at least 11 months to repay are included in the back ratio. The minimum payment is used when calculating the time needed to repay. For example, a car loan that will reach maturity in seven months need not be included in the ratios.

For revolving debt, such as a credit card, conforming guidelines require the use of 5% as the minimum payment, unless the creditor requires a higher minimum. This information can be found on the borrower's monthly statement and on his or her credit report.

Determining an acceptable debt ratio for a particular borrower is dependent upon their credit reputation and the stability of their income. A person with good credit and a stable income might be permitted to have a 50% or higher back ratio, while someone who is self-employed and has a spotty credit history might be limited to 36%.

For test purposes, you should assume standard conforming ratios of 28% and 36%, unless told otherwise in the instructions for the question. If the question refers to an FHA mortgage, the qualifying ratios you should use are 29% and 41%. The VA only uses a back ratio, which is 41%.

QUALIFYING CALCULATIONS

Loan-to-Value

There are two loan-to-value (LTV) calculations. The first describes the relationship between the first, or primary, mortgage and the property's value. This is the LTV. The second describes the relationship between all liens and encumbrances and the property value. This is called the combined loan-to-value, or CLTV.

The LTV formula is as follows:

$$\{\text{loan amount}\} \div \{\text{property value}\} = \{\mathbf{LTV}\}$$

The CLTV formula is as follows:

1. {first loan balance}+{second loan balance}+{all other lien balances} = {**total encumbrance**}

2. {**total encumbrance**} ÷ {property value} = {**CLTV**}

A property with only one mortgage or lien will only have an LTV. The CLTV applies only when subordinate financing is or will be in place.

POINTS AND PREMIUMS

There are several calculations made by determining a percentage of the loan amount. These include discount points, mortgage insurance, yield spread premium (YSP), and prepayment penalties. The calculations are made by multiplying the appropriate percentage, entered as a decimal, by the loan amount.

Discount Points

Discount points, or just "points," are equal to 1% of the loan amount. On a basic calculator, the equation for one discount point would be as follows:

$$\{\text{loan amount}\} \times \{0.01\} = 1 \text{ point}$$

Basis Points

Basis points are the unit of measure by which pricing changes in the secondary lending market. A basis point is one hundredth of one percent (0.01%) of the loan amount. On a basic calculator, the equation for one basis point would be as follows:

$$\{\text{loan amount}\} \times \{0.0001\} = 1 \text{ basis point}$$

QUALIFYING CALCULATIONS

Yield Spread Premium

A YSP is typically given in points. For example, a lender might offer 0.75 points for a specific yield. To calculate the premium, you multiply the points by the loan amount. In this example, the formula is as follows:

{loan amount} X {0.0075} = premium

Mortgage Insurance Premiums

The upfront mortgage insurance premium (MIP) on an FHA loan, the funding fee on a VA loan, and single premium private mortgage insurance (PMI) are all calculated in the same way. They are given as a percentage of the initial loan amount and calculated by multiplying the premium by the loan amount. The formula is as follows:

{loan amount} X {MI in points} = premium

PER-DIEM INTEREST

Per-diem, or daily interest, is calculated by dividing the annual interest rate by the number of days in a year, then multiplying the result by the outstanding balance of the loan. In some states, you will use 360 days, but other states require the use of 365 days. Others allow the use of either number. Be sure you know what your state requires before making the calculation.

The formula is as follows:

1. {interest rate} ÷ 360 = {**daily interest rate**}

2. {daily interest} X {loan balance} = {**per-diem interest**}

If the loan is amortized, the per-diem interest will change every month as the loan balance declines. For the estimates included on a Good Faith Estimate, the calculation is made on the anticipated loan amount.

Per-diem interest is collected at closing to put the loan on schedule. For example, if a loan is closing on the 20th day of a month, the closing agent will collect 10 days of per-diem interest to pay the interest cost until the end of the month.

QUALIFYING CALCULATIONS

BREAK-EVEN POINT

A borrower considering a refinance or a permanent buydown must know how long it will take to recover the cost of the refinance or buydown. Without this information, the cost-effectiveness of the transaction cannot be evaluated. Fortunately, the calculations are simple.

For a permanent buydown, the PI payment is first calculated at the market rate, and then at the buydown rate. The difference between the two payments is the monthly savings. To finish the calculation, divide the cost of the buydown by the monthly savings. This will yield the number of months until the break-even point is reached.

For example, if a borrower wanted to know how long it would take to recover the cost of a permanent buydown plan that reduced the note interest rate from 6.50% to 5.75% on a $150,000 mortgage loan amortized for 20 years, and if the fee for the buydown was three points, the math would look like this:

Payment @ 6.50%:	$1,118.36
Payment @ 5.75%:	$1,053.13
Difference:	$ 65.23

Buydown Cost:	$150,000
	x 0.03
	$ 4,500
	÷ 65.23
Months to Break-even	68.99

This same procedure can also be used to determine the break-even point on the cost of a refinance. In both cases, the most important step is to determine whether the borrower will retain the loan long enough to recover the costs. In this example, if the borrower planned to sell the home in less than 69 months, he or she should be advised against the permanent buydown.

It is difficult to make a permanent buydown make sense financially. Most people do not stay in their home, or keep their mortgage, long enough to recapture the costs. A rate and term refinance can present similar concerns, especially in light of state predatory lending laws. These laws often require that the lender demonstrate a net tangible benefit to the borrower. Some define that benefit very narrowly, requiring that the borrower reach the break-even point in as little as 24 months.

QUALIFYING CALCULATIONS

For example, suppose that 12 months ago the Cole family received a high-cost ARM loan of $180,000, which is now at 9.50%. Their current balance is $178,890.00. They have improved their credit and now qualify for a loan at 7.50% fixed for 30 years. The cost of refinancing will be $5,200, which will be added to the balance. To determine the break-even point you must compare the payments at two different loan amounts. The math looks like this:

Current Balance:	$178,890.00
Finance Costs:	+ $ 5,200.00
New Loan Amt:	$184,090.00
Original Loan Payment:	$1,513.54
Proposed Loan Payment:	- $1,287.18
Difference:	$ 226.36
Finance Costs:	$5,200.00
Savings:	÷ $ 226.36
Months to break-even:	18.55

This refinance would make good economic sense and meet the requirements of even the most stringent state regulations. It makes even more sense when you consider the change from an ARM to a fixed-rate mortgage.

PREPAYMENT PENALTIES

Prepayment penalties are usually given as a percentage of the original loan amount. The amount of the penalty usually declines as the loan matures. For example, there might be a 3% penalty in the first year, 2% in the second year, 1% in the third, and no penalty thereafter.

To calculate the prepayment penalty you have to know the original loan amount and the rate of the penalty at the time the loan is being paid off. The formula is as follows:

{original loan amount} X {penalty rate} = {prepayment penalty}

Many states limit the amount of a prepayment penalty, so be sure to consult the law for the state you are dealing with before discussing prepayment penalties with a borrower.

QUALIFYING CALCULATIONS

ARM Adjustments

Worst-case Scenario

Borrowers (and test writers) will frequently ask you to calculate the maximum amount that an interest rate on an ARM could rise in a given time period. This is often referred to as a "worst-case" scenario. To perform the calculation, you will need to know the following:

- The starting interest rate
- The first adjustment date
- The frequency of adjustments thereafter
- The periodic rate cap
- The lifetime rate cap
- The time frame of interest

Test writers will often provide you with the index and margin, but they are not needed for a worst-case calculation. You simply assume that the rate will rise the most it can rise for each adjustment period. The start rate and caps, not the index and margin, control this.

To begin the calculation, determine the maximum interest rate by adding the lifetime rate cap to the start rate. This is the most the interest rate could ever be.

{start rate} + {lifetime cap} = {**maximum rate**}

The next step is to determine how many adjustments could occur in the given time frame. For example, a 3-1 ARM stays stable for three years, then adjusts every year thereafter. The amount of each adjustment is limited by the periodic rate cap and the lifetime rate cap.

Therefore, if the question regarded the interest rate in the fifth year, you would know that the rate would have already adjusted twice. The rate would have adjusted once at the end of the third year, which would have been applied to the fourth year payments, and once at the end of the fourth year, which would have been applied to the fifth year payments.

To calculate the rate in the fifth year, follow these steps:

1. {number of adjustments} X {periodic cap} = {**periodic adjustment**}

2. {start rate} + {periodic adjustment} = {**new rate**}

The last step is to compare the new rate with the maximum rate. If the new rate is lower than the maximum rate, then the new rate is the correct

QUALIFYING CALCULATIONS

answer. If it exceeds the maximum rate, then the maximum rate is the correct answer. Read these questions very carefully before attempting to answer them. They can be tricky.

Sample Rate Calculations

John and Mary Smith are borrowing $280,000 toward the purchase of a home. The loan is a 3-1 ARM with a start rate of 5.625%, a periodic rate cap of 2% thereafter, and a lifetime rate cap of 6%. What is the highest interest rate that could be charged in the fifth year of the mortgage?

Step 1: Maximum Rate

(starting rate) 5.625% + (lifetime rate cap) 6% = (max rate) **11.625%**

Step 2: Adjustment Periods

In a 3-1 ARM, the first adjustment occurs at the end of the third year and applies to the fourth year. The rate adjusts each year thereafter. In this example, the rate would have adjusted twice—once after the third year and once after the fourth year.

The calculation is as follows:

Step 3: Maximum Rate for Adjustment Period

2 X 2% = **4%** (maximum periodic adjustment)

5.625% + 4% = **9.625%** (new rate for fifth year)

Step 4: Comparison with Maximum Rate

9.625% $\leq$ 11.625%

Using the Margin and Index

You might be asked a question in which the margin and index are given, as well as a hypothetical change in the index that occurs at some specified time. This type of question requires the consideration of both the change in the index and the limitations on the rate changes imposed by the caps.

In our previous example, the margin on the loan might be 2.75% and the index might have risen to 5.50% at the time the second adjustment occurred. In this case, the actual new rate would have been computed by adding the margin and index, then comparing the result to the maximum rate.

QUALIFYING CALCULATIONS

The calculations are as follows:

$$2.75\% + 5.50\% = \mathbf{8.25\%}$$

$$\mathbf{8.25\%} \leq 9.625\%$$

Because 8.25% is less than or equal to 9.625%, the new rate for year five would be 8.25%.

A Word of Caution

Borrowers often feel very anxious about how much their rate might rise. The worst-case scenario can be used to provide substantial comfort for the borrower, but it must be used very carefully. Remind borrowers that the maximum allowable rate is not the rate they are likely to receive. However, if they cannot see a way to handle the maximum allowable rate, they may want to reconsider their choice of an ARM loan.